GW01117104

Language and Identity

Also available from Bloomsbury

Language Acquisition and Language Socialization,
edited by Claire Kramsch
Language, Culture and Identity, Philip Riley
Learning Strategies in Foreign and Second Language Classrooms,
Ernesto Macaro
Pedagogy of Hope, Paulo Freire
Second Language Identities, David Block
Teacher Cognition and Language Education, Simon Borg

Language and Identity

Discourse in the World

Edited by David Evans

Bloomsbury Academic
An imprint of Bloomsbury Publishing Plc

B L O O M S B U R Y
LONDON • NEW DELHI • NEW YORK • SYDNEY

Bloomsbury Academic
An imprint of Bloomsbury Publishing Plc

50 Bedford Square   1385 Broadway
London   New York
WC1B 3DP   NY 10018
UK   USA

www.bloomsbury.com

BLOOMSBURY and the Diana logo are trademarks of Bloomsbury Publishing Plc

First published 2015

© David Evans and Contributors 2015

David Evans has asserted his right under the Copyright, Designs and Patents Act, 1988, to be identified as the Editor of this work.

All rights reserved. No part of this publication may be reproduced or transmitted in any form or by any means, electronic or mechanical, including photocopying, recording, or any information storage or retrieval system, without prior permission in writing from the publishers.

No responsibility for loss caused to any individual or organization acting on or refraining from action as a result of the material in this publication can be accepted by Bloomsbury or the author.

British Library Cataloguing-in-Publication Data
A catalogue record for this book is available from the British Library.

ISBN: HB: 978-0-5673-3816-7
ePDF: 978-0-5670-4779-3
ePub: 978-0-5675-6614-0

Library of Congress Cataloging-in-Publication Data
A catalog record for this book is available from the Library of Congress.

Typeset by Deanta Global Publishing Services, Chennai, India
Printed and bound in Great Britain

I would like to dedicate this book to my wife, Dominique, my daughter Sandra and my son Thomas who have provided me with endless encouragement in this project. Also to the academic staff of the Education Faculty of Liverpool Hope University amongst whom the spirit of enquiry, debate and research were kindled.

Deo Gratias

Dr David Evans

Table of Contents

Contributors   ix

Part 1   Theoretical Overview

1   Introduction   *David Evans*   3

2   The Identities of Language   *David Evans*   15

3   How Language Shapes Social Perception   *Philippe Chassy*   36

Part 2   Languages, Discourses and Identities in the World

4   Quebec's Shift from Ethnic to Civic National Identity: Implications for Language Attitudes Among Immigrants in Montreal   *Ruth Kircher*   55

5   Trilingualism and Uyghur Identity in the People's Republic of China   *Mamtimyn Sunuodula, Anwei Feng and Bob Adamson*   81

6   'Queensland for Ever & Augus un ballybug go braugh': The Expression of Identity in Nineteenth-Century Irish Emigrant Letters   *Marije van Hattum*   105

7   Indigenous Languages, Cultures and Communities in the Amazon: Strengthening Identities   *Alex Guilherme*   123

Part 3   Critical Pedagogies

8   The Language of Leisure and Physicality: Constructing and Re-constructing Identity   *Wendy Bignold*   145

9   Drama and the Identity of the Language Learner   *Bernie Hughes*   166

10   Towards a Cultural Paradigm of Alterity in Modern Foreign Language (MFL) Learning   *David Evans*   188

| 11 | English Language Teacher Identity: A Framework for Teacher Learning and Professional Development *Richard Kiely* | 207 |
| 12 | Conclusion *David Evans* | 229 |

Index   231

Contributors

Bob Adamson is professor of curriculum studies at Hong Kong Institute of Education. He is head of Department of International Education and Lifelong Learning and director of the Centre for Lifelong Learning Research and Development.

Wendy Bignold is associate dean international at Liverpool Hope University. Her research interests are in youth identity and international education.

Philippe Chassy is lecturer in psychology at Liverpool Hope University.

David Evans is fellow in education at Liverpool Hope University. His research interests are in language/identity within education, pedagogy and youth development, and more widely, multilingual identities, marginalized languages and cultures.

Anwei Feng is Professor in Language Education and Head of the school of Education, University of Nottingham, Ningbo, China.

Alex Guilherme is lecturer in education studies at Liverpool Hope University where he is director of the Paulo Freire Research Centre for Critical Pedagogy. Alex has published extensively on the topic of dialogical education as a tool for reconciliation between communities in conflict. He has also published in philosophy and theology on Spinoza, Fichte and Schelling.

Marije van Hattum is lecturer in English at the University of Lausanne, Switzerland.

Bernie Hughes is senior professional tutor for modern foreign language teacher education at Liverpool Hope University.

Richard Kiely is associate professor of applied linguistics and language education at the University of Southampton. His main research interest is language teacher learning, which he explores from identity and communities of practice perspectives.

Ruth Kircher is lecturer in English language at Liverpool Hope University.

Mamtimyn Sunuodula is Area Studies librarian in the School of Government and International Affairs at Durham University.

Part One

Theoretical Overview

1

Introduction

David Evans

Language and Identity: Discourse in the World is a book that connects linguistic expression and non-verbal communication with a range of identities. Indeed, a widely defined view of language, encompassing signs, semiotics, gesture etc., can be viewed as discourse. Within discourse, language is much more than words and phrases and disembodied sounds but rather the coming to life of social interaction where sentences may be incomplete, punctuated by the voices of others or by gaps, silences, intonations, accent and accompanied by bodily gestures and facial movements. In short, language is embodied and expresses ways of being in the world through the creation of meanings which relate to us in terms of identity. Identity here should be seen as self-concept, and the point of this book is to show how self-concept is constituted by the meanings of language and how it is reflected by language, not just in small-scale social interactions but also in larger linguistic–political discourses. Halliday (2003) views language and grammar within linguistic discourse as serving two main purposes – the transmission of knowledge/information and the construction of relationships. In the first he refers to language as 'ideational' and in the second as 'relational'. Other proponents of discourse such as Fairclough (1989, 1992), who are more inclined towards social sciences and the links to social structures as opposed to a more narrowly defined view of language, would argue that language shapes the knowledge and information that it expresses and from which it cannot be extricated. Viewed from such a perspective, language not only reflects and expresses relations, ideas and information but also actually plays a large part in constructing them.

The book argues that the meanings that substantiate self-concept or identity are both created through language and expressed by language. Halliday, a linguist rather than a social scientist, refers to language as 'construing human experience'

(2003: 275). An image that I use on occasions in the book is that of language therefore being a 'double-edged sword' which can both liberate and constrain identities and as such is a very powerful tool in the creation of meaning.

Identities are considered, in the book, under many aspects and many, but not all, are politically, culturally and socially marginalized. The commonalities between disparate identities in such diverse locations as the Amazonian jungle of Brazil, urban spaces in Britain and the Uyghur province of China are indeed marginalized identities. However, emancipation of marginalized cultural identities can be brought about through a sociopolitical and sociocultural valorization of language and discourse. Discourse can therefore go beyond the interactional, constructing larger-scale meanings at sociocultural and sociopolitical levels.

Language is then a 'double-edged sword'; constraining identity by erecting boundaries between 'them and us' be they geographical or sociocultural, and liberating identity by offering fresh opportunities to cross barriers and boundaries. Critical pedagogy is also an essential feature of this book and proposes a solution and a redress for marginalized language and discourse. Critical pedagogy supports the agency and intentionality of identity confronted by a discursive, ideological hegemony in language and education. It seeks to offer an alternative to the 'banking system' of pedagogy (Freire 1970) which favours instrumental outcomes and is committed to promoting liberated personal identity within a context of social justice. Freire proposes problem-posing education where people 'develop the power to perceive critically *the way they exist* in the world *with which* and *in which* they find themselves; they come to see the world not as a static reality, but as a reality in process, in transformation' (Freire 1970: 64). Individuals can liberate themselves in the language choices they make and in the linguistic–cultural opportunities they embrace. There are cultural and linguistic positions and projects we see people undertaking in the chapters of this book. They seek, through language and cultural opportunity, a means of transforming identity, sometimes marginalized but sometimes not.

Themes of the book

Language as political–cultural capital

Bourdieu and Passeron (1977) and Norton (2000) argue that language is a cultural and symbolic capital. Some languages contain a more highly valued sociopolitical and economic currency than others. We see this in the case examples of the predominance of Mandarin Chinese over Uyghur, of English over French and also immigrant languages in Montreal, and Brazilian Portuguese over Amazonian tribal languages. In this latter case we witness how a change in language policy contributes to restoring a former indigeneous identity. We also see the tensions in language–culture attitudes, particularly in the Montreal and Uyghur case studies, between perceived economic benefits and the social needs of affiliation and allegiance. This is where language resides at the level of sociopolitical discourse with its divisions and social tensions. Many of these examples show how language shapes and reflects identity, not just within lexicogrammar and concepts but also around language as discourse.

Discourse

Foucault (1972) argues that discourse is much more than signs and language. Rather, it is about the way in which the world is ordered through social practices. For Foucault knowledge is discursively constituted through social practices suffused by relations of power and ideology. Thus, language within discourse creates social realities through linguistic–cultural concepts (as outlined by Philippe Chassy in Chapter 2). These social realities form the basis for each culture's epistemology. The corollary of Foucault's position is that had social practices and discourses been different, then the types of knowledge and reality we experience now would have been different. Of course, powerful discourses colonize the less powerful, and powerful languages supersede the less powerful, resulting in the demise or sidelining of local knowledge-culture and even the death of languages. Fairclough (1989, 1992) who proposes a much less totalizing view of discourse than Foucault nonetheless accepts that there are some areas of knowledge that are 'talked' into existence. These areas are created by the discursive language we use. In this way, human relations are psychologized through the social practice of counselling or human behaviours are 'performatized' through management accountability practices. Such knowledge is then relative to the discursive formation that constitutes it.

For this discursive constitution of knowledge to take place, a discourse has to be powerful enough to displace former social arrangements; for example a counselling discourse may have the power to penetrate educational practices and become an integral part of pedagogy – similarly, a performance management discourse of accountability involving the setting and auditing of targets may be able to penetrate professional practices in education among school and university teachers. These are two discourses which have come from different areas of social life and have colonized a place in educational discourse. Language and discourse hegemony is therefore created through power relations between groups of social actors within their communities, and we see in this book how this can create marginalized languages, discourses and identities.

Alterity

Respect and promotion of alterity (or 'Otherness') are implicit in the pedagogical philosophy in this book. The philosophy of Levinas outlines the need for the understanding and appreciation of the 'Other'. Levinas (1989) criticizes a Western intellectual propensity to colonize the Other, to make the Other a Sameness. Consequently in understanding the Other we appropriate it and make it our own by internalizing it into our understanding. In this sense, to understand something is to render external reality the same as ourselves. Levinas proposes a respect for the Other in his ethics as a first principle of philosophy and metaphysic of Otherness or alterity. Levinas expounds a notion of ethics being the a priori condition for knowledge rather than the a posteriori condition of knowledge. In this regard ethics come first in respect of knowledge of the Other rather than afterwards. We can perhaps see how this philosophy of Otherness could influence the way in which minority languages and cultures might be viewed, as something to be inherently nurtured in respect of diversity. This means of course acknowledging the existence of external reality as opposed to reality simply being an extension of one's own subjectivity. Of course, culture in this regard needs to be seen as a dynamic process of ongoing human relations rather than a static fixed product or commodity. Culture needs to be viewed as fluid and evolving and discourse as open rather than closed. Levinas views alterity as irreducible and, of course, this radical view perceives the whole world outside one's own consciousness as the Other. This view, however, is problematic as it limits any engagement with the Other since all engagement leads to a potential colonization.

While maintaining a notion of alterity, we can look to Bakhtin in terms of the construction of identity within a dialogic relationship with the Other (Bakhtin 1981). According to Bakhtin, language and identity are constructed in the encounter between oneself and the Other. Therefore we internalize the language of others and, through our interpretative powers and agency, re-frame and reuse the language of others. Consequently, our identity contains something of the identities of the Other. Bakhtin states as follows, 'the ideological becoming of a human being . . . is the process of selectively assimilating the words of others' (1981: 341). Within the individual therefore there is a constant dialogical negotiation between the individual's own meanings and the meanings of the external world. Therefore we can be changed by the external world and in a dialectical relationship we can, in our social groups, change the world. The moral tension here is between changing the world and at the same time respecting the alterity of cultures. Thus in terms of the politics of language, minority languages and identities need to be nurtured for diversity and yet individuals surely still need to have access to globally powerful languages in the interests of their own socio-economic opportunities. There is here a strong argument for multiple identities in language-culture where people can use both local and global languages, and we see a move towards this situation in **Chapter 3** where many Uyghurs look to develop a trilingual language identity.

Critical pedagogy

In the pedagogical **Part 3** we start, in Chapter 8, by seeing that learning and teaching concern the transformation of identities in the exploration of self through leisure. We continue, the subsequent chapters, by discovering one's 'third place' (Kramsch 1998, 1993) in the journey of exploration towards foreign language-culture as opposed to socio-economic instrumentality. Harrist and Richardson (2011) express a view that '. . . we tend to collapse the cultural and moral dimensions of life into merely technical and instrumental considerations' (2011: 342). They furthermore warn that we are left 'without ways to keep our individual and collective lives from being co-opted and dominated by modern systems of production and bureaucratic domination' (2011: 343). They therefore express a Levinasian view that social action should be relational rather than instrumental. However, arguably the pedagogical model that best suits a model of empowerment of individual identity and of all individuals collectively in a spirit of emancipation and social justice is that of the Critical Pedagogy of Paolo Freire.

Freire (1970) criticizes the banking model of education where the educational system inculcates knowledge and skills into a subjugated and passive audience. Here the oppressed internalize the pedagogical agenda of the dominant as the dominant bank knowledge and skill for the instrumental purposes of maintaining a status quo. Freire advocates a problem-posing model of education where social reality is problematized so that hidden agendas can be made visible and subject to critical analysis. He proposes this model for education to develop the intentionality of social actors. Individuals are endowed with intentionality to act upon the world for social justice whereas a banking system dispossesses individuals of this necessary agency and thus turns recipients of education into instruments where a functional objectivity robs them of capacity to act. The banking system immobilizes the socially dispossessed.

Freire proposes a construction of knowledge and skill with teachers and learners in a shared learning enterprise. In the following sections, the themes that are covered above are discussed in synopsis.

Part 1 is theoretical, explicating, in **Chapter 2**, the two sides of language: the interiority of language in terms of lexicogrammar and the exteriority of language in discourse in its interface with the social world. In this chapter, **David Evans** focuses on Halliday's systemic functional linguistics outlining the interrelationship between the interiority and exteriority of language. In **Chapter 3 Philippe Chassy** relates the neuropsychological functioning of language to socioculture in the context of the Sapir–Whorf hypothesis. We learn how languages contain social realities that are not easily translatable between linguistic and national cultures. The chapter explains how lexicogrammar constructs concepts which contain sociocultural realities. In fact the 'Concept' is key in mediating between lexis, grammar and culture.

Part 2 presents ethnic communities navigating a route between languages and cultures; for example, in Montreal, immigrants and their descendants have a hard choice to make between French, which is the official language of Quebec, and English, which is not only the language of upward mobility in Canada and the rest of North America but also the global lingua franca. A similar situation prevails in the Uyghur region of north-west China where the politically dominant Mandarin Chinese language overshadows Uyghur, the local language of preference, and English is seen by some as offering a wider global and economically liberated identity. One thing that seems certain is that ethnic native languages often concede social precedence to socio-economically dominant languages, although in Chapter 6 we do glimpse a partial reversal of this trend through government intervention in Brazil. Nevertheless, generally we see that language contains a politico-economic currency in much the same way as economic capital (Bourdieu and Passeron 1977).

This section presents the studies of these cases of marginalized and emancipatory language identities over several continents, past and present – they are as follows: tribal language communities in the Amazonian jungle of Brazil, immigrant communities in Montreal, the Uyghur population of north-west China and the historical Irish diaspora to Australia in the nineteenth century. We are able to see evidence for the theoretical considerations of language and identity, made manifest in these empirical chapters. Often, there is ideological and political struggle to revalorize marginalized language or, alternatively, personal struggle to adapt to the perceived dominant language and culture. **Chapter 4**, written by **Ruth Kircher**, discusses language and identity issues with regard to the numerous immigrants and individuals of immigrant descent in Montreal, the urban centre of the Canadian province of Quebec. As English is not only the language of upward mobility in the rest of Canada and North America but also a global lingua franca that affords international possibilities of economic success, immigrants and their descendants traditionally tended to integrate into Montreal's anglophone community. However, in an attempt to ensure the future of the French language in Quebec, recent language planning measures have tried to integrate them into the city's francophone community instead. While the resulting ethnic diversification of the French-speaking community in Montreal was initially not unproblematic, a shift now seems to have occurred from the traditional, ethnic conception of Quebec identity towards a more inclusive, civic conception. Chapter 4 discusses the implications that this shifting sense of identity has had for the language attitudes held by immigrants and individuals of immigrant descent in Montreal.

Language, as we then see, in its daily and wider political use is much more than words, phrases and grammar. Language and discourse contain sociopolitical, socio-economic capital, social relations of power and are, as already mentioned, 'a double-edged sword' for both a wider, more emancipated identity and a means of constraining identity. In **Chapter 5**, **Mamtimyn Sunuodula and Anwi Feng and Bob Adamson** write about the struggles for linguistic and cultural political identity in north-west China between the Uyghur ethnic minority and the dominant ethnic majority Han Chinese. We see how language can constrain identity in the Uyghur's perception of the encroachment of Mandarin Chinese but also how language can offer possibilities for the opening up of identity, a possibility offered by learning English.

In the 1950s, the Uyghur minority population was able to establish the Uyghur language as an official regional language of China. The language was approved by the Chinese authorities for use in regional institutions including education and schools. However, in the process of nation-building and economic modernization, mainstream Chinese language and culture have encroached on

Uyghur linguistic–cultural identity as the Chinese state has sought to create a stronger unified national identity around the official language. This shows how linguistic and cultural identity in global contexts can become sites for political tension as ethnic communities struggle to preserve and enhance their political identity. In the Chinese situation, an empirical study involving higher education students reveals a level of complexity with regard to identity since the majority acknowledge that, although they have a strong desire to preserve Uyghur cultural identity through the Uyghur language, they still recognize the need to learn Mandarin Chinese for socio-economic self-betterment. Paradoxically, the learning of English, in a move towards trilingualism, offers an opportunity for the Uyghurs to resist linguistic hegemony, as they can develop an international identity. Provided that they can access adequate resources to learn English, the Uyghurs can find themselves on an equal footing with the Han population in their aspirations to develop an overarching globalized identity. This, therefore, demonstrates the emancipatory possibilities of language in its ability to power alternative identities – in this case, a globally powerful language can liberate by providing users with a powerful identity.

In **Chapter 6, Marije van Hattum** demonstrates a historical narrative where the use of Irish written dialect in letters home can reflect a former cultural identity. Marije narrates and analyses the relationship between language and identity in the lived experience of Irish diaspora to Australia in the nineteenth century. The written language that emerges from Irish emigrants' letters sent back to the 'Old' country from Australia reinforces a former identity which persists alongside their new identity. The Irish emigrants have a strong desire to accommodate to the new language and culture and their native dialects become influenced by their new contexts in the colony of settlement. However, Marije shows, through her analysis of writing in their letters home to Ireland, that the new and the old identities can co-exist alongside each other within a dual identity of Irish Australian. This chapter expresses the view taken by this book that individuals can take on dual and multiple identities which do not need to be mutually exclusive.

A not dissimilar situation in **Chapter 7** where **Alex Guilherme** writes about a return to a former identity through the re-use of native tribal languages among the Amazonian Indians of Brazil. This is currently occurring through a sociopolitical revalorization of Amazonian Indian languages within the school system, inspired by the critical pedagogy of Paolo Freire. Here former indigenous identities that had been suppressed by a dominant Brazilian/Portuguese language and culture have now been liberated to the extent that a modern state can possibly allow.

These language and identity chapters in **Part 2** point to a contemporary theme in juxtaposed linguistic communities which is the need to explore capacities for bi-lingual and multi-lingual cultural identities, often between heritage and new linguistic–cultural identities. This theme is prescient of the interrelationship that will be covered in Chapter 2, between Sameness and Other, the dialogism of Bakhtin and possibilities of multiple identities in an emergent culturally hybrid third place. Notions of cultural and linguistic multiple identities and hybridity are all areas for further research.

Part 3 addresses the discourses of critical pedagogy. This section relates to the previous **Part 2** in the context of foregrounding and promoting marginalized discourses faced with what often seems to be the hegemony of dominant culture. In this third section, we see how, in various educative and developmental contexts, students and teachers can be liberated by being allowed to interpret the education and schools project together as equal partners. Education can then take place at a culturally deeper level, freed up from the more immediate socio-economic exigencies, often promoted by a 'banking' system of education which instrumentalizes learning (Freire 1970). Students, who are disconnected from the hegemonic mainstream and marginalized by dominant culture, can find new motivations and revitalized identities in discovering their own 'third space' in the learning process (Kramsch 1993, 1998). This means re-interpreting their learning activities in terms of their own life perceptions as creative individuals. This may involve different ways of perceiving their subjects or ways of being within a developmental discourse.

In **Chapter 8, Wendy Bignold** writes about learners seeking new motivations and identities in exploring alternative discourses for physical education away from the perennial mainstream of football and rugby. She writes about the 'unplanned' existential language of unicycling where youth creatively and spontaneously redefine adult urban environments and in doing so contribute to redefining their own identity. Young people playfully make use of the spaces that have been 'seriously' planned by the adult professional and corporatized world. The more playful, creative urban leisure activities of unicycling and others such as skateboarding and parkours stand as alternative discourses to the more corporately organized and ubiquitous football and rugby. This entails the use of a different linguistic vocabulary and non-linguistic discourse of dress, posture, gesture, style, facial expression and music. This, then, becomes a culture and an alternative way of being, walking and talking. Wendy relates this culture to identity, defined as self-concept which in turn contains notions of self-esteem and confidence. She shows that these inner features of the identities of young people can be motivated by alternative cultural and leisure discourses and the positive effects of these arrangements can result in a better academic engagement back in the traditional world of schooling.

The chapter gives a vibrant sense of youth community, bonding in a shared identity – the lived experiences in the narratives of two research participants suggest a genuine warmth and joy in constructing unique identities through unicycling. In this opening chapter of Part 3 which is devoted to critical pedagogies, we gain a sense of learning as transformative in becoming a different and unique person through activity. This sets the scene for Chapters 9, 10 and 11 which focus pedagogy on the development and transformation of learner identities.

Chapters 9 and 10 outline ways in which identity issues occur in modern foreign language (MFL) education. In **Chapter 9, Bernie Hughes** writes about the existential construction of identity by students who find their own 'third place' through drama in the study of an MFL. From their own agency students are able to experiment with the cultural otherness of different identities within this safe third place afforded by drama. This third place becomes its own cultural discourse of playfulness and experimentation where a blend of hybrid identities may be constructed, in a place between the first place of one's own culture and the second place of the 'Other'.

Drama of course has its own intrinsic advantages of building self-confidence through risk-taking in a safe environment. Bernie shows how drama role play acts as a bridge between native language and culture and foreign language and culture. Trainee primary foreign language teachers can then use drama to compensate for gaps in their linguistic competence by combining existing and developing language knowledge with non-verbal language of gesture and movement. Much as in **Chapter 8**, non-verbal communication encourages a discourse where agency and existence in the moment create a liberated identity and a refreshingly educative process.

In **Chapter 10, David Evans** contrasts the inner culture of foreign language and the notion of 'third place' (Kramsch 1993, 1998) with the more external socio-economic ideologies in language learning. He proposes alternative pedagogical conceptualizations involving student appropriation of foreign language and culture as opposed to the external imposition of stereotyped notions of dominant language-culture. Students need to appropriate language-culture for their own needs, ways of being and seeing the world. However, they also need to acknowledge the 'Otherness' or alterity of foreign language and culture in a process of active discovery and here foreign language education is conceived as an exploration of the Otherness or alterity of culture within and around language. Appreciating alterity rather than colonizing the Other, therefore, has a moral and even spiritual dimension which has escaped the more conventional pedagogy of the building blocks of words, phrases and transactional grammar in what Freire (1970) would label a banking model for education.

In **Chapter 11, Richard Kiely** writes about issues of identity in the development of teachers in the teaching of English to speakers of other languages (TESOL). He addresses a discourse of teaching as performance and as cultural performativity through which teachers learn and extend their skills. He argues that this discourse has progressed from earlier accounts of language teacher identity based on mastery of the subject (English). The former technical rational model of language mastery and pedagogic skills expertise often excluded the social, interactional and interpersonal dimensions of teaching as areas where teachers learn and extend their personal and professional capacity.

Richard therefore frames language pedagogy as performing a cultural identity in a professional setting, and as such language teaching (as well as language learning) is an exploration of identity. He draws on Wenger's Communities of Practice theory (Wenger 1998) where learning through work is a process of identity formation, led by the imagined self in a social and professional context. Consequently second language teacher education can develop a focus on the performance of identities of teachers as language professionals, engaging with identity as a process of becoming and changing rather than as a fixed product. This pedagogic discourse, he argues, is transformative since it contributes to personal cultural development as well as linguistic expertise where both teachers and students are inevitably changed by learning situations.

This book, then, not only presents marginalized language and identity existing outside the hegemonic mainstream but also shows the creative and transformational opportunities for identity offered by language and language education. This gives agency, intentionality and critical voice to cultural minorities. Minority languages can coexist alongside dominant language within a notion of multiple identities in language-culture. Identity in terms of different languages-cultures is therefore not an issue of the 'either/or' of unitary identity but the 'both/and' of multiple identities. This addresses both issues of revalorizing minority and dying languages-cultures while at the same time promoting equality of access to the more socio-economically influential languages. Both propositions should be viewed in a framework of empowerment through a developmental and critical pedagogy.

Governments will always want the interests of the state to be the major stakeholder in the processes and outcomes of education. This is nothing new: whose interests were served by Education Act of 1870? Was it those of the state or of children recently delivered from the factories and mines? Certainly both in the long term, as each stakeholder has their priority within education as a contested site for ideology. However, educators have a responsibility to their students to assist them in the pursuit of meaning and development in the same way that the doctor is responsible for the well-being of each patient, as opposed to the notion of providing a healthy workforce for the economy of the nation.

The underlying philosophy of the book addresses notions of sociocultural justice, delivered through the linguistic opportunity and also the educational opportunity to transform identity through language and discourse. Hopefully, readers will be able to judge for themselves the extent to which language, discourse and critical pedagogy are able to play a significant part in this developmental project.

References

Bakhtin, M. (1981), *The Dialogic Imagination: Four Essays*, ed. M. Holquist. Austin: University of Texas Press.
Bourdieu, P. and Passeron, J. (1977), *Reproduction in Education, Society and Culture*. London: Sage.
Fairclough, N. (1989), *Knowledge and Power*. London/New York: Longman.
—(1992), *Discourse and Social Change*. Cambridge: Polity Press.
Foucault, M. (1972), *The Archeology of Knowledge*. London: Routledge.
Freire, P. (1970), *Pedagogy of the Oppressed*. London: Continuum.
Halliday, M. A. K. (2003), *On Language and Linguistics*. London: Continuum.
Harrist, S. and Richardson, F. C. (2011), 'Levinas and hermeneutics on ethics and the Other'. *Theory and Psychology* 22(3): 342–58.
Kramsch, C. (1998), *Language and Culture*. Oxford: Oxford University Press.
—(1993), *Context and Culture in Language Teaching*. Oxford: Oxford University Press.
Levinas, E. (1989), *The Levinas Reader*. Oxford: Blackwell.
Norton, B. (2000), *Identity and Language Learning: Gender, Ethnicity and Educational Change*. London: Longman.
Wenger, E. (1998), *Communities of Practice: Learning, Meaning and Identity*. New York: Cambridge University Press.

2

The Identities of Language

David Evans

> **Editor's Introduction**
>
> This chapter provides an overview of different models of language and identity. A particular feature of the chapter is the relationship between the inside of language and its outward interface with social structures. Do social structures shape lexicogrammar in terms of identity? How are meanings generated from within language and then come to be shaped by the individual's position in society, in terms of what can be said and what must remain unsaid? Such questions are addressed within notions of discourse and a proposed unified theory of systemic functional linguistics (SFL).

This chapter sets out to demonstrate the centrality of language in the construction of identities. I will examine the position of language in relation to identities with regard to different accounts of cultural life: sociocultural, objective rational mind and existential self.

First, sociocultural identity refers to identity shaped through social language within a social context; secondly, the identity of objective rational mind talks of objective grammatical language reflecting a rational view of the individual. This is language as the outcome of reason. Finally, within an existential view of language one's subjective being constantly interacts with the fluidity of language meanings and interpretations.

I present the notion of identity as the idea, sense and perception of self or self-concept. According to the language models above identity may be a relatively stable unitary self-concept or evolving and changing multiple self-concepts and subjectivities. In this chapter self is therefore conceived within a continuum which has a fixed, unitary identity at one point or multiple, changing identities or selves at the opposite point of view. I will explore language and identity at different levels corresponding to the three respective accounts of cultural life mentioned above: (1) ideological identities within discourse evoked by writers such as Foucault and Fairclough including developments from systemic functional linguistics originated by Halliday, (2) generic categories of identity within the grammatical structures of language referring to Descartes and Chomsky and (3) spiritual and existential identities evoked by Heidegger and Derrida. The purpose is to gain a wide-ranging and widespread view of the language–identity relationship from a variety of perspectives.

Language will therefore be considered from the different perspectives of structuralism, social constructivism and post-structuralism, analysing the different versions of identity emerging from these models.

Philosophically, language can be viewed in two significantly different paradigms; first as separate from self, although connected to it and amenable to analysis as an objective phenomenon. Secondly, language can be seen as inhabited by self, which co-constructs the world within discourse, through which self, in turn, is also constructed. Vygotsky (1962) expresses these two basically opposite paradigms as follows: 'A look at the results of former investigations of thought and language will show that all theories offered from antiquity to our time range between identification, or, fusion of thought and speech on the one hand, and their equally absolute, almost metaphysical disjunction and segregation on the other' (Vygotsky 1986: 2). This chapter will endeavour to explore a middle ground between these two poles of language in 'structural-constructivist' attempts to find a unified theory of language and identity.

The first paradigm described above, that of structuralism, is a Cartesian view of language espoused by Chomsky (1975) in particular. Here, the structures of language in grammar belong to the individual within an innate mental structure as part of rational mind. However, the individual does not existentially inhabit language. Language can be rationally analysed and can, as an objective tool of mind, analyse and describe a pre-existing world.

The second opposing view of language is a sociocultural one contained in the notion of discourse. Here, language is integrated into the individual's subjective perception and construction of the world. The individual cannot be extricated from language and in fact the individual's identity is, at least to some extent, contained within language. Unlike the first paradigm, language does not have a rational neutrality but is intrinsically 'shot through' with ideologies and relations of power. Meaning is not objectively contained within language but within agency.

Whatever the text, meaning is occasioned by individuals within discourses and always reflects a particular ideological standpoint. As Kilpert (2003) points out, 'to use language is to put a construction on experience' (2003: 165) and, quoting from Halliday and Martin (1993: 8), 'the language is not passively reflecting some pre-existing conceptual structure; on the contrary, it is actively engaged in bringing structures into being, such language does not simply correspond to, reflect or describe human experience; rather, it interprets, or, as we prefer to say "construes" it' (Kilpert 2003: 166).

Universal Grammar

Chomsky (1975) refers to language as a mirror of the mind. 'Thus language is a mirror of mind in a deep and significant sense. It is a product of human intelligence, created anew in each individual by operations that lie far beyond the reach of will or consciousness' (1975: 4). This places language beyond individual agency, and indeed Chomsky proposes the notion of Universal Grammar, which is an initial structure for language, deeply embedded and innately built into the human species. It is 'Universal Grammar' which, according to Chomsky, accounts for human acquisition of language within such a short space of time. There is therefore a specific capacity for language within the mind, which receives and processes language from outside the mind with apparently very little difficulty. Chomsky compares the time it takes to learn one's own language fluently with the act of gaining a similarly comprehensive knowledge of physics, where the latter would take much longer because, unlike language, we are not biologically programmed to learn physics.

Chomsky, however, does not take into account the difficulty many people have in learning a second language in later life, which might bear more relationship to learning a science such as physics once the optimal time for language learning has passed. The point he is trying to make, nevertheless, is that humans are programmed to learn language, whatever the language(s), in much the same way as they are programmed to take on any other biological function. The simple fact, as proposed by Chomsky, is that children in their developmental process can learn any language due to their possession of Universal Grammar. This is because all specific grammars pertaining to human languages are derived from Universal Grammar, and in this respect, all grammars of human languages resemble one another at a deep level, even if, at the surface, the word orders and other linguistic features may differ. Chomsky defines Universal Grammar as follows: 'as the system of principles, conditions and rules that are elements or properties of all human languages not merely by accident, but by necessity' (1975: 29). Universal Grammar is then an 'innate property of the human mind' (1975: 34). Chomsky's account of language acquisition is derived from a Cartesian view of human innate and rationally structured identity and consequent theory of knowledge. Chomsky maintains that 'learning is primarily a matter of filling in detail within a structure that is innate' (1975: 39).

Descartes's theory of knowledge

Descartes argued that the structures for knowledge in the outside world had corresponding structures inside the head as part of the cognitive fabric of mind. In *Meditations* and *Discourse on Method*, Descartes had affirmed the 'I' of the mind as the knowing agent in the Cogito. As he stated in *Meditations*, even if the outside world were a dream or illusion, the mere fact that he can doubt or speculate on its reality proves his existence as Mind if not as body:

> I am a thinking thing, that is one that doubts, affirms, denies, understands a few things, is ignorant of many others, wills this and not that and also imagines and perceives by the senses; for as I have already remarked, although the things I perceive or imagine do not perhaps exist, yet I am certain that the modes of thinking . . . , considered purely and simply as modes of thinking, do exist inside me. (Descartes 2008: 25)

Therefore in spite of the empirical, sensory world all around him, Descartes is able to analyse its veracity through the innate structure of a thinking mind. Descartes goes on to connect this thinking mind to the outside world. He makes a causality argument connecting himself to the outer world, where he claims that effects in his mind must contain the same level of reality as the causes outside his mind. He maintains, as follows, that an idea in his mind cannot come from nothing: 'But, by the same token, the idea of heat, or of the stone, cannot exist in me, unless it is produced in me by some cause in which there is at least as much reality as I conceive to be in the heat or in the stone' (Descartes 2008: 29). The causality structure corresponding between the inside of the mind and the outside mean that knowledge is rather uncovered than discovered, in that we reveal what is already structurally possible and latently knowable.

Chomsky (1975) models this Cartesian epistemology with regard to language acquisition. Individuals already possess a skeletal inner structure for language, and this simply awaits completion from the actual language itself. Much as in Cartesian epistemology, nothing really new is learnt, and certainly nothing is learnt which does not have a system in place already awaiting its arrival. (In the 'Third Meditation', Descartes goes on to apply his cause–effect epistemology to account for religious faith and the existence of God. However such philosophical enquiry is just slightly outside the scope of this chapter!) This view of an a priori inner language structure, finding its linguistic match in the language of the outside world, is contested by Kilpert (2003), who maintains that there is no such thing as a linguistic inner–outer match but that language has to be constructed; language has to construct categories *ab initio* on its own as they are not already there in the world awaiting activation.

Chomsky, by contrast, uses his theory of Universal Grammar to explain why children learn their native language(s) so quickly and effortlessly: because, in fact, the job is already done in the deep mental structures. However, he does not refer to sociocultural and ideological agency or intentionality in terms of meaning and identity. Meaning resides in the grammatical structures of languages and can be rationally analysed through the structure of the sentences. In this model of structuralism, meaning is created by the sentences and the grammatical possibilities for semantics within sentences. However, identity in terms of the agency of intentionality is hidden from view, much as in official documents. Here the impersonal voice and passive voice are often used with expressions such as in the following examples: 'it is expected that . . .', or 'it was felt that . . .', or 'the subsidies were withdrawn from claimants on the grounds that . . .', or 'the British were seen to be . . .'. This is a way of placing meaning firmly and seemingly rationally within the text and at the same time disguising agency and intentionality. Human identity here becomes a generic grammatical, linguistic concept, structured by the use of grammar and the arrangements of words. He states as follows: '. . . once the system of language and other cognitive structures are developed by the mind, the person has a certain range of choices available as to how to use these systems' (1975: 77). Here in this statement there seems to be some implication of a limited agency, and yet structures still determine what can and cannot be said rather than agency; if the individual has an identity, it is a generic one contained within the grammatical and linguistic structures of sentences and utterances. He furthermore states that 'deep structures give all the information required for determining the meaning of sentences' (1975: 81).

Post-structural accounts of language and identity

Post-structuralist models of language account for meaning in much wider contexts than the structures of sentences. Derrida (1967), drawing on and also critiquing the work of Saussure (1966), acknowledges the difference between the two different systems of written and spoken language, or 'Langue' and 'Parole', in Saussurean terms. According to Derrida, in traditional logocentric philosophy, 'Parole', or spoken language, is the only authentic language in that it is the only language that truly reveals human identity. This is because 'the voice, producer of the first symbols, has a relationship of essential and immediate proximity with the mind' (1967: 11).

Derrida therefore argues that spoken language has been seen as closer to the meaning of being and the Logos. He maintains, as follows, that 'the sign and divinity have the same place and time of birth. The age of the sign is essentially theological' (1967: 14). Rayment–Pickard's (2003) observation on this is that theology, throughout history, has been woven into human grammar. This view of word, sign and grammar is then the relation of language to ideal transcendental meanings from Logos or the word of God. Derrida maintains that throughout history linguistic identity is primarily spiritual in the voice before written language detracts from this primary divine connection. According to Derrida, the written sign is secondary and merely a representation of speech. Writing has taken us away from the Logos because of its secondariness and abstraction, whereas speech is seen as calling into being the presence of objects or the 'signified'. In this view of language then, speech evokes presence and, as Derrida acknowledges, traditional writing in its secondariness postpones presence into a future time known as deferral. Here meanings are never definitive but subject to endless interpretations as the written text always moves through futures. Even when a text is read and interpreted in a present time there is always a future when the interpretation could change. Writing is thus only an 'exterior representation of language' (Derrida 1967: 31). Writing as a 'deviation from nature' (1967: 38) and as a rupture with the Logos is criticized by Derrida, who argues for a new form of writing that might occupy the same status as speech.

Much in the same way as Derrida, Heidegger views spoken language as a spiritual identity invoking the presence of 'being'. Heidegger (1993) argues that individuals have their 'being' within language and language allows the world to come into being. 'Thus we are within language, at home in language, prior to everything else' (Heidegger 1977, 1993: 398). He maintains that speech is a matter of showing or pointing, which is bringing to presence all things that are in our concerns; language operates by pointing and reaching out to every area of presence, letting what is present appear. Furthermore he goes on to say that speakers come to own their speech and belong to what they say. This means that the essence of individuals lives within the speech acts rather than transcending them. He states, as follows, 'We, human beings, in order to be who we are, remain within the essence of language to which we have been granted entry. We can therefore never step outside it in order to look it over circumspectly from some alternative position' (1993: 423), and further on, Heiddeger argues that we belong to language rather than language belonging to us, referring to language as the 'House of Being' (1993: 424).

Ultimately then, if as humans we belong within language, language must carry a very significant part of our identity. This model of language and identity can be seen as diametrically opposed to Chomskyan structuralist views of language in which speakers and listeners are notional beings rather than living and breathing beings. Yet there is an important point which is shared by these polar opposites, represented on the one hand by the structuralism of Saussure in particular, outlined in the next section, and on the other by Derrida and Heiddeger. Although the former maintains that language is the structural meaning and the latter that language is spiritual or existential 'Being', both share a view of words which function as pointing or indexing devices. The word is then not synonymous with the object it describes or, in other words, the signifier is not identical to the signified.

Saussurean structuralism

For Ferdinand de Saussure (1966), the word as signifier is only connected with the signified object by conventional association. There is no necessary link, and this association is contingent upon the arrangement and conventional meanings of supporting adjacent words. Words therefore stand in relationship to each other not only by similarity but also by opposition; therefore, a particular word means one thing because it does not mean something else. This means that words denote and delineate difference as well as association. They stake out a territory and lay claim to a category, associating with an object or group of objects yet differentiating between a particular category and its adjacent categories. Thus a tree is a tree partly because it is not a bush as well as due to its categorical resemblance to other trees; when the word for 'oak' appears, this means that it is not a 'birch' or a 'poplar'. In terms of human gendered identity, the designation of male is such, not just because of maleness but also because of lack of femaleness. The signifier–signified connection is then as much about what the word-object is *not* as it is about its similarity. Structuralism basically treats language as a labelling process, defining and refining word meanings in their oppositions to related word meanings. However, in Saussurean 'structuralism', there is an acknowledgement that language does not have a priori meaning but is conferred meaning by conventional associations between words and objects – the signifier and the signified. A word then can evolve a different meaning over time. Saussure sums up language as follows: '. . . language has neither ideas nor sounds that existed before the linguistic system but only conceptual and phonic differences that issued from the system. The idea . . . that a sign contains is of less importance than the other signs that surround it' (Saussure 1966: 120).

Both post-structuralist and Saussurean models concur that language has no internal substantive meaning and the word meanings themselves can change over time. In the latter model, meanings can only be held in place by the support of the surrounding linguistic structure and do not have an a priori direct referent outside of the linguistic system.

Both in Heideggerian and Saussurean terms, language-identity tells us more about being in the world rather than the nature of the signified objects – it tells us more about the nature of identity in how we perceive the world rather than about the world itself. Language may be closer to the structures of mind than to the structures of the outside world. When we use words, our usage may tell us more about our perceptions and ideologies than about the realities of the outside world. In opposition to Descartes, Kant, in the *Critique of Pure Reason*, argues that the '*noumenon*' of the world, or the world as it is, lies beyond our grasp and is only 'knowable' through the empirical data conveyed by sense perceptions. Language therefore does not give us the world as it really is, only how we perceive it to be.

This Saussurean version of structuralism facilitates the progression towards notions of discourse where language connects more to the individual/collective mind than to the objective external world. There is perhaps a sense in which we co-create the world ourselves through language. Foucault (1972) argues that this is done through discursive social practices.

Discourse and social practice

In post-structuralism, meaning no longer resides within the structures of language in terms of words, sentences and grammar. These items may help to transmit meaning but they do not of themselves generate meaning. Meaning in post-structuralism is generated through language by agency and power in the social world. Agency creates signs, symbols, social practices, images, gestures, tone of voice, silences and also text, which may be words and images combined rather than continuous script. All this is in a state of flux from situation to situation, and the same arrangement of words, meaning one thing in one situation, may mean something else in a different situation depending on who is talking and the power relations in the situation. To know what an utterance might mean, the post-structuralist does not analyse the structure of grammatical semantics but the prevailing situational context, the semiotics of symbols, images, power interactions and relationships between participants. This is analysis at the level of discourse.

Foucault (1972) goes further, arguing that discourse is much more than signs and language. It is rather about the way the world is ordered through social practices. According to Foucault, analysing discourse is 'a task that consists of not... treating discourses as groups of signs... but as practices that systematically form the objects of which they speak' (Foucault 1972: 54). Although language is at the heart of discourse, language is not viewed as inward facing in the search for meaning within lexical and grammatical items, but rather outwards to who is speaking, the position they are speaking from and the effects they are trying to produce. Meaning is therefore actively constructed rather than passively uncovered – but meaning is also often constructed through the power of dominant discourses. The importance in the connection between the language of discourse and identity is that identity is not a grammatical construction determined by what language can allow us to say but rather by what we are enabled to say by our own position in social structures in small-scale or large-scale discourses. Since there are many discourses in which we may participate, small and large, separate as well as interconnecting, the notion of identity may well be multiple rather than unitary. In fact, it may well be more appropriate to refer to social selves as subjectivities, as individuals move from situation to situation. Wertsch (1991) refers to voices of the mind as heteroglossia, where participants in discourse use language from other discourses, causing an overlap in identities or subjectivities. This is because, as Chouliaraki and Fairclough (1999) point out, we internalize other voices from dominant discourses and express them in our own voice at interactional level. As an example of this, I would refer to the powerful hegemonic discursive practice of advertising, which is able to penetrate into smaller less powerful interactional discourses. We often hear people in their daily lives repeating the jingles from television adverts or wearing advertising logos on tee shirts and other clothing. Individuals thus take brand names into their daily interactions.

Discourses can be powerful and can constrain individuals by dictating what can be said and what cannot be said. There can therefore be a powerful determinism within notions of discursive. Edwards and Usher (1994) state that power/knowledge relations lie in discourses and can define what can and cannot be said, who can speak and who must remain silent. Discourses have the power to create meaning and, through the knowledge they claim, they can state what is true and what is false. Edwards and Usher (1994) point out that individuals located within discourses remain unaware of it. They state that discourse speaks but is yet silent – it is an absent presence, yet a powerful one. Edwards (1998) points out that although discourses are localized in time and sociocultural place, they offer absolute and universal perspectives within their own terms of reference. There is therefore a certain determinism at the heart of a discourse and it is only when viewed from the outside that its truth may be seen as relative to other discourses.

At a much larger scale, Foucault refers to the totalizing effect of discourse, which over time has historically oriented societies towards forms of knowledge through language and social practices. Knowledge and consciousness are therefore shaped by the larger discursive structures or 'Orders of Discourse' in which societies reside. This implies that if the discourses had taken a different historical route – an ideologically different one in terms of, for example, religion or politics – then forms of knowledge might have been different.

Forms of knowledge are, then, constructed through language, social relations and social practices. This is a very different epistemology to the one proposed by Descartes, which places knowledge objectively outside of language. Knowledge, including scientific knowledge in Foucauldian terms, is a product of prevailing discourses.

This determinism with regard to knowledge and identity within Foucault's totalizing system of discourse invokes an age-old debate around free will.

The crucial issue with regard to free will or determinism in identity in relation to language is to consider whether individual identity resides on the inside or outside of language.

If the individual and identity are contained within language, then it can be said that the individual and perceptions of the world are constructed by language. Now the individual him/herself may actively use language to contribute to or co-construct the social world in his/her social groups, but it is always the case that individuals are using and understanding language borrowed from more powerful discourses with pre-established meanings. Individual agency is therefore operative within larger discourses in processes of interpretation of meanings, where semantic possibilities have been pre-established. Free will might then be constrained by the larger discourse.

In this discursive view of language, meanings are created in an intersubjective world rather than within the brain-based Universal Grammar of the isolated individual. Cultural meanings are constructed out in a social world that involves power relations in order to secure meaning. We will see how the ideological power for meaning develops within language/discourse in subsequent sections.

Social constructivism, intersubjectivity and cultural identity

Bakhtin (1981) does much to individualize language and promote the notion of agency in his concept of 'dialogism'. This suggests that in choosing words and in framing them into (grammatical) statements, speakers will have an eye to the possible interpretations of interlocutors. The listener in this sense will co-create the choice of language and meaning in conjunction with the speaker. Thus, speakers tend to construct their messages and meanings with an eye to their audience. The production of cultural messages and meanings therefore are not generated in the head or brain of the individual but outside the brain, within the intersubjectivity between oneself and others. Vygotsky (1962) had already claimed all meanings to be social before they became individualized through language. Bakhtin refines this by saying that all meanings are born on the edge of the encounter between the individual and others. When the individual speaks she/he has a dual attention divided between the inner workings of language and the audience, be this individual or collective. The dynamic of linguistic meaning may be constituted by both the intentionality of the speaker in terms of his/her ideology and the grammatical possibility. It is in this encounter where we might explore identity in the interface between grammar and intention, inner and outer language, and between the determinism of linguistic constraints and the creative free will of the individual. Fairclough (1989) brings the inner- and outward-facing aspects of language together in his notion of Critical Discourse Analysis (CDA), which aims to analyse how language works in its transmission of ideological identity.

Fairclough – discourse and social power relations

Fairclough's (1989) view is that we are both inside and outside of language. Nevertheless powerful discourses can construct parts of the social world that previously did not exist – such as bureaucratic practices, practices of management/performance accountability, counselling etc. However we are sufficiently outside of language to have free will to create a metalanguage of analysis since, for Fairclough, discourse is only one social practice among many others. He terms this metalanguage activity CDA – Critical Discourse Analysis (Fairclough 1989).

Chouliaraki and Fairclough (1999) advance a structure–agency model of language which combines inner structuralist semantic possibilities with outward-facing language. Their particular model of CDA brings together in an analytical practice the two disciplines of critical social science and linguistics, which they term SFL – Systemic Functional Linguistics. This presents us with a unified theory of language. They define this as a 'dialectic of the semiotic and the social in a wide variety of social practices . . .' (1999: 17). Chouliaraki and Fairclough are not discourse idealists who view the entire social world as a product of language and discourse, and as they state, 'We believe that it is important for critical social science to incorporate discourse in its theorizing but to do so in a non idealistic way which does not reduce social life to discourse' (1999: 28). They acknowledge, therefore, objectivity in the world, in that the world is not just an aggregation of subjectivities but actually does exist outside of language. They view knowledge consequently as a dialectical product of subjectivity and objectivity. They state as follows: 'critical social science constructs, as the objective of scientific research, the dialectical relationship between objective relations and structures on the one hand, and the practical dispositions of subjects engaged in practices on the other' (1999: 30). The operations of discourse therefore demand the interrelations between the linguistic as objective structure and the social as subjectivity. The subjectivity of agency does not have complete free will since it is constrained, as well as enabled, by objective structures. Overall, Chouliaraki and Fairclough advocate a dialectical theory of language which they label 'Constructivist-Structuralist' (1999: 37).

Within this model of language, Chouliaraki and Fairclough retain the Saussurean structuralism, where possibilities for meaning derive from inside the linguistic system and where semantic derivation is produced by the interrelation of words and signs rather than necessary a priori meanings. This linguistic ground provides the basis for the dynamic, interactionist and productive language of discourse. Discourse is shaped by the underlying relatively stable inner linguistic structures, and yet over time, discourse acts back on these structures to cause them to evolve in response to the social demands of language. The fact that the structures of language in Saussurean linguistics are disconnected from a priori links to objects allows this dialectic to take place. Unlike Chomskyan a priori Universal Grammar, grammar in SFL is ultimately responsive to the long-term demands of social situations, rather than intrinsic rationality. Therefore grammar, in SFL, is both reproduced and transformed by the social functions of discourse. Language therefore contains a grammatical system that interrelates with its surrounding discourse. The discourse around the system inevitably involves the identities of the speaking subject. It reflects and reinforces the social position of the speaking subject, and it also allows the speaking subject to enact some agency in the generation of language. With regard to the linguistic structure within this dialectic, its grammatical possibility allows the speaking subject to express a variety of generic identities such as nominal subject, gender, number, future tense, conditional possibility, subjunctive doubt and past tense narration. Identity of this generic nature is built into the bedrock of language and then afterwards, more specifically to the individual, 'played out' and 'fleshed out' in the dynamic performance of interactional discourse. Again the demands of social situations, as already mentioned, act back on grammatical structure. A model of SFL as explained so far can be seen in the following figure.

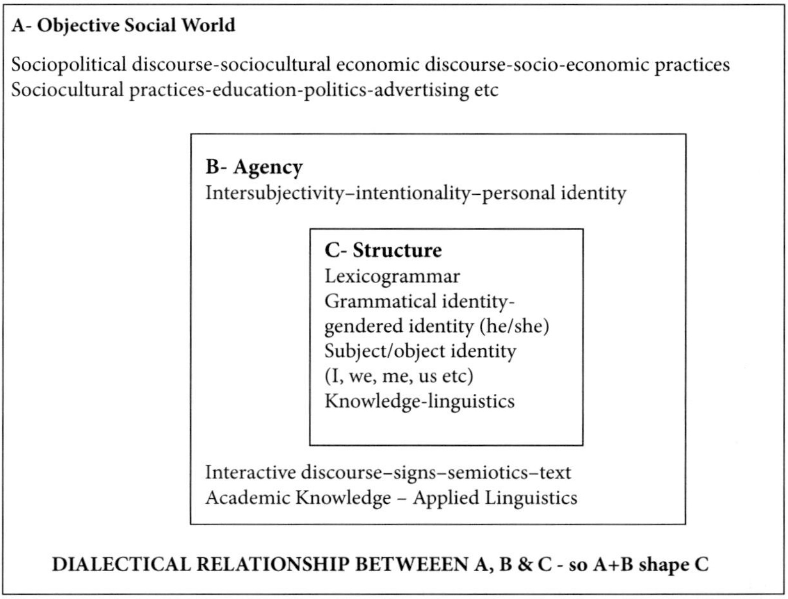

A- Objective Social World
Sociopolitical discourse-sociocultural economic discourse-socio-economic practices
Sociocultural practices-education-politics-advertising etc

> **B- Agency**
> Intersubjectivity–intentionality–personal identity
>
> > **C- Structure**
> > Lexicogrammar
> > Grammatical identity-
> > gendered identity (he/she)
> > Subject/object identity
> > (I, we, me, us etc)
> > Knowledge-linguistics
>
> Interactive discourse–signs–semiotics–text
> Academic Knowledge – Applied Linguistics

DIALECTICAL RELATIONSHIP BETWEEEN A, B & C - so A+B shape C

Figure 2.1 Model of systemic function linguistics. My diagrammatic representation based on Chouliaraki and Fairclough (1999).

Rationale of systemic functional linguistics

This linguistic theory is advocated by Chouliaraki and Fairclough (1999) as a unified theory of language that connects critical social science to the interior of language itself. SFL defines language as a semiotic system where meaning is connected to spoken and written characters through the medium of lexicogrammar. Lexicogrammar, or vocabulary and grammar, does not connect directly to the outside world but is an enabling device containing the fullest range of relatively stable semantic possibilities at a particular time. These semantic possibilities become semantic actuality when activated by the production of spoken or written text. The meaning, the written and spoken characters and the lexicogrammar all form part of language as a semiotic system interacting with the demands of social functions. These social functions and the meanings that they construct act back upon the semiotic system in an interactive dialectic to modify, over time, lexicogrammatical structures. This is because grammar, in the production of language, constructs the world not only as idea but also relationally, in contextualizing social relations between users of language. The social is therefore built into grammar and can, historically, modify grammar. An example of this, in Spanish, French and other languages, is in the informal and formal forms of address of Tu/Usted and Tu/Vous. Here the grammatical usage of subject pronoun depends exclusively on the relational connection between speakers and interlocutors. Equally the gender of the language user will also, in French and Italian, affect certain past participle endings in the written language, as the ending agrees with the gendered subject.

Chouliaraki and Fairclough's SFL closely resembles the model proposed by Halliday (1978) and, as Kilpert (2003: 3) states, SFL is a theory which 'has grown out of Halliday's work over the past four decades' (2003: 159). He differentiates between language as knowable system and language as behaviour. Halliday is a linguist rather than a social scientist, whose object of study is the functions of language rather than Discourse Analysis. For Halliday, system and behaviour in language have to be interconnected since language exists in its use: '... there can be no social man without language, and no language without social man' (1978: 12). Furthermore, he states that 'the individual's potential for linguistic interaction with others implies certain things about the internal make-up of the individual himself' (1978: 13). The inside and the outside of language are then connected. Language connects to individual identity, and it is only through language that individuals can interconnect, forming social groups and whole societies.

The linguistic analysis of Halliday is language in action rather than the Chomskyan ideational and therefore context-free view of language. His linguistic system is, then, functional since language exists to serve social functions and demands. Halliday's system places the semantic system, therefore, as the originator of meaning, providing a meaning potential which is activated through lexicogrammar. The semantic system is the total possibility for meaning intention, but this can only be realized in the lexicogrammatical system. The semantic system implies agency, and therefore the potentiality for identity occurs in the interaction between semantics and lexicogrammar. The final delivery of meaning takes place through the graphic systems of writing and the phonic systems of speech.

For Halliday, the whole semiotic system containing semantics, grammar and phonics is connected to the social system through registers containing field, tenor and mode. Field is the social context of language, tenor refers to the relationships involved between participants, and mode refers to the channels of communication such as face-to-face, telephone, texting and internet. The register is also mediated by dialect; register and dialect are closely interrelated to form discourse in the shaping of identity. It can be argued that some registers are only accessible through certain dialects. This evokes identities of social class where standard dialects, for example, carry high social standing, giving access to the most powerful discourses and, by contrast, where local dialects may be stigmatized and give access only to local registers and low status discourses.

Language is then, to summarize, both a system and a discourse, and Halliday's functional linguistic model can be summarized in Figure 2.2.

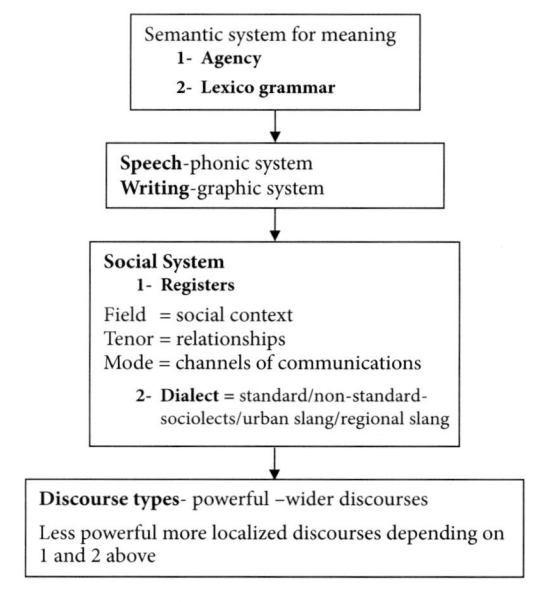

```
┌─────────────────────────────────────┐
│   Semantic system for meaning       │
│        1- Agency                    │
│        2- Lexico grammar            │
└─────────────────────────────────────┘
                  ↓
┌─────────────────────────────────────┐
│   Speech-phonic system              │
│   Writing-graphic system            │
└─────────────────────────────────────┘
                  ↓
┌─────────────────────────────────────┐
│   Social System                     │
│        1- Registers                 │
│   Field  = social context           │
│   Tenor  = relationships            │
│   Mode   = channels of communications│
│        2- Dialect = standard/non-standard-│
│            sociolects/urban slang/regional slang │
└─────────────────────────────────────┘
                  ↓
┌─────────────────────────────────────┐
│   Discourse types- powerful –wider discourses │
│   Less powerful more localized discourses depending on │
│   1 and 2 above                     │
└─────────────────────────────────────┘
```

Figure 2.2 Halliday's linguistic model.

Language as cultural capital; language as ideological capital

We now need to consider the more outward-facing aspects of language and social identities as opposed to the inner features of language.

Norton (2000) argues that language practice is connected to symbolic and cultural capital and that this underpins identity. A speaker, therefore, speaks from a particular social position belonging to a social network and having access to symbolic resources drawing upon socio-economic power and knowledge. Drawing upon work by Bourdieu and Passeron (1977), Norton argues that cultural capital involves forms of thought and knowledge that pertain to certain social groups which are deemed to possess a higher value than other forms of knowledge and thought. Some language types, in terms of lexicogrammar, are deemed to have more value than others. Within the same language, these more valued types would constitute standard language with its own grammar and pronunciation. In terms of languages generally, some languages themselves are more valued than others due to socio-economic value and or historical prestige. English, French and Spanish are regarded as world languages due to their historical colonial empires and current economic possibilities; they therefore enjoy primacy on schools' teaching curricula. These languages, and especially English, are languages of political and economic power, conflated with geographical spread, and are consequently more readily learnt than, for example, Scandinavian, Central European or African languages.

Blackledge (2005) argues that language choice is bound up with language ideology, power relations and political influence. A high-status language is one that has political and cultural capital and, much like a highly valued monetary currency, everyone wants to learn it for professional, socio-economic and/or sociocultural return. Blackledge points out that Anglophones in Quebec are now keen to learn French, just as many continental Europeans are keen to learn English, because of the sociopolitical ascendancy of the language in that particular area (cf. Chapter 4 on 'Language and Identity in Quebec' by Ruth Kircher).

There is, then, sociocultural capital within languages, as there is between languages. Linguistic–cultural capital is represented by standard language, grammar and pronunciation. In France, for example, this written standard is legally embodied by the Academie Francaise, which enforces a hegemony within the media, political and education systems. Those whose identity ideologically occupies a sociopolitical life world removed from this hegemony may well speak alternative discourses. Anti-establishment discourses such as hip-hop in the English-speaking world or Verlan in the French-speaking world are examples of this. Verlan is a 'sociolect' or cultural dialect that has evolved in the milieu of immigrants and the unemployed who have been pushed to the fringes of French society. The language is constituted by reversing the syllables of French words, adding lexical items from North African and Eastern European immigrant communities as well as aspects of American hip-hop. Those who speak it self-consciously position their identities within a new social identity with an alternative linguistic–cultural capital, away from the perceived power of French hegemonic linguistic identity. The internal grammar of such dialects may well differ from standard grammar. Conjugations in English-based urban dialect may differ so that it is possible to say 'we is' rather than 'we are' and also syntax constructions such as 'innit' as a catch-all phrase rather than 'aren't I' or 'isn't she'.

Nevertheless, Gieve and Clark (2006) argue that individuals are able to take on a multiplicity of linguistic–cultural identities since identities are multiple and fluid rather than static and linear. We will see in the forthcoming case-study chapters how dual or multiple languages/dialects and identities can co-exist and are indeed taken on by those seeking new sociocultural, socio-economic identities while retaining older ones. Chapters 4, 5, 6 and 7 explore possibilities for dual/multiple identities.

The issue of language as cultural capital is extremely important in identity formations. Chouliaraki and Fairclough (1999) point out that linguistic capital mediates other forms of capital transforming them into symbolic capital. Linguistic capital is 'the power conferred upon a particular linguistic form, style or dialect associated with the legitimacy and prestige of particular social positions – it is crucial in the conversion of other forms of capital into symbolic capital' (Chouliaraki and Fairclough 1999: 101). Chouliaraki and Fairclough name other forms of capital as economic, social and cultural. Capital refers to the resources at one's disposal in society as an expression of one's capacity to act in the context of identity. Identity here is being able to act; what can I do rather than who am I? It could be argued that linguistic capital is itself a cultural capital in terms of the language type one uses – be this a high-prestige standard variation of a national language or a globally powerful language. Language is indeed an internal semiotic system but it is also connected to the user through the social system and is, as such, mediated by relations of prestige and power. Hasan (2005) argues that language as a social practice is inscribed with social relations, social divisions and hierarchies. According to Hasan 'standard language is simply "the measure of its domination"', (2005: 293) and standard official language normalizes the dominant linguistic habitus. She goes on to define 'habitus', a term conceptualized by Bourdieu (1977), as a set of linguistic structural dispositions shaping the way in which the individual speaks. Habitus provides then the social conditions for language use. People speak from the position they occupy in society and their utterances are shaped by the social structures of their experience.

Chouliaraki and Fairclough underpin habitus with the notion of 'Field', again drawing upon Bourdieu, defined as a social order in which capital is distributed and composed in terms of a mix between economic, social and cultural. Examples of 'field' would be education, politics, sport, television, advertising and marketing which provide for the wider orders of discourse which shape individual and group habitus in vocabulary, grammar and ways of constructing utterances. Fields connected to powerful socio-economics, cultures and prestige account for powerful languages and standard dialects of power.

However Hasan (2005) criticizes Bourdieu for making over-deterministic connections of causality between language and socio-economy. She accuses Bourdieu of only regarding the external value of language conferred by political economy and undervaluing the inward composition of language in terms of linguistic construction of meaning from the inner semantic possibilities. Of course language has both the inward-facing semantic possibilities for the construction of meaning through lexicogrammar and the outer features of sociocultural agency for the actualization of meaning which are both combined in SFL. It would therefore also be wrong to regard language as disconnected from external social structures and geo-political discourses as though language were simply a self-contained and autonomous unit.

Conclusion

Language and identity exist on many different levels. Chomsky (2009) points out that the essential difference between humans and animals is 'exhibited most clearly by human language' and by the ability 'to form new statements which express new thoughts and which are appropriate to new situations' (2009: 59). Language then encompasses a generic human identity. Chomsky refers to a Cartesian view, which proposes that this identity is based on reason rather than on physiological attributes. This means that the biological functions which allow humans to emit speech sounds do not account for the rational and creative content of spoken language. Language goes beyond basic stimulus–response mechanistic communication characterized by animals. Humans have a capacity to create language which is not necessarily based on the immediacy of need. Chomsky states as follows: '. . . human language is free from stimulus control and does not serve a merely communicative function, but is rather an instrument for the free expression of thought and for appropriate response to new situations' (2009: 65). Chomsky furthermore points out that freedom from instinct underpins human rationality. This means that language-identity is characterized by reflection rather than instinct. This echoes work from the completely different language–identity paradigm of Vygotsky. Vygotsky (1986) argues that higher order thinking is impossible without language. Of course, Vygotsky argues that language-thought comes from the social world, from within intersubjectivity, before penetrating the individual mind. Cartesian linguistics proposes, however, that the inner mind houses its own rationality and rational templates for meaning. Linguistic human identity, in the Chomskyan model, possesses therefore an a priori nature rather than a Vygotskian sociocultural nature. This means that language already has a rational, ideational template within the mind even before any particular language is learnt. This inner linguistic template then needs to be activated by actual language in the outer world. Language is therefore 'acquired' rather than actively learnt. Identity, from this perspective, is characterized by never learning completely new knowledge but learning what we already know. Notions of identity are essentialist within language, in having been already created for a pre-existing knowledge which only needs to be uncovered.

Sociocultural perspectives on language and identity view identity differently, as constructed by human agency through language and discourse. Saussurean linguistics are significant in this perspective in disconnecting the signifier from the signified. This meant that words signify something by conventional agreement rather than by a priori necessity. The meaning no longer resides in the word or sentence but in the conventional social agreement on usage. Language then tells us more about our own identities rather than about signified objects. It is with Saussurean structuralism that discourse eventually becomes possible, constituting our sociocultural identities through language and sign.

Objects are not 'there' in themselves but are social constructs created by the language we use.

The crucial issue within the discursive model of language is the issue of whether identity rests on free will or is determined. Are we totally within the large language and semiotic discourses, as in the Foucauldian model, or is identity co-constructed by ourselves in a social constructivist dialectic with these powerful discourses? The former seems totalizing and deterministic, whereas the latter gives us some measure of free will.

Fairclough and Chouliaraki (1999) and, before them Halliday (1978), propose a unified linguistic theory of SFL which acknowledges human agency and the relationship between the social world and lexicogrammar. Discourse is only one social practice among many, and individuals, through discourse analysis, have the agency to interrogate the discourses they visit. SFL provides the linguistic theory and rationale for such an analysis.

We see then that different aspects of identity are shaped by different models of language.

The more generic facets of human identity are contained in grammatical structures such as gender, subject/object identities, singular and plural, formal and informal etc. The more interactive and intersubjective language becomes, in the encounter with the social world, the more identity itself becomes personalized in the semiotic-social dialectic. Here, identity is less generic and more particular, located in ideological settings. Identity is at its most particular and personal in interactive social situations, such as work, school and family, where individuals actively negotiate their multiple identities or subjectivities as they move within and between different linguistic contexts, lexicogrammars and discourses.

References

Bakhtin, M. (1981), *The Dialogic Imagination: Four Essays,* ed. M. Holquist. Austin: University of Texas.
Blackledge, A. (2005), *Discourse and Power in a Multilingual World.* Amsterdam/Philadephia: John Benjamins Publishing Company.
Bourdieu, P. (1977), *Outline of a Theory of Practice.* Cambridge: Cambridge University Press.
Chomsky, N. (1975), *Reflections on Language.* New York: Pantheon Books.
—(2009), *Cartesian Linguistics: A Chapter in the History of Rationalist Thought.* Cambridge: Cambridge University Press.

Chouliaraki, L. and Fairclough, N. (1999), *Discourse in Late Modernity: Rethinking Critical Discourse Analysis*. Edinburgh: Edinburgh University Press.

Clark, R. and Gieve, S. N. (2006), 'On the discursive construction of "The Chinese Learner"'. *Language, Culture and Curriculum* 19(1): 54–73.

Derrida, J. (1967), *Of Grammatology*. Baltimore: John Hopkins University Press.

Descartes, R. (2008), *Meditations on First Philosophy*, trans. M. Moriarty. Oxford: Oxford University Press.

Edwards, R. (1998), 'Mapping, locating and translating: A discursive approach to professional development', *Studies in Continuing Education* 20(1): 1–23.

Edwards, R. and Usher, R. (1994), *Post-modernism and Education*. London: Routledge.

Fairclough, N. (1989), *Language and Power*. London/New York: Longman.

Foucault, M. (1972), *The Archeology of Knowledge*. London: Routledge.

Halliday, M. A. K. (1978), *Language as Social Semiotic: The Social Interpretation of Language and Meaning*. London: Edward Arnold.

Hasan, R. (2005), *Language, Society and Consciousness*. London: Eqinox.

Heidegger, M. (1993), *Basic Writings*. New York: Routledge.

Kant, E. (1993), *The Critique of Pure Reason*, ed. Vasilis Politis. London: Everyman.

Kilpert, D. (2003), 'Getting the full picture: A reflection on the work of M. A. K. Halliday'. *Language Sciences* 25: 159–209.

Norton, B. (2000), *Identity and Language Learning: Gender, Ethnicity and Educational Change*. London: Longman.

Rayment – Pickard, H. (2003), *Impossible God: Derrida's Theology; Transcending Boundaries in Philosophy and Theology*. Aldershot: Ashgate Publishing Ltd.

Saussure, F. de (1966), *Course in General Linguistics*. New York: McGraw-Hill.

Vygotsky, L. S. (1962), *Thought and Language*. Cambridge, MA: MIT Press.

—(1986), *Thought and Language*. Cambridge, MA: MIT Press.

Wertsch, J. V. (1991), *Voices of the Mind: A Sociocultural Approach to Mediated Action*. Cambridge, MA: Harvard University Press.

3

How Language Shapes Social Perception

Philippe Chassy

> ### Editor's Introduction
>
> Philippe Chassy discusses the Sapir–Whorf Hypothesis that social reality can only be accessed through language. Within language the foundation for this reality is the formation of concepts. Concepts are formed through the vocabulary and grammar of language and contain sociocultural realities. These realities, formed through language, change from language to language and therefore they cannot be accurately mapped on to each other in translation. Philippe demonstrates this empirically in the way different languages and cultures construct their own numbering systems and therefore different ways of conceptualizing number.

Introduction

Social groups often use symbols (logos, banners) to claim their identity. The symbols identify members within the group and state publicly the group identity to the outside world. Yet, an essential marker of one's group identity is the words used to communicate social realities. Language, conceived as a functional inheritance of a civilization's history, not only reflects the identity of the individual but also constrains the perception of social realities. The perceptual filters superimposed by language on social realities bias how individuals build a representation of the situation. This idea, expressed very early by Sapir and Whorf, has been extensively investigated by psychologists for more than 50 years. In this chapter, I will attempt to recast the insights of the two leading psycholinguists by exposing a new, data-driven view on the question. Evidence from spatial and numerical cognitions will be used to illustrate how language filters can impair intergroup communication. The ensuing discussion will focus on the evidence from social psychology showing how identity-related linguistic filters generate conflicts between groups.

Linguistic relativity

Whether language shapes our perception of reality has been debated for centuries. The question that lies behind this is whether our description and understanding of reality are accurate. If different languages provide a different access to reality, it might be that no language is able to provide an accurate picture of it. Our perception of reality would thus be systematically biased. Two pioneers in linguistics, Edward Sapir and Benjamin Lee Whorf, have put forth the idea that we access reality solely through language (Sapir 1929; Whorf 1956). In the words of Sapir (1929): 'Human beings do not live in the objective world alone, nor alone in the world of social activity as ordinarily understood, but are very much at the mercy of the particular language which has become the medium of expression for their society' (209–10). The ideas of Sapir on linguistic relativity have been taken up and developed by Whorf (1956) in his work comparing English and a language called Hopi. The evidence has led Whorf to postulate that language does not only distort but literally shapes our understanding of the world. Such a bold statement has been the focus of intense research for over half a century. In its strict interpretation, it implies that our perception of the world would then be limited to the tools that language offers to us. We would be blind to aspects of reality that cannot be captured by language. This interpretation of Whorf's statement will be referred to as the strict relativistic hypothesis. A softer interpretation is that under some circumstances, there is an interaction between language and perception. Language would distort but not undermine our perception of the world. This interpretation will be referred to as the soft relativistic hypothesis. The present chapter will evaluate the validity of both hypotheses. We will finally discuss how language contributes to identity.

A cognitive stance on the question of language will inform about which mechanisms underpin language processing and so will enable identification of potential sources for language-dependent differences in the perception of reality. The cognitive architecture presented in Figure 3.1 will serve as the framework to understand how language contributes to our understanding of reality. We can

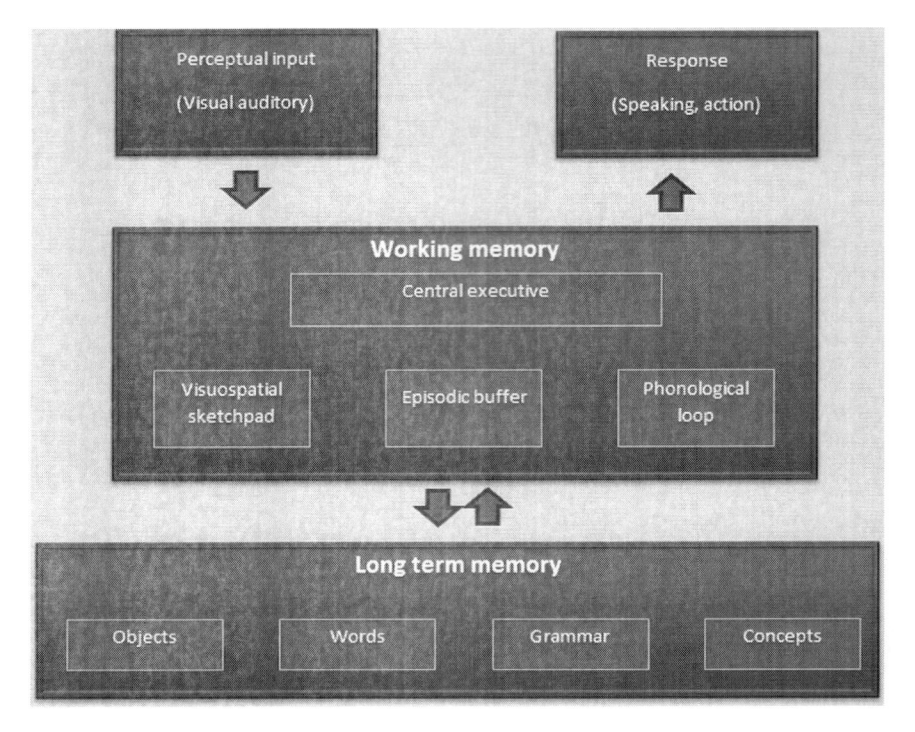

Figure 3.1 Schematic architecture of the human mind.

distinguish two forms of memory. One form, termed working memory, actually refers to the ability to keep information active and to manipulate it. For example, when we need to keep in mind a new phone number to dial it, it is working memory that keeps active the memory trace of this new information. It is in this psychological space that reality is interpreted. Working memory is made of four components (Baddeley 2003). One component is the phonological loop. Its role is to hold verbal information active and to transform this information upon request. The second component is the visuospatial sketchpad. It serves the same function for visuospatial information: maintaining and transforming mental images. A third component, termed the episodic buffer, integrates the information from the phonological loop and the visuospatial sketchpad to provide conscious experience. The fourth component is a supervising system called the central executive. It is in charge of several processes, including regulating the information flow among the various components of working memory.

The second form, termed long-term memory, is the repository of our knowledge. Squire (2004) has provided a taxonomy based on the properties of knowledge. He distinguishes declarative from non-declarative knowledge.

The latter refers to what is known but cannot be verbalized. Riding a bike is a classic example of such form of knowledge. Explaining to someone else how to ride a bike does not actually teach them how to ride a bike. Declarative knowledge refers to information that can be verbalized. It is here that we find all the knowledge that is associated with language. Figure 3.1 shows the various elements of declarative memory that play a role in language processing. The concept is the actual semantic content, a word is used to refer to it and grammar is the set of rules used to combine words and thus concepts.

The world is understood by accessing semantic information encapsulated in concepts. A concept in its simplest form is an internal representation of a class of objects. Let us consider, for example, the concept of 'chair'. The concept encapsulates all the elements that contribute to make a chair what it is and also includes all the attributes of a chair. When I see or hear about a chair, the concept is activated in my memory, and all features and attributes are accessible. Concepts are retrieved from memory to interpret perceptual input or contribute to the production of a sentence. For example, the sentence 'the dog is running' will activate in memory two key concepts that will contribute to its understanding: the one of *dog* and the one of *running*. Once retrieved from memory, these concepts will be integrated following grammar rules so as to reflect their relationship. Another sentence like '*men and women are equal*' will activate the concept of '*men*', '*women*' and '*equality*' in the listener. *Equality* is an abstract concept since it does not refer to a class of physical objects. Abstract concepts are used to create mental representations of realities that are beyond the grasp of direct perception. Concepts, whether referring to concrete or abstract objects, are used as bricks to reconstruct a representation of reality. It is through this lens that we understand the world. These concepts are more likely to display interindividual variance since they do not refer to an object that would limit interpretations. Since concepts are learnt, we can expect that the same reality can be understood or formalized by different concepts.

Spatial cognition refers to the ability to process spatial information. Often, it is about navigating in a new environment or remembering locations. From the point of view of cognitive neuroscience, spatial information is processed by a brain region called the hippocampus (Broadbent et al. 2004). This region has been shown to create spatial maps within minutes of exploration of a new environment. Since this anatomical structure is common to all individuals, regardless of their culture, it is not expected that individuals would show variation in the perception and description of space. Yet, striking differences in describing spatial relations have been demonstrated.

Figure 3.2 A public garden of Toulouse, France. (source: www.Toulouse-Tourisme.com).

Figure 3.2 is a photograph taken in a public garden of the city of Toulouse (South of France). How would you describe the position of the bridge with respect to the pavilion? Personally, I would say that the bridge is at the left of the pavilion. This description would sound appropriate for a huge portion of the planet but not for all individuals. In some communities it would sound incorrect. One of the communities using a different spatial frame is located in the north of Australia. The inhabitants of the Arrernte region speak Arandic. In this language, you describe the location of objects in cardinal coordinates. That is, you use two axes, north-south and east-west, to tell where something is located. Consequently, if a member of this community were to find himself or herself in this garden for a visit, he or she would likely describe the bridge as standing east of the Pavillon. Similarly, should a bird land on the shoulder of a person, members of the Arandic community would describe the bird as being on the 'north shoulder' rather than on the left shoulder. We can also describe things with respect to cardinal coordinates in English and all languages that belong to the Western culture. What is interesting is that we do not do it; otherwise we might confuse our interlocutor. Let us consider the following example: 'to find the closest metro station you need to walk northbound for 50 metres and then turn east, walk eastbound 20 m and then turn south'. It would take some time to actually make sense of the message by reframing the spatial relationship in our coordinates (i.e. left, right, etc . . .). It implies that the members of these communities not only describe space with a different reference but also that their representation of space might actually differ insofar as they frame spatial relationships in a rigid cardinal system.

The question that is raised at this point is whether a difference in the language used to describe spatial relations reflects a difference in understanding reality. A series of studies have been conducted by Pederson et al. (1998) to explore the spatial cognition of several communities using different spatial referencing systems. The central idea of the experiment is neat: the participants will be shown a sequence of ordered objects and they will have to retrieve from memory where the objects are standing with respect to each other and their location in space. Between exposure to the stimulus and recall, the frame will be rotated by 180 degrees. To illustrate this idea let us have a look at Figure 3.3.

Figure 3.3 shows the sequences of three objects ordered along a north–south axis. The circle implements the position of an observer who is standing at the left of the objects. For a Westerner the verbal description would be that A is at the left of B, which itself stands at the left of C. For a member of the Arrernte community, the objects A, B and C are aligned from north to south. So far, if an Englishman or an Arandic speaker reports the position of objects to another member of their community, no differences will be noted. But, let us assume that the observer makes a U-turn. Then for an Englishman, the objects A, B and C will still be next to one another with object A standing at the left and object C standing at the right. If we draw that on a frame, we find that the disposition of objects along the north–south axis has been inverted as compared to its original location. For an Arandic speaker, the location of objects will be the same, with A standing north and C south. Hence, after the observer has moved, the distribution of object will change for an English speaker and not for an Arandic speaker. Pederson et al. (1998) have actually carried

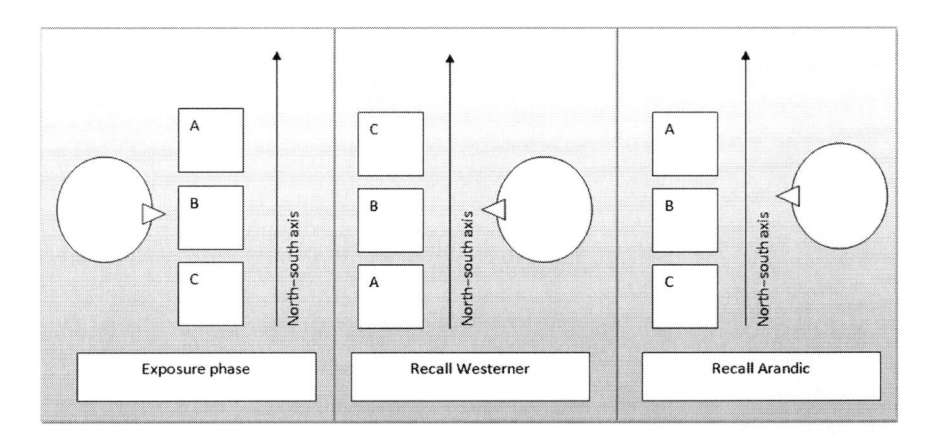

Figure 3.3 Experimental paradigm.

out this experiment with animals as objects. The authors have demonstrated that communities using a relative frame (here Dutch and Japanese speakers) memorize objects differently than communities using a cardinal frame (e.g. Arandic). The result of this framing of information in spatial memory is that members of the two communities will disagree on the arrangement of objects after the 180 degree rotation has taken place. English speakers will think that Arandic speakers do not set things properly, with A standing at the left. However, Arandic speakers will think that English speakers do not understand since A is supposed to be the northern object. This is a good illustration of why different communities might sometime disagree on the description of events, with all communities being honest!

The example of spatial cognition unravels a key weakness in the strict interpretation of the relativistic hypothesis. It is not language that is the issue but the framing in the inner eye. We can use another format than words to produce thoughts. Shepard and Metzler (1971) have demonstrated that rotating a shape mentally takes a time that is proportional to the angle of rotation. That is, it takes more time to rotate the shape by 120 degree than 60 degree. The ability to rotate mentally objects actually relies on information coded in a visuospatial format. Processing information in this format does not require the use of verbal information. The visuospatial format is the format used to process geometrical problems, or for representing chess position in the mind. A study by Kosslyn et al. (1978) has demonstrated that the time taken to travel virtual spaces (e.g. on a map of an imaginary island) is proportional to the distance it represents. This constituted another source of early evidence pointing towards a visuospatial system separated from the verbal system. Subsequently, functional magnetic resonance imaging research has shown that the neural networks in charge of processing 'virtual space' are the same as those involved in the actual perception of space (Ganis et al. 2004). When information is in visuospatial format, verbal information plays a minimal role. It merely translates the result of the visuospatial operation to communicate it to another party but does not play a role in the processing of the information.

We have shown so far that language is not the only format in which individuals can think. Moreover, we have uncovered that words and internal images interact. That words have a striking capacity of influencing our internal representation of events is shown by a series of studies relating to eye-witness testimony. Since eye witnesses have long been considered to provide evidence central to convicting suspects in a crime, psychologists have tested whether their memory of events is as reliable as the jury supposes. Elisabeth Loftus conducted a series of experiments that were designed to test the stability of the memory trace. In one experiment, the participants were shown a car at a crossroad. Later on, the participants were asked whether they remembered the stop sign or the traffic light. Still later on, the participants were asked to retrieve from memory the image of the car at the crossroads and to describe it verbally. Interestingly, those who had been asked about the stop sign were more likely to report a stop sign, and those participants who were asked about the traffic light were more likely to report one. In other words, asking a question that includes false information has distorted the memory. The words have basically invaded the image. In another study, Loftus and Palmer (1974) showed slides of car crashes and asked the participants to estimate the speed of the cars. 'They compared the estimated speed given by participants, who were asked a series of questions regarding how fast the cars were going when they hit each other.' The authors designed the questions with a variety of words (collided, bumped, smashed) and found out that the impression of speed was influenced by the verb in the question.

The studies reviewed so far have made us aware that what seems to be a difference in language is sometimes a difference in concept. How well I understand something is reflected in the language, but it is not language itself that makes the difference between two perceptions. There are subtle links between language and the understanding of reality.

Our understanding of reality consists mostly in retrieving elaborated records, termed concepts, from memory. These concepts are used to interpret the perceptual input. The more elaborated the concept, the better the understanding of the person.

Numbers in the minds

Counting natural numbers like 1, 2, 3, 4, 5, 6, 7, 8 and 9 is one of the basic steps in education. Since we all need the numerals to carry out a wide range of tasks, it seems natural to us to know the numerals. But is it that natural? Numbers and their mental manipulation are the result of years of training. As usual, if something is learnt then it is likely that it can display interindividual variation due to differences in familial and educational settings. A society that has developed independently from the one using Arabic numerals or a society that does not require as much mathematics as current Western societies might not rely on a similar numeric scale. Our mathematical system is base 10. Hence, 84 refers to 8 times 10 units plus 4. It has been shown that the community of Yoruba in Nigeria uses a different counting structure (Mann 1887). In Yoruba 16 is not 10 + 6 but rather 20 − 4. It has been argued that this different system of counting shows that natural numbers are a cultural construct (Watson 1990). For reasons I will expose later, I have to challenge this view. Actually, this base of 20 has some resemblance with how numbers were sporadically counted in France during the seventeenth century. In his drama *l'Avare*, Molière writes 'six-vingts' (i.e. six-twenty) to mean 120 (Moliere 1668/2009). In French, even today, 80 is spelt 'quatre-vingt', which literally means 'four-twenty'. In line with this counting system, the French for 94 is 'quatre-vingt-quatorze', which translates literally as 'four-twenty-fourteen'! Strikingly, other French-speaking countries such as Switzerland and Belgium do spell 94 as *nonante quatre* (i.e. ninety four). If the words used to describe natural numbers differ from one language to the other, they still represent the same quantities. That is, the notion of twenty is the same in, say, English and Yoruba. That the base is different does not influence much the representation of numbers. Computers use a base of 8 or 16 and have no problem computing much faster and with greater accuracy than human beings. That is, whether we talk about eighty or 'four-twenty', we deal with the same quantity, and communication is possible. The differences in numerical systems become striking when they reflect a difference in conception of quantities.

The Mundurucu have a system denoting one, two and . . . many! That is, if you ask a person how many children he or she has, you will get one, two or many as an answer. This striking counting system has been deeply investigated by the anthropologist Pierre Pica (Pica et al. 2004). To what extent does such a numerical system impair communication between civilizations? The issue relates to a fundamental question in mathematical cognition: the internal representation of magnitudes. Do Mundurucu members make the difference between, let say, 20 and 25, with the same accuracy as mathematically educated people do? The answer might seem obvious at first; we are inclined to say yes since they will notice that a pack of 25 apples has more apples than a pack of 20. Yet, from the point of view of internal representations, things might not be as clear. Actually, the degree of discrimination between quantities should not be as tuned for Mundurucus as it is for Westerners (Dehaene et al. 2008). Members of another community, called the Piraha, exhibit similar features in their mathematical system (Everett 2005).

The neural mechanisms underpinning these differences in representing natural numbers mentally are informative of why such differences emerge. The evidence suggests that numbers are represented as space in the brain. The evidence from neuroimaging experiments shows that a subsection of the parietal lobe, the intraparietal sulcus (IPS henceforth), codes for quantities (Nieder and Dehaene 2009). It is believed that quantities are coded by assemblies of neurons that are tuned with experience to respond to natural numbers. This is likely to be the result of neural plasticity, a process whereby the neurons readjust their weight through dynamical (short-term) or structural (long-term) changes. As research in developmental psychology informs us, the process of mastering the basics of mathematics takes years. Several studies have shown that learning natural numbers and mastering the notion of quantities induce changes in neural dynamics. These mathematical basics are important since they potentially underpin the emergence of abstract mathematical concepts, as demonstrated by the fact that the IPS is recruited when participants process abstract quantities such as negative numbers (Chassy and Grodd 2012). If we consider that some communities do not have words to describe numbers higher than two, should we conclude that they cannot master counting beyond three? That is unlikely. What is probable is that the capacity of processing elementary arithmetic operations is impaired. The fact is that the notion of number depends on a system that represents quantities increasing linearly as a logarithmic progression. This basically means that, for a non-educated individual, the difference between 20 and 19 is smaller than the difference between 3 and 2. The representation of quantity is distorted. So, even if the members of these communities do discriminate high quantities, it is possible that their internal representations of these quantities are not very accurate. Consequently, communicating efficiently on abstract mathematical concepts might be impossible.

Language and identity

Concepts in their network

Interpretation of reality is made through the retrieval of concepts to interpret the data. We have seen a case wherein words mask a difference in concept. That is, non-educated individuals have more limited mathematical capabilities because the notion of number is not as accurate as it is for trained individuals. Under some circumstances, the concepts are shared across two cultures, but the connotations might differ slightly, distorting the interpretation of the message. This distortion stems from the organization of concepts in long-term memory. Collins and Quillian (1969) have formalized the structure of long-term memory as a network wherein concepts are linked by hierarchical relationships. For example, the concept of 'canary' belongs to the category of 'bird' but 'bird' does not belong to 'canary'. In this perspective, if you see a canary the concept of *canary* will be activated and the knowledge about the concept *bird* will also be activated. However, if you think about birds, the concept *bird* will be activated but the concept of *canary* will not, since it is subordinate to the one of bird. Quickly, evidence has accumulated to show that semantic memory is a 'scale free' network (Collins and Loftus 1975). Any concept can be connected to any other concept. Hence, the semantic content of a concept and the concept's connections depend upon the experience of the individual. A problem can appear when different cultures are trying to communicate: the fact that the set of connections of one concept in one language is different from the set of connections for the same concept in another language leads to different interpretations. Armstrong (2004) has conducted an interesting study on the translation of the show *The Simpsons* from English to French. Analysing the impact of the connotations associated with the accents of the characters, Armstrong shows that the actual inferences about the characters might differ between a US and a French audience. Mr Burns has an upper-class accent in both countries. In the American version it is close to a British accent, which has specific connotations linked to US history. In French it is upper class, but the historical baggage is not associated with the accent. Since the concepts connected to the posh accent in the US listener are different from those in a French listener, each country makes different inferences about the nature of Mr Burns and thus interprets the show in slightly different ways.

Another overarching memory structure, the proposition, codes whether statements (semantically connected concepts) are true or false. Many propositions are stored, and the cognitive apparatus has the power to examine new propositions. For example the sentence, 'The car of John is so fast that it can fly' can be examined and rejected. What makes interpretation possible is the parsing of the sentence into a grammar structure. Syntax is the way we know how concepts are supposed to be related to each other. The fact that syntax has the ability to connect concepts underlines the fact that not all words in a sentence have an equal value. Some words refer to concepts, some embody the connections between concepts and other words are less useful. An example of a word of a lesser importance is the article. For a speaker of French, the word car is feminine (*une voiture*) but for a Spanish speaker it is masculine (*un coche*). These differences between articles do not impair the understanding of the situation since the words do not carry meaning. When differences appear on words of semantic relevance, then communication might be impaired. In Spain, you say good afternoon sometimes up to 20:00, while in France the concept of afternoon starts at 12:00 but finishes around 18:00 or 19:00, when evening starts. Hence if a French speaker tells a Spanish speaker that they should meet at the beginning of the evening there might be confusion about the time.

Language as claim for identity

The previous sections have showed that language differences can reflect a difference in framing information or in conceptual understanding. Such evidence constitutes a demonstration that reality is understood through concepts. This section is devoted to showing that the same mechanisms are actually at work when an individual builds his or her identity within a group.

Human beings are gregarious animals: They need to be part of a group. The group provides both security and also an identity. By adopting the group's identity, its values, its codes, the individual will perceive the world through the concepts that underpin the group. The social world is then going to be structured by these concepts. In line with this, the members of a group tend to align their thoughts with the group's norm, and those who will not run the risk of being ostracized. Since groups set norms that the members have adopted, the members of the same group are perceived as good. For the same reasons, the members of other groups are perceived homogeneously as less desirable. This is a foundation for identity. Groups require members to share the same values. One of them is, of course, the language in use. Language carries more than just symbols: it also carries the values on which a group or a society is built. It is thus not surprising that, to claim an identity, often groups put forth a different language. History is full of examples wherein groups have claimed their identity through the use of a different language. Two cases can be compared to see how identity and language are linked and used for political purposes.

The first case will be the one of Occitan. What is now France geographically, politically and culturally was in the eleventh century a series of counties, one of them being the kingdom of France. In the Paris region, people spoke a language that was to become French. But, in many places, other languages were used, for example Occitan in Toulouse. At that time, there were regular wars between the Count of Toulouse and the king of France. Like many other regions, Toulouse has been conquered or bought by the king of France along the centuries. Yet, in the middle of the nineteenth century, several millions of inhabitants were still unable to communicate in French. In 1881, the French minister Jules Ferry organized primary schools across France. He also made the school compulsory and free! The point was obviously to make everyone speak in French. The childhood memories of Marcel Pagnol (1895–1974) are full of examples where people have problem mastering French and usually communicate in a local language (Pagnol 2004a, 2004b). Many dialects have been erased by school training. Today, a tiny minority of inhabitants speaks Occitan fluently. The local TV channel broadcasts in French, and publications, whether classic or academic, are exclusively in French.

The other case I am examining is the one of Catalan and Castellano (the actual name for Spanish). Catalan is spoken in the south-west of France and in Catalonia, the autonomic community located north-east of Spain. Catalan is a language that has been spoken for centuries in the region. It is now an official language of the autonomic community. Teachings at the University of Barcelona can be in Catalan. Similarly, Catalan is spoken in the streets, the shops, it is present in official documents, and university textbooks are in Catalan. General Francisco Franco took power after a cruel civil war (1936–39). The city of Barcelona was one of the last republican bastions to oppose resistance to the army of the nationalists. After his victory, supported by Hitler's armies, Franco used repression to destroy the Catalan identity. One of the first decisions he made was to banish the language from official documents and communications in business. All documents and communications were then in Castellano. Catalan towards the end of Franco's reign was more tolerated. The language survived and, when Franco died, the identity of the Catalans regained its force. In this context, one understands that the rivalry between F.C. Barcelona and the Real Madrid goes far beyond the pitch. Nowadays, the autonomic community of Catalonia is strong and powerful. It is innovative in science and is financially sound. It is thus not a surprise that the Catalan government thinks about separation: the very hallmark of national identity!

The differences between the French and Spanish examples are striking. Where the local language has been erased or at least reduced to a cultural folklore, the local identity has been lost. I do not claim that it is the elimination of the language that has caused the elimination of the identity, but we can notice that they are concomitant. In Spain, the Catalans have known how to protect their language and their cultural heritage in difficult times, and now the Catalan identity is very strong.

Language as indicator of identity

Language is often used to claim a group identity. For example, language has long been known to be a marker of social status (Romaine 2002). Indeed, having a higher rank in society is reflected by a different way of speaking. Interestingly, groups sometimes purposefully change words to accentuate their distinction from other groups. Typically, teenagers use words that will not be understood by their parents to mark their difference. This use of language is very common. Yet it has a perverse effect. It is that some dialects or accents might lead people to classify their interlocutors into categories based solely on the language or the accent. It is here that stereotypes meet language. Kinzler and DeJesus (2012) have interviewed children aged 5 or 6 about the northern and southern accents in the United States. They did not really find noticeable differences. The children are simply too young to categorize people according to accents. They repeated the experimental procedure with children aged around 10. Then, the children have attributed the label of nice to the southern accents and of smart to the northern accent. Here, we can see that language properties (accent) were associated with concepts ('nice' vs. 'smart') that led the children to judge the temperament of the speaker. What is striking is that the stereotype is shared by both children from the north (Illinois) and the south (Tennessee) of the United States. The words used to classify speakers denote a structuration of reality, here the psychological attributes of people based on their pronunciation of English. Such evidence supports the view that we use language to identify the groups to which a speaker belongs.

Conclusions

Now that we have reviewed the evidence of how language contributes to our perception of reality, we are in a position to make a judgement about the Whorfian hypothesis. We have shown early in this chapter that many differences attributed to language are actually differences in concepts, be it spatial or numerical cognition. When confronted with simple, clear situations individuals of different language perceive the same reality. It is not the perception of reality per se that is changed by language but how it is reconstructed. The example of spatial cognition has demonstrated that the same situation can be described by using different frames of reference. This piece of discussion has also shown that the coding in memory is different and thus that the reconstruction of the memory is going to differ. The discussion about numerical cognition has taught us that the development of cognition and of the language that goes with it might sometimes hide subtle but measurable differences in how the world is perceived. In both cases, it is a difference in internal representation that induces a difference in language description but not the contrary. However we have seen instances wherein language actually affects the perception of others. It is here that we can lend some credit to Whorf's view that language shapes reality. By using one word instead of another, as we have seen politicians do, we can introduce a subtle nuance in the person's representation of the situation. We will not determine the person's thought, as the strong version of the Whorfian hypothesis would suggest, nor will we change the set of values that underpins the person's way of thinking, but we definitely can orient thinking. In this sense, and within the limits set in this chapter, we can say that language is a marker of identity and also contributes to shape our social perception of the self and of others.

References

Armstrong, N. (2004), 'Voicing "The Simpsons" from English to French: A story of variable success'. *The Journal of Specialised Translation* 2: 97–109.

Baddeley, A. D. (2003), 'Working memory: Looking back and looking forward'. *Nature Reviews Neuroscience* 4: 829–39.

Broadbent, N. J., Squire, L. R. and Clark, R. E. (2004), 'Spatial memory, recognition memory, and the hippocampus'. *Proceedings of the National Academy of Sciences* 101(40): 14515–20.

Chassy, P. and Grodd, W. (2012), 'Comparison of quantities: Core and format-dependent regions as revealed by fMRI'. *Cerebral Cortex* 22(6): 1420–30.

Collins, A. M. and Loftus, E. F. (1975), 'A spreading-activation theory of semantic memory'. *Psychological Review* 82(6): 407–28.

Collins, A. M. and Quillian, M. R. (1969), 'Retrieval time from semantic memory'. *Journal of Verbal Learning and Verbal Behavior* 9: 240–7.

Dehaene, S., Izard, C., Spelke, E. and Pica, P. (2008), 'Log or Linear? Distinct Intuitions of the Number Scale in Western and Amazonian Indigene Cultures'. *Science* 320: 1217–20.

Everett, D. (2005), 'Cultural Constraints on Grammar and Cognition in Pirahã: Another Look at the Design Features of Human Language'. *Current Anthropology* 46: 621–46.

Ganis, G., Thompson, W. L. and Kosslyn, S. M. (2004), 'Brain areas underlying visual mental imagery and visual perception: An fMRI study'. *Cognitive Brain Research* 20: 226–41.

Kinzler, K. D. and DeJesus, J. M. (2012), 'Northern=smart and Southern=nice: The development of accent attitudes in the United States'. *Quarterly Journal of Experimental Psychology* 66(6): 1146–58.

Kosslyn, S. M., Ball, T. M. and Reiser, B. J. (1978), 'Visual images preserve metric spatial information: Evidence from studies of image scanning'. *Journal of Experimental Psychology: Human Perception and Performance* 4(1): 47–60.

Loftus, E. F. and Palmer, J. C. (1974), 'Reconstruction of auto-mobile destruction: An example of the interaction between language and memory'. *Journal of Verbal Learning and Verbal Behaviour* 13: 585–9.

Mann, A. (1887), 'Notes on the numeral system of the Yoruba Nation'. *The Journal of the Anthropological Institute of Great Britain and Ireland* 16: 59–64.

Moliere (1668/2009), *L'avare*. Paris, France: Garnier Flamarion.

Nieder, A. and Dehaene, S. (2009), 'Representation of number in the brain'. *Annual Review of Neuroscience* 32: 185–208.

Pagnol, M. (2004a), *La gloire de mon pere*. Paris: De Fallois, Collection Fortunio.

—(2004b), *Le chateau de ma mere*: Fortunio.

Pederson, E., Danziger, E., Wilkins, D. G., Levinson, S. C., Kita, S. and Senft, G. (1998), 'Semantic typology and spatial conceptualization'. *Language* 74(3): 557–89.

Pica, P., Lemer, C., Izard, V. and Dehaene, S. (2004), 'Exact and approximate arithmetic in an Amazonian indigene group'. *Science* 306: 499–503.

Romaine (2002), 'Language and social class', in N. J. Smelser and P. B. Baltes (eds), *Encyclopedia of the Social and Behavioral Sciences*. Oxford: Pergamon Press, pp. 8308–12.

Sapir, E. (1929), 'The status of linguistics as a science'. *Language* 4: 207–14.

Shepard, R. N. and Metzler, J. (1971), 'Mental rotations of three dimensional objects'. *Science* 171: 701–3.

Squire, L. R. (2004), 'Memory systems of the brain: A brief history and current perspectives'. *Neurobiology of Learning and Memory* 82: 171–7.

Watson, H. (1990), 'Investigating the Social Foundations of Mathematics: Natural Number in Culturally Diverse Forms of Life'. *Social Studies of Science* 20(2): 283–312.

Whorf, B. L. (1956), 'Some verbal categories of Hopi', in J. B. Carroll (ed.), *Language, Thought, and Reality: Selected Writings of Benjamin Lee Whorf*. Cambridge, MA: MIT Press, pp. 112–24.

Part Two

Languages, Discourses and Identities in the World

4

Quebec's Shift from Ethnic to Civic National Identity: Implications for Language Attitudes Among Immigrants in Montreal

Ruth Kircher

> ### Editor's Introduction
>
> Ruth Kircher's chapter focuses on language attitudes and identity issues among adolescent first- and second-generation immigrants, compared to non-immigrants, in Montreal. Specifically, the chapter examines whether Quebec's shift from an ethnic to a more civic conceptualization of national identity has led to individuals of all backgrounds sharing a social identity as Quebecers, thus considering French their common in-group language and holding positive attitudes towards it, particularly in terms of the solidarity dimension.

Introduction

Quebec is Canada's only province with a francophone rather than an anglophone majority. Much of the province is, linguistically and ethnically, relatively homogeneous. Quebec's urban centre Montreal, however, is home not only to many francophones but also to comparatively large anglophone and allophone communities (52.1 per cent, 13.5 per cent and 32.9 per cent, respectively, as well as 1.5 per cent who have both French and English as their mother tongues; Statistics Canada 2011 Census), with 'allophones' being the term used in the Quebec context to describe those whose mother tongue is a language other than

French or English. These allophones are immigrants as well as individuals of immigrant descent who tend to concentrate in the Montreal metropolitan region because it offers better economic opportunities than the rest of the province, and because it allows them to maintain the in-group networks that provide the cultural and financial support needed to adjust within the host community (Bourhis 2001). Montreal's allophones constitute a highly heterogeneous group that comprises immigrants of different generations, individuals from diverse countries of origin and numerous ethnicities, and speakers of a vast variety of mother tongues. Many of the city's francophone and anglophone inhabitants are also immigrants or individuals of immigrant descent.

In recent decades, Quebec has undergone a shift from an ethnic to a more civic conceptualization of national identity (Oakes and Warren 2007). An ethnic national identity is based on common ancestry and shared cultural heritage, whereas a civic national identity is manifested in a common loyalty to a territory and rooted in a set of political rights, duties and values (Roshwald 2006). The issue of how Quebec's shifting conceptualization of belonging has affected the language attitudes held by Montreal's immigrant population ties in with the province's central language conflict – that is, the desire of the francophones to protect their mother tongue from the threat of English. As a consequence of Montreal's linguistic and ethnic diversity, the city holds a special status within Quebec and it is generally assumed that this is where the future of French in the province will be determined – and the integration of Montreal's allophone immigrants and their descendants into the francophone (rather than the anglophone) linguistic community has become a strategically significant means of stemming the long-term decline of the French-speaking population (Bourhis 2001). This integration process was induced by language legislation in the 1970s. A number of studies (e.g. Bourhis et al. 2010) have investigated the host community's acculturation orientations *towards* immigrants in the context of this shifting conceptualization of belonging in Quebec. However, the author is not aware of any studies that have researched the attitudes held *by* these immigrants and their descendants.

The purpose of this chapter is thus to begin filling this gap in the research literature by examining the attitudes that young Montreal first- and second-generation immigrants, compared to non-immigrants, hold towards French and English. Due to the close link that exists between language and social identity, attitudes towards particular languages are generally considered to be reflections of individuals' attitudes towards the speakers of those languages (Ryan et al. 1982). Based on the social psychological literature, such attitudes are here understood to comprise beliefs, feelings and behaviours (Garrett 2010). The findings of the study presented here will be discussed with regard to the two main evaluative dimensions of language attitudes, that is, status and solidarity. A language with high status is one that holds significant utilitarian value, while a language that is evaluated highly on the solidarity dimension is one that elicits feelings of attachment and belonging to a particular social group (Ryan et al. 1982). It should be noted that due to the non-representative nature of the participant sample, no claims are made regarding the generalization of this study's findings to the Montreal population at large. The aim of this work was simply to gain an insight into the attitudes of this particular participant sample, which can then serve as a basis for further, more representative research. Nevertheless, the findings can be seen as a tentative indication of how successful Quebec's language and immigration policies have been.

Following a brief overview of the socio-historical background, this chapter will describe the methodology and materials employed in the current study before presenting and discussing its results, and commenting on their implications for future policy and planning measures.

Socio-historical background

Up until the middle of the twentieth century, the vast majority of French-speaking Quebecers were *Québécois de souche*, 'old-stock' Catholic francophones who could trace their ancestry back to the regime of New France, as Quebec was called between the arrival of Jacques Cartier in 1534 and the cession of the territory to the British in 1763. The majority of francophones lived in the rural areas of the province, where they had little contact with Protestant anglophones and the English language. Even the francophones living in Montreal rarely mixed with the city's anglophones: 'French and English lived in separate areas, formed different classes, engaged in different economic activities, had different religions, different languages, and different schools and other institutions' (Heller 1985: 76). It was thus possible for the francophones to uphold an ethnic interpretation of Quebec national identity that was founded on the pillars of French descent as well as traditional Catholic – and primarily rural – values.

While Montreal's anglophones were numerically a minority, they long constituted an economic elite, which held a disproportionate number of well-paid jobs in the city's upper echelons and even controlled key sectors of the national

Canadian industry (Dickinson and Young 2003). Consequently, for a long time, Montreal anglophones could live and work exclusively in English without ever needing to learn French; the city's francophones, however, were obliged to learn and use English in order to advance economically (Levine 1997).

In the late nineteenth and early twentieth centuries, the rapid urbanization and industrialization of Quebec society made it increasingly difficult for the francophones to uphold their ideology of what is known as *la survivance*: 'a Church-based "defensive" strategy of cultural survival based on avoiding contamination by urban, English Montreal and maintaining French-Catholic purity in the homogeneous environments of rural and small-town Quebec' (Levine 1990: 33). Moreover, by the late 1950s, a new middle class of francophones had emerged in Montreal and found itself increasingly frustrated by the conditions in the city, considering linguistic assimilation an unacceptable price to pay for economic mobility. The members of this new middle class thus began to reconcile Quebec francophone identity with the realities of a modern, urban society (Dickinson and Young 2003). Yet while they rejected traditional Catholic values in favour of secularism and statism, their sense of national identity was still very firmly rooted in their shared French ancestry.

A further development that significantly shaped Quebec, and especially Montreal society in the twentieth century, was immigration. In two great waves – between 1901 and 1931, and 1945 and 1961 – Montreal became a multiethnic city. During the first decades of the century, the newcomers were primarily Italians and Eastern European Jews who moved to Quebec to escape economic and political turmoil; in the postwar period, many of the immigrants were from southern Europe and the Slavic countries, as well as Jews from all over Europe (Dickinson and Young 2003). As mentioned above, these immigrants tended to concentrate in the Montreal metropolitan region, and while some of them had either French or English as their mother tongue, most of them were allophones.[1]

While the author is not aware of any previous studies that have investigated the attitudinal differences between different generations of immigrants compared to non-immigrants in Montreal, it is possible to draw inferences from their linguistic behaviour – for, as noted above, behaviour is one of the components that constitute an attitude. At least up until the mid-1970s, the city's allophone immigrants overwhelmingly opted for English as their main language of public usage (Dickinson and Young 2003). Based on the assumption that 'the language used by the majority of allophones will be the one that is considered to be more *useful*' (Carpentier 2004: 1), this suggests that the allophone immigrants attributed more status to English than to French. This notion is supported by the fact that up until the 1970s, the majority of allophone immigrants chose English-medium education for their children: they regarded command of English as essential in order to advance economically, and English-medium schooling was the primary agency through which they prepared their children for this (Levine 1990). Overall, the allophone immigrants' linguistic behaviour up until the mid-1970s thus suggests more positive attitudes towards English, at least in terms of the status dimension.[2]

As a consequence of the majority of allophone immigrants adopting English as their new language, up until the mid-1970s, Montreal's francophone community remained essentially composed of *Québécois de souche*, and its only sources of growth were natural increase and the migration of rural francophones – whereas the anglophone community quickly turned into a multicultural and multiethnic one whose strength was bolstered significantly by the allophone immigrants (Breton 1988). Evidently, the anglicization of allophone immigrants and their descendants posed a threat to the future of French in Montreal, and thus in Quebec – particularly in the light of the precipitous plunge that the francophone birth rate had taken over the last half-century as a result of the aforementioned industrialization and urbanization (Bourhis 2001). The issue of immigrant anglicization therefore became one of the focal points of language conflict in the subsequent decades.

Before the 1960s, there had been little serious and sustained political debate about language rights in Montreal, but by the end of the decade, the language question had come to dominate the city's social and political life. This change began with what has come to be known as the Quiet Revolution, a turbulent period that was characterized by the francophones' desire to dislodge the anglophone elite and 'reconquer' Montreal as the French-speaking metropolis of Quebec (Levine 1997). Much pro-French language legislation has been implemented since then – most importantly the Charter of the French Language, commonly known as Bill 101, which in 1977 reinforced the status of French as the only official language of Quebec as well as stipulating that French was to become the main language in several areas of public life. The stipulations of Bill 101 that had the strongest impact on the allophone immigrants and their descendants were those regarding the language of education, because it became obligatory for allophone children to attend French-medium primary and secondary schools, with only few exceptions. This was effectively the beginning of the integration of allophone immigrants and their descendants into the francophone community.

Bill 101, as well as further language legislation, has aided Quebec francophones significantly in their 'reconquest' of Montreal: the city is no longer dominated – economically or linguistically – by its anglophone minority, and the integration of allophone immigrants and their descendants into the francophone community has come a long way. However, this success is fragile. Due to Quebec's proximity to the largest anglophone markets of the world, French continues to be threatened by the status that English holds as the language of socio-economic advancement in the rest of Canada and the United States. Moreover, in the context of increased globalization, French now also faces the challenge of English as the global lingua franca (Stefanescu and Georgeault 2005). The integration of allophone immigrants and their descendants into the francophone linguistic community therefore remains crucial for ensuring the future of French in Montreal, and thus in Quebec (Levine 1997).

Initially, this integration process was not unproblematic, and the ethnic diversification of the French-speaking community in Montreal that had been brought about by the stipulations of Bill 101 resulted in a culture shock – primarily because it entailed the necessity to forge a new francophone identity that encompassed not only the *Québécois de souche* but also the emerging French-speaking ethnic minority groups (Levine 1997). Yet over time, this integration gave rise to an opening up of Quebec national identity in order to accommodate the hitherto unknown ethnic pluralism among the francophones. By the beginning of the twenty-first century, things had changed so much that researchers attested 'a common will [among the population] to work towards an inclusive social project, to construct a common life space and to lower the barriers that divide Quebec society according to ethnic origin' (Gouvernement du Québec 2001: 4). It is now generally acknowledged that a shift did indeed occur from the traditional, defensive, *ethnic* conception of national identity whose basis of inclusion consisted of French ancestry as well as Catholic and rural cultural values (Breton 1988), towards a more development-oriented, inclusive and *civic* conception of national identity 'which unites people from various ethnic groups around common values and institutions' – with the French language as one of the central elements (Oakes and Warren 2007: 14).

Many allophone immigrants and their descendants have adopted French – as their main, second or third language – and they do use it in the public sphere. However, 'the majority of immigrants and their children feel it is important to know both English *and* French because they realize, as do most of the other people with whom they are in contact, that life in a modern Quebec society that is open onto the world requires knowledge of both languages. Immigrants' use of French is [thus] not as widespread as it could be' (Pagé and Lamarre 2010: 2). This suggests that while French is viewed more favourably now than it used to be, positive attitudes towards English, at least in terms of the status dimension, remain prevalent. However, evidently, the insight provided by linguistic behaviour alone is limited, and a more comprehensive understanding of the language attitudes held by Montreal's immigrants and their descendants is desirable – in terms of both the status *and* the solidarity dimension. As noted above, a language that is evaluated highly on the solidarity dimension is one that elicits feelings of attachment and belonging to a particular social group – that is, a language that 'acquires vital social meaning and comes to represent the social group with which one identifies' (Ryan et al. 1982: 9). If the shift from ethnic to civic national identity had the impact desired by the provincial government, it would be expected that Montrealers of all ethnic and migration backgrounds have a shared social identity as Quebecers, and that they hold more positive attitudes towards French on the solidarity dimension because it is their shared in-group language. The study presented here aims to find out whether this is indeed the case, as well as ascertaining young Montrealers' language attitudes on the status dimension.

Method

The methods chosen for this study were one direct and one indirect method of attitude elicitation, namely a questionnaire and a matched-guise experiment. This choice was motivated by the fact that direct and indirect methods frequently yield rather different results since they pertain to different 'levels of analysis' (Ryan et al. 1987: 1076).

The purpose of direct methods of attitude elicitation such as questionnaires is typically recognizable, and as most individuals try to put themselves in a good light, findings obtained by means of direct methods tend to reveal what is considered to be socially acceptable and desirable.

The major strength of indirect methods such as the matched-guise technique, however, lies in the elicitation of spontaneous attitudes that are much less sensitive to reflection and social desirability biases. The technique was developed by Wallace Lambert and his associates in the late 1950s (Lambert et al. 1960). In the basic set-up of a matched-guise experiment, recordings are made of a number of perfectly bilingual speakers (in this context, French and English) who each deliver the same passage of text twice, once in each of their languages. Prosodic and paralinguistic features of voice, such as pitch and speech rate, are kept constant as far as possible across the different recordings. The participants who then listen to these recordings remain unaware of the fact that they are hearing the same speakers twice, in matched guises. Instead, they are under the impression that they are listening to a series of different speakers. They do know, however, that all speakers are delivering the same message. The effects of both the voices of the speakers and their messages are thus minimized, and other potentially influential factors such as physical appearance are excluded. Using voice cues only, the participants are then asked to rate personality characteristics of the speakers on semantic scales for certain traits (such as intelligence, dependability and kindness). To avoid the influence of social desirability biases, the real purpose of the experiment is withheld. Any differences in reaction to the different recordings of the same speaker are presumed to be based on the participants' attitudes towards the different languages used. It is generally accepted that in studies of this kind, much more private reactions are revealed than in standard measures of attitudes such as questionnaires.

Ryan et al. (1987) note that if only one type of measurement is employed, it is rarely possible to make any definitive statements about language attitudes. In the present study, it was therefore decided to use a combination of these methods in the hope that a comparison of the findings would enable a more complete understanding of the complexity of the social and linguistic situation in Montreal.

Participants

All participants of the present study were students at Colleges of General and Vocational Education. These colleges constitute a type of post-secondary education institution exclusive to the province of Quebec, attendance of which is obligatory for those individuals who have completed primary and secondary education and who wish to enrol in a university. The participant sample for this study was drawn from different classes at two French-medium and two English-medium colleges. Usable data were collected from 161 students whose mean age was 18.3 years.[3]

The overall participant sample contained more females (70.1 per cent) than males (29.9 per cent). However, there was no evidence of significant non-orthogonality. Based on their own and their parents' place of birth, the participant sample was subdivided according to immigrant status (henceforth: IS), that is, first generation immigrants (26.7 per cent), second generation immigrants (36.6 per cent) and non-immigrants (36.6 per cent).[4] Based on Statistics Canada's (2009) definition of mother tongue (henceforth L1) as the first language a person learnt at home in childhood and still understands, and taking into account that some respondents may declare that they learnt two or more languages simultaneously, the participant sample was also subdivided into four L1 groups: those whose L1 was English (and in some cases another language) (henceforth anglophones), those whose L1 was French (and in some cases another language) (henceforth francophones), those who had both English and French (and in some cases another language) as their L1 (henceforth English–French bilinguals) and those whose L1 was a language/languages other than English or French (henceforth allophones). The respondents from all L1 groups had good knowledge of both English and French. As noted above, allophones who are L1 speakers of Romance languages have been found more likely to integrate into Quebec's francophone community – and this integration pattern could be an indication of more positive attitudes towards French on their part. Ideally, the allophones should therefore have been subdivided further into those who had a Romance language as their L1 and those who had a non-Romance language as their L1. However, such a subdivision would have resulted in smaller cell numbers, which in turn would have made the statistical analysis more problematic. The author thus decided against this.

As shown in Table 4.1, each L1 group included first-and second-generation immigrants as well as non-immigrants. In the light of the historical background, it is not surprising that the majority of first-generation immigrants were allophones, most second-generation immigrants were anglophones and most non-immigrants were francophones.

In a number of cases, the respondents' IS had a main effect on their language attitudes, and these main effects are discussed below. The small numbers of respondents in the cells constitute a likely explanation for the fact that no systematic or meaningful patterns were revealed by those few instances in which IS interacted with L1. For reasons of space, and in order not to detract from the most relevant results, these interactions are therefore not discussed.

Table 4.1 Cross-tabulation of L1 and IS, and results of Chi-square test

L1	1st generation immigrants			2nd generation immigrants			Non-immigrants		
	N	Ne	%	N	Ne	%	N	Ne	%
English	5	12	11.6	28	16.6	47.5	12	16.5	20.3
French	4	14.7	9.3	14	20.2	23.7	37	20.2	62.7
English and French	2	3.5	4.7	5	4.8	8.5	6	4.8	10.2
Other	32	12.8	74.4	12	17.6	20.3	4	17.6	6.8
Total	43	43	100	59	59	100	59	59	100

Missing cases = 3 $\chi^2 = 79.02$; df = 6; sig. = 0.000

Procedure

The research instruments were administered to all students in a given class at the same time, and the procedure took one lesson in total. At the English-medium colleges, the author spoke to the students in English and administered all materials in English; at the French-medium colleges, the author spoke French and administered all materials in French. At the beginning of the class, the matched-guise experiment was conducted, and then the language attitudes questionnaire was administered.

Materials

Questionnaire

The background section of the questionnaire ascertained the participants' IS as well as their age, sex and L1. The main section contained items that elicited attitudes towards English and French in terms of status and solidarity by means of five-point interval questions, with 1 meaning 'completely agree' and 5 meaning 'don't agree at all'.

A language that is perceived to have high status is defined as one that is, *inter alia*, associated with economic opportunity and upward social mobility (Echeverria 2005). The items 'Knowing English/Knowing French will increase my opportunities to find employment' were thus designed to elicit attitudes with respect to economic opportunity, and the aim of the items 'English/French is a language that is important to know in order to get far in life' was to ascertain attitudes with respect to upward mobility. Based on the assumption that a language's suitability to modern society implies its usefulness, the items 'English/French is a language that is well suited to modern society' sought to investigate the utilitarian value that the respondents attributed to English and French – another important characteristic of languages that are associated with status and social recognition (Gardner and Lambert 1959).

As noted above, a language that is evaluated highly on the solidarity dimension, in contrast, is one that elicits feelings of attachment and belonging because it is one's in-group language (Ryan et al. 1982: 9). As it can be assumed that it is mainly with in-group members that individuals share their joys as well as their concerns, the items 'English/French is a language that lends itself well to expressing feelings and emotions' sought to find out to what extent this was the case. The items 'Knowing English/French is a significant part of Canadian cultural heritage' aimed to find out to what extent the languages elicited feelings of attachment and belonging to the English and/or French language communities, that is, at the level of social identity. In order to obtain a more complete picture, the items 'Knowing English/French is an important part of my personal identity' were used to ascertain the extent to which the languages were important to the respondents at the level of individual identity.

The questionnaire data were analysed by means of analyses of variance (ANOVAs) that used IS and L1 as the independent, between-subject variables. Independent samples t-tests were subsequently performed to compare the respondents' evaluations of English and French, and to ascertain whether the resulting differences were statistically significant.

Matched-guise experiment

The stimulus recordings employed for the matched-guise experiment were the same as those used in a previous study that had investigated the language attitudes held by Montreal anglophones and francophones (Genesee and Holobow 1989). The researchers describe their selection process as follows:

> Recordings in each of three guises – Canadian English, Quebec French and European French – were made of five 'trilingual' males. . . . All speakers spoke middle class language varieties. . . . The recordings were then presented in random order to 20 male and female undergraduate psychology students from McGill University who were asked to judge the first language and nationality of each speaker. These judgments were used to select three of the five speakers for inclusion in the study. The three speakers who were selected were judged to be

native speakers in each of their guises by at least 85% of the students. (Genesee and Holobow 1989: 23–4)

The order of the recordings was randomized and two other samples from different speakers were added to the beginning, as practice voices. The text used was a short news item from a bilingual airline magazine (personal communication with Fred Genesee). The study presented here employed recordings of each of the speakers in three different guises – namely Canadian English, Quebec French and European French – because it constitutes part of a larger research project that investigated not only attitudes towards English compared to French, but also attitudes towards Quebec French compared to European French. Yet while there were differences in participants' attitudes towards these two different varieties of French compared to each other (Kircher 2012), the same evaluative pattern emerged for Quebec French compared to English as it did for European French compared to English. For the purpose of this chapter, the two varieties were thus combined, and the term 'French' is used here in a sense that includes both of them.

The participants were asked to give their ratings of each recording on a 16-point scale with 0 meaning 'not at all' and 16 meaning 'very'. Five of the scales pertained to status-related traits: intelligence, dependability, education, ambition and leadership. The other five scales pertained to solidarity-related traits: kindness, humour, warmth, likeability and sociability. All of these evaluation traits had previously been employed in numerous other investigations of language attitudes in Montreal, including Lambert et al. (1960) as well as Genesee and Holobow (1989).

After combining the ratings of the speakers, the matched-guise data were analysed by means of repeated measures ANOVAs that used IS and L1 as the independent, between-subject variables.

Results

Attitudes on the status dimension

While the respondents from all IS groups rated both languages positively on the status dimension, Table 4.2 shows that they tended to evaluate English even *more* positively than French. The respondents from all IS groups alike considered English to be significantly better suited to modern society. They also judged knowledge of English more likely to increase their opportunities of finding employment, and in the case of the first-generation immigrants and the non-immigrants this was statistically significant. Moreover, all three IS groups thought knowledge

Table 4.2 Independent samples t-test of the different IS groups' evaluations of English and French on the status dimension. Means: 1 = completely agree, 5 = don't agree at all

Item	Language evaluated	IS	N	Mean	t	df	sig.
English/French is a language that is well suited to modern society	English	1st generation immigrants	43	1.4	−5.814	58	0.000
	French		43	2.4			
	English	2nd generation immigrants	59	1.3	−6.058	97	0.000
	French		59	2.3			
	English	non-immigrants	59	1.5	−4.048	116	0.000
	French		59	2.2			
Knowing English/French will increase my opportunities to find employment	English	1st generation immigrants	43	1.2	−2.743	71	0.008
	French		43	1.5			
	English	2nd generation immigrants	59	1.5	−0.972	116	0.333
	French		59	1.7			
	English	non-immigrants	59	1.2	−2.183	104	0.031
	French		59	1.5			

(Continued)

Table 4.2 (Continued)

Item	Language evaluated	IS	N	Mean	t	df	sig.
English/French is a language that is important to know in order to get far in life	English	1st generation immigrants	43	1.8	−2.680	84	0.009
	French		43	2.5			
	English	2nd generation immigrants	58	1.9	−2.332	115	0.021
	French		59	2.3			
	English	non-immigrants	59	1.9	−0.555	116	0.580
	French		59	2.1			

Table 4.3 Evaluations of speakers in different guises in terms of status traits. Means: 0 = not at all, 16 = very[5]

Trait	N	Mean/ English	Mean/ French	F	df	sig.
Intelligence	142	10.8	8.4	43.723	1(133)	0.000
Dependability	133	10.3	8.0	34.135	1(124)	0.000
Education	143	10.8	8.8	30.387	1(134)	0.000
Ambition	143	8.7	7.3	15.274	1(134)	0.000
Leadership	137	9.8	6.8	34.288	1(128)	0.000

of English to be more important in order to get far in life, and in the case of the first- and second-generation immigrants this was statistically significant.

Table 4.3 presents the results of the repeated measures ANOVAs that were performed on the status data obtained by means of the matched-guise experiment. As the respondents' IS did not have a significant effect, only the total means are presented here. The findings show the same trend as those of the questionnaire: regardless of their IS, the respondents evaluated English even more favourably than French – and this was statistically significant with respect to all five status traits, that is, intelligence, dependability, education, ambition and leadership.

The outcomes of both the questionnaire and the matched-guise experiment thus indicate that the first- and second-generation immigrants and the non-immigrants in this study all held more positive attitudes towards English than towards French on the status dimension.

Attitudes on the solidarity dimension

While the respondents from all IS groups also rated both English and French positively on the solidarity dimension, Table 4.4 shows that again, there were differences in their evaluations of the two languages. All three IS groups stated that they considered French to lend itself better to expressing feelings and emotions, with the difference being statistically significant for the non-immigrants and the first-generation immigrants. The non-immigrants also stated that they thought French to be a significantly more important part of Canadian cultural heritage, and they deemed it to be significantly more important to their personal identity. The only other statistically significant finding was the second-generation immigrants deeming English to be more important for their personal identity. Apart from the latter finding, the overall results of the questionnaire thus suggest that the respondents from all IS groups held more positive attitudes towards

Table 4.4 Independent samples t-test of the different IS groups' evaluations of English and French on the solidarity dimension. Means: 1 = completely agree, 5 = don't agree at all

Item	Language evaluated	IS	N	Mean	t	df	sig.
English/French is a language that lends itself well to expressing feelings and emotions	English	1st generation immigrants	43	2.2	+2.670	84	0.009
	French		43	1.7			
	English	2nd generation immigrants	59	2.1	+0.173	116	0.863
	French		59	2.0			
	English	non-immigrants	59	2.2	+4.354	89	0.000
	French		59	1.4			
Knowing English/French is a significant part of Canadian cultural heritage	English	1st generation immigrants	43	1.8	−0.227	84	0.821
	French		43	1.9			
	English	2nd generation immigrants	59	1.9	−1.299	116	0.197
	French		59	2.1			
	English	non-immigrants	58	2.3	+3.785	98	0.000
	French		58	1.6			

Knowing English/French is an important part of my personal identity						
1st generation immigrants	English	43	2.3	−0.555	84	0.580
	French	43	2.5			
2nd generation immigrants	English	59	1.7	−3.003	116	0.003
	French	59	2.4			
non-immigrants	English	59	2.6	+4.088	101	0.000
	French	59	1.6			

Table 4.5 Evaluations of speakers in different guises in terms of solidarity traits. Means: 0 = not at all, 16 = very

Trait	N	Mean/ English	Mean/ French	F	df	sig.
Kindness	143	10.3	8.6	18.862	1(134)	0.000
Humour	144	8.7	6.3	33.800	1(135)	0.000
Warmth	142	9.9	7.2	43.574	1(133)	0.000
Likeability	140	10.6	8.1	43.469	1(131)	0.000
Sociability	142	10.6	7.8	45.476	1(133)	0.000

French in terms of the solidarity dimension, and that these positive attitudes were particularly pronounced among the non-immigrants and – slightly less so – among the first-generation immigrants.

The results of the repeated measures ANOVAs that were performed on the solidarity data obtained from the matched-guise experiment are shown in Table 4.5. Again, only the total means are presented here as IS did not have a significant effect. Unlike the questionnaire results, the matched-guise findings show that regardless of their IS, the respondents evaluated English more favourably than French – and this was statistically significant with respect to all five solidarity traits, that is, kindness, humour, warmth, likeability and sociability.

The solidarity-related findings of the questionnaire and the matched-guise experiment are thus diametrically opposed, with the questionnaire results suggesting that the respondents from all three IS groups (and particularly the non-immigrants and the first-generation immigrants) held more positive attitudes towards French, and the matched-guise results indicating that all respondents held more positive attitudes towards English in terms of solidarity.

Discussion

The findings suggest that the young first- and second-generation immigrants as well as the non-immigrants who participated in this study attributed at least a certain amount of status to the French language. As noted above, up until the mid-1970s, English was the only language required for economic advancement in Montreal whereas French had very little utilitarian value in the city. In 1977,

Bill 101 reinforced the status of French as the only official language of Quebec and made it the main language of several areas of public life in the province – and while it is difficult to establish cause-and-effect relationships when evaluating the impact of legislation on attitudes, the status that the young Montrealers of different ISs in this study attributed to French does seem to suggest the efficacy of measures such as Bill 101.

However, while the respondents attributed a certain status to French, the results of both the questionnaire and the matched-guise experiment clearly indicated that the participants of all ISs evaluated English even *more* positively on the status dimension. The same attitudinal trend was already indicated by the linguistic behaviours outlined in the background section. As discussed previously, French in Quebec remains threatened by English due to the function of the latter as the language of socio-economic advancement in the rest of Canada and the United States, as well as its role as the global lingua franca of our times. Despite the aforementioned 'reconquest' of Montreal, English consequently continues to be a pivotal language in public and private communication among many Montrealers, and it exerts a strong power of attraction – particularly so among young people who still have to forge their way in the working world. The fact that the adolescent first- and second-generation immigrants as well as the non-immigrants in this study held more positive attitudes towards English than towards French on the status dimension can be interpreted as a reflection of this. Moreover, the fact that these more positive attitudes towards English were evidenced by the findings of both the matched-guise experiment and the questionnaire suggests that the respondents not only held these attitudes at a more private level, but also considered them to be socially acceptable.

Regarding the solidarity dimension, the findings obtained by means of the different methods of attitude elicitation in this study differed significantly: the overall results of the questionnaire suggested that all IS groups held more positive attitudes towards French, and that these positive attitudes were particularly pronounced among the non-immigrants and the first-generation immigrants. The matched-guise results, however, indicated that regardless of their IS, the respondents evaluated English significantly more favourably on the solidarity dimension. As noted above, it is not uncommon for direct and indirect methods of attitude elicitation to yield dissimilar and sometimes even contradictory results. Ryan et al. (1987: 1076) explain that this is by no means an issue of relative methodological merit, but that it is due to the fact that the different methods simply produce results at different levels of analysis: 'direct and indirect methods lay claim to quite different layers of experience and as such manifest sometimes quite contradictory, yet highly rational, attitude constellations'. It is therefore not entirely surprising that the outcome of the questionnaire and that of the matched-guise experiment should differ from each other – however, the question is what the rationale behind this difference might be. As in the case of the findings pertaining to the status dimension, it is likely that the explanation lies in the socio-historical context.

As mentioned previously, the integration of allophone immigrants and their descendants into the francophone community has for some time now been strategically important – particularly as a means of pursuing the provincial government's goal to make French the 'common public language' in the province, that is, the language of public communications used by Quebecers of all ethnic and linguistic backgrounds (Oakes 2005). Quebec language planners soon realized that while status planning measures such as Bill 101 may have succeeded in increasing the *utilitarian* value of French in the province, there are also significant benefits in encouraging an *affective* attachment to the host society and its language because this can constitute an additional source of motivation for the use of French (Gouvernement du Québec 2001). Governmental efforts to create such an affective attachment to Quebec and the French language were particularly noticeable with regard to allophone immigrants. These efforts were mirrored not only in official rhetoric but also in practice – be it in the free French classes for adult immigrants and the 'welcoming classes' for school-aged children, or Quebec's overall model for the integration of its immigrants. Known as interculturalism, this model involves 'the meeting of cultures, their mutual interpenetration and the reciprocal recognition of their respective contributions, within a common civic culture and a French-speaking framework' (Anctil 1996: 143). In effect, this means that newcomers to Quebec are – or at least should be – welcomed without being expected to assimilate to the majority culture as long as they accept certain basic conditions, including the use of French in their public communications. As Oakes and Warren (2007: 149) note, Quebec as a host aims to provide its guests with 'the key to the house' – that is, the French language – 'so that they can make themselves totally at home'. The choice of interculturalism as the official model for Quebec thus ties in with the aforementioned shift regarding the conceptualization of belonging in the province – that is, from the traditional, ethnic conceptualization of national identity whose basis of inclusion consisted of French ancestry as well as Catholic and rural cultural values, towards a more development-oriented, civic conceptualization of national identity which is independent of descent and ethnicity but instead places importance on common values and institutions.

As noted above, findings obtained by means of direct methods of attitude elicitation often reveal what the respondents consider to be socially desirable. It is therefore possible that the questionnaire results were caused by the non-immigrants' and the first-generation immigrants' feeling that they *should* hold these comparatively positive attitudes towards French in terms of solidarity – possibly as a result of the governmental efforts to create an affective attachment to Quebec and the French language. The non-immigrants and the first-generation immigrants might be especially susceptible to this: the former because they were brought up in the knowledge of how hard their parents' generation had to fight for French language rights, and the latter because they are a particular focus of many of the aforementioned governmental efforts. The questionnaire results pertaining to the solidarity dimension could thus be interpreted as reflecting social desirability biases.

As explained previously, the major strength of indirect methods such as the matched-guise technique lies in the elicitation of spontaneous attitudes that are less sensitive to reflection and social desirability biases than directly assessed attitudes. Consequently, the underlying assumption is that in studies of this kind, more private reactions are revealed. If the questionnaire results were indeed indicative of social desirability biases, it remains to be explored what precisely the more private reasons were that caused the respondents to evaluate English more favourably than French in the matched-guise study. However, it is likely that they relate to social identity, and elsewhere, the author posits two possible explanations: firstly, a Montreal-based identity that encompasses English as the common in-group language, and secondly, an international youth identity that is expressed with the help of English (Kircher 2014). These two are not mutually exclusive, and either one of them or a combination of both could be what caused the respondents to hold more positive attitudes towards English than towards French on the solidarity dimension.

Regardless of the precise nature of the social identity (or identities) underlying the respondents' attitudes on the solidarity dimension, the findings of this study allow for tentative conclusions to be drawn regarding the implications that Quebec's shift from an ethnic to a civic conceptualization of national identity has had on the language attitudes of immigrants in Montreal. The outcomes of both methods of attitude elicitation indicate that overall, the first- and second-generation immigrants share the general attitudinal trends of the non-immigrants.

This applies not only to their notions of what is considered socially acceptable and desirable, as measured by the questionnaire, but also to their privately held attitudes, as measured by the matched-guise experiment. This could be seen to suggest that the immigrants also shared the non-immigrants' aforementioned social identity (or identities) underlying these attitudes. On the one hand, this would mean that the shift from ethnic to civic national identity was successful because common ancestry and shared cultural heritage do not appear to be significant determinants of these adolescents' identities. The respondents appeared to identify in the same manner regardless of their ethnic and migration backgrounds. On the other hand, it seems that their shared social identity is not Quebec-based, as had been desired by the provincial government, but rather Montreal-based and/or founded on membership in a particular age group – and that it encompasses English rather than French as its in-group language. This could be seen to show that the governmental efforts to make French an integral component of a Quebec-based, civic identity shared by individuals of all ethnic and migration backgrounds were not as fruitful as had been hoped.

Conclusion

In conclusion, it can be said that the adolescent Montrealers who took part in the study presented here attributed at least a certain amount of status to the French language, and that this is likely to be a result of status planning measures such as Bill 101. However, all three IS groups evaluated English even more positively than French on the status dimension, which can most probably be attributed to its role as the global lingua franca as well as its function as the language of socio-economic advancement in the rest of North America.

Regarding the solidarity dimension, the questionnaire results suggested that the respondents of all three IS groups held more positive attitudes towards French. The results of the matched-guise experiment, however, indicated more positive attitudes towards English among all three IS groups. A likely explanation for these discrepant findings is that the questionnaire results were influenced by social desirability biases, and that the findings of the matched-guise experiment were due to the respondents' social identity (or identities). The fact that the immigrants shared the non-immigrants' privately held attitudes as well as their notions of what is considered socially acceptable and desirable is tentatively interpreted as a sign of all participants sharing the social identity (or identities) underlying these linguistic evaluations. This would signal both a success and a failure with regard to Quebec's shifting conceptualization of belonging: on the one hand, the adolescents identify in the same manner regardless of their ethnic and migration background – but on the other hand, their primary self-identification does not appear to be that of Quebecers who consider French to be their common in-group language.

Evidently, it is impossible to establish a definite cause-and-effect relationship when evaluating Quebec's shifting conceptualization of belonging and the language attitudes held by immigrants in Montreal – particularly in the absence of studies that investigated immigrants' language attitudes before this shift took place. Further research is certainly necessary to explore the attitudinal differences between different generations of immigrants compared to non-immigrants, as well as the precise reasons underlying these attitudes. In future work, a clear distinction should be made between those allophones who have a Romance language as their L1 and those who do not; larger participant samples should be employed to ensure sufficiently large subgroup sizes; qualitative as well as quantitative data should be collected, and the effect of variables such as the respondents' age should also be investigated. Such future investigations would enable an even more complete and nuanced understanding of the attitudinal differences between different generations of immigrants compared to non-immigrants in Montreal, and how they have been affected by Quebec's shift from a purely ethnic to a more civic conceptualization of national identity. Particularly in the light of recent developments such as the debates about the Quebec Charter of Values (between May 2013 and April 2014), the situation is now likely to be even more complex.

If it emerges that the findings of the present study are indeed representative, this would have implications for future language policy and planning measures aiming to protect and maintain French in Quebec. In the light of the role English plays in North America as well as globally, it is doubtful that any measure could increase the status of French beyond that of English. Yet, as Cargile et al. (1994) note, attitudes on the solidarity dimension can be crucial determinants of why languages persist, regardless of their status. Ensuring that Quebecers of diverse backgrounds have an affective attachment to French might thus not be an *additional* way improving the prospects of the language, as had been thought initially, but it might in fact be the *primary* way in which this can be achieved. However, further and different measures than the ones implemented hitherto would be required to create a Quebec-based identity that involves French as the common in-group language and thus leads to such an affective attachment.

Acknowledgements

I am grateful to Fred Genesee for allowing me to use his recordings in my matched-guise experiment, and to Ruxandra Comănaru and Leigh Oakes for their insightful comments on an earlier version of this chapter. I also gratefully acknowledge the financial assistance of a Doctoral Award from the Arts and Humanities Research Council, a Queen Mary Research Studentship, a Wingate Scholarship, a Prix du Québec from the Délégation Générale du Québec, as well a Graduate Student Scholarship from the International Council for Canadian Studies.

Notes

1 Since the 1960s, too, tens of thousands of immigrants from various origins have moved to Quebec each year. Since 1991, when the Canada-Quebec Accord relating to Immigration and Temporary Admission of Aliens was instated, the Quebec government has had an increased measure of control over the selection of these newcomers. While Canada retains responsibility for the admission of family reunion migrants and refugees, Quebec now has the exclusive right to select all economic migrants. This means that the provincial government has been able to privilege knowledge of French as a key criterion in the selection of many of its newcomers (Bourhis 2001). However, large numbers of allophones also continue to arrive each year.

2 Evidently, not all allophones displayed identical language usage patterns. Various factors appear to have had an effect, including their mother tongue: Romance language speakers, for example, have always been more likely to adopt French as their main language than non-Romance language speakers (Conseil supérieur de la langue française 2007). The trends described here therefore have to be understood as generalizations.

3 The original sample included 164 participants. However, three of them did not provide information regarding their immigrant status and they were thus excluded from the analysis presented here.

4 The first generation immigrants had moved to Quebec from various countries: America, Argentina, Bangladesh, Bolivia, Bulgaria, China, Colombia, France, Haiti, Kuwait, Lebanon, Mexico, Moldova, the Netherlands, Pakistan, Peru, the Philippines, Romania, Russia, Saudi Arabia, Sri Lanka, Thailand, Turkey, the Ukraine and Vietnam.

5 On the final page of the evaluation sheets used in the experiment, the participants were asked for their opinion regarding the purpose of the study, and whether

they thought that there was anything unusual about the voices they had heard. The purpose of these questions was to enable the researcher to ascertain whether any of the participants had guessed the actual aim of the study. Four of them did indeed guess the real objective as well as realizing that the same speakers were reading the text in different guises. Since the participants' ignorance with regard to the methodology is a precondition to the elicitation of valid results by means of matched-guise experiments, these participants were removed from the analysis of the matched-guise data, resulting in a sample of 157 respondents.

References

Anctil, P. (1996), 'La trajectoire interculturelle du Québec: la société distincte vue à travers le prisme de l'immigration', in A. Lapierre, P. Smart and P. Savard (eds), *Language, Culture and Values in Canada at the Dawn of the 21st Centuy/Langues, cultures et valeurs au Canada à l'aube du XXIe siècle*. Ottawa: International Council for Canadian Studies/Carleton University Press, pp. 133–54.

Bourhis, R. Y. (2001), 'Reversing language shift in Quebec', in J. A. Fishman (ed.), *Can Threatened Languages be Saved? Reversing Language Shift, Revisited: A 21st Century Perspective*. Clevedon: Multilingual Matters, pp. 101–41.

Bourhis, R., Montaruli, E., El-Geledi, S., Harvey, S. P. and Barrette, G. (2010), 'Acculturation in multiple host community settings'. *Journal of Social Issues* 66: 780–802.

Breton, R. (1988), 'From ethnic to civic nationalism: English Canada and Quebec'. *Ethnic and Racial Studies* 11(1): 85–102.

Cargile, A. C., Giles, H., Ryan, E. B. and Bradac, J. J. (1994), 'Language attitudes as a social process: A conceptual model and new directions'. *Language and Communication* 14(3): 211–36.

Carpentier, A. (2004), *Tout est-il joué avant l'arrivée? Étude de facteurs associés à un usage prédominant du français ou de l'anglais chez les immigrants allophones arrivés au Québec adultes*. Quebec: Conseil de la langue française.

Conseil supérieur de la langue française (2007), *Les accommodements raisonnables en matière linguistique. Mémoire présenté à la Commission de consultation sur les pratiques d'accommodement reliées aux differences culturelles*. Quebec: Conseil supérieur de la langue française.

Dickinson, J. and Young, B. (2003), *A Short History of Quebec,* 3rd edn. Montreal/Kingston: McGill/Queen's University Press.

Echeverria, B. (2005), 'Language attitudes in San Sebastian: The Basque vernacular as challenge to Spanish language hegemony'. *Journal of Multilingual and Multicultural Development* 26(3): 249–64.

Gardner, R. C. and Lambert, W. E. (1959), 'Motivational variables in second-language acquisition'. *Canadian Journal of Psychology* 13(4): 266–72.

Garrett, P. (2010), *Attitudes to Language*. Cambridge: Cambridge University Press.
Genesee, F. and Holobow, N. E. (1989), 'Change and stability in intergroup perceptions'. *Journal of Language and Social Psychology* 8(1): 17–39.
Gouvernement du Québec (2001), *Le français, une langue pour tout le monde*. (Report of the Commission des États généraux sur la situation et l'avenir de la langue française au Québec.) Quebec: Gouvernement du Québec.
Heller, M. S. (1985), 'Ethnic relations and language use in Montreal', in N. Wolfson and J. Manes (eds), *Language of Inequality*. Berlin: Mouton, pp. 75–90.
Kircher, R. (2012), 'How pluricentric is the French language? An investigation of attitudes towards Quebec French compared to European French'. *Journal of French Language Studies* 22(3): 345–70.
—(2014), 'Thirty years after Bill 101: A contemporary perspective on attitudes towards English and French in Montreal'. *Canadian Journal of Applied Linguistics* 17(1): 20–50.
Lambert, W. E., Hodgson, R. C., Gardner, R. C. and Fillenbaum, S. (1960), 'Evaluational reactions to spoken language'. *Journal of Abnormal and Social Psychology* 60(1): 44–51.
Levine, M. V. (1990), *The Reconquest of Montreal: Language Policy and Social Change in a Bilingual City*. Philadelphia: Temple University Press.
—(1997), *La reconquête de Montréal*. Montreal: VLB éditeur.
Oakes, L. (2005), 'French as the "common public language" in Québec', in I. Lockerbie, I. Molinaro, K. Larose and L. Oakes (eds), *French as the Common Language in Québec: History, Debates and Positions*. Quebec: Éditions Nota bene, pp. 153–94.
Oakes, L. and Warren, J. (2007), *Language, Citizenship and Identity in Quebec*. Houndmills, Basingstoke: Palgrave Macmillan.
Pagé, M. and Lamarre, P. (2010), *L'intégration linguistique des immigrants au Québec*. Montreal: Institut de recherche en politiques publiques.
Roshwald, A. (2006), *The Endurance of Nationalism: Ancient Roots and Modern Dilemmas*. Cambridge: Cambridge University Press.
Ryan, E. B., Giles, H. and Hewstone, M. (1987), 'The measurement of language attitudes', in U. Ammon, N. Dittmar and K. J. Mattheier (eds), *Sociolinguistics: An International Handbook of Language and Society*. Berlin: Walter de Gruyter, pp. 1068–81.
Ryan, E. B., Giles, H. and Sebastian, R. J. (1982), 'An integrative perspective for the study of attitudes towards language variation', in E. B. Ryan and H. Giles (eds), *Attitudes Towards Language Variation: Social and Applied Contexts*. London: Edward Arnold, pp. 1–19.
Statistics Canada (2009), *Mother Tongue of Person*: http://www.statcan.gc.ca/concepts/definitions/language-langue01-eng.htm.
—(2011), *The 2011 Census*: http://www12.statcan.gc.ca/census-recensement/index-eng.cfm?HPA.
Stefanescu, A. and Georgeault, P. (2005), 'Conclusion', in A. Stefanescu and P. Georgeault (eds), *Le français au Québec: les nouveaux défis*. Montreal: Fides, pp. 589–608.

5

Trilingualism and Uyghur Identity in the People's Republic of China

Mamtimyn Sunuodula, Anwei Feng and Bob Adamson

> ### Editor's Introduction
>
> In some ways similar to the last chapter, this chapter looks at the sociopolitical implications for identity faced with language choice. The difference in this chapter is that the choices are faced with the uninvited encroachment of Han Mandarin language and culture upon an unwilling Uyghur population. Uyghurs feel they have to learn Mandarin as their own language no longer enjoys institutional recognition. However, in similarity with the last chapter English represents a global opportunity for economic success and an empowerment to rival Mandarin. We see, in this chapter, that language is a 'double-edged sword' in that it can liberate identity as well as impose constraints on identity.

Prologue

There are 55 officially recognized ethnic minority groups in the People's Republic of China (PRC). One such group, the Uyghurs, is made up of Turkic people living in Northwest China, predominantly in the province of Xinjiang. Historically, this group has never been strongly assimilated into the majority Han culture; indeed, the political, economic and social policies of the central and regional governments have engendered tensions – at times violent – between the Uyghurs and the Han in Xinjiang, as some Uyghurs have perceived the policies as threatening the integrity of their culture and language. However, to characterize the relationship between Uyghurs and Han as uniformly and mutually hostile would be a misrepresentation of a far more nuanced reality. This chapter (co-authored by a Uyghur, a Han Chinese and an Englishman) explores the complexities and tensions surrounding language and Uyghur identity. Language issues are particularly sensitive and, as a result, instructive of the broader attitudes and practices relating to identity. The Uyghur language forms an essential part of ethnic identity, while Chinese – which is promoted for national unity – offers opportunities for educational, economic and social advancement. English provides international connectivities that enhance and complexify notions of identity. The chapter explores language in education policies in Xinjiang to reveal official attitudes and practices, and the attitudes and practices of Uyghurs regarding their self-identity.

Introduction

Contrary to popular impressions of homogeneity held outside of the PRC, there are 55 officially recognized ethnic minority groups in the country, in addition to the majority Han. These ethnic groups are very diverse in terms of history, culture and language. They number some 113.79 million people (National Bureau of Statistics of China 2011) living in 155 ethnic autonomous areas, many of which are located near the country's borders to the south-west, west, north-west, north and north-east. All ethnic minority groups are subject to the same central legislature and laws as Han Chinese and enjoy the same constitutional rights. However, decentralization of some aspects of state policy (such as the provision of education) has led to considerable variation in the relationship between individual minority groups and the local, regional and national government (Schluessel 2007). This relationship has also varied over time, as state policy has veered between coercive assimilation to acceptance of diversity. To some extent, this variation can be attributed to sociopolitical and cultural factors, such as the prevailing political climate, as well as the historical tendency of individual minority groups towards or away from assimilation with the Han, and their sense of identity and linguistic vitality (Adamson and Feng 2009).

Language issues are particularly sensitive and, as a result, instructive of the broader attitudes and practices relating to cultural identity in the PRC. Chinese and minority languages are accorded different status (Adamson and Feng 2009). Chinese is 'the language of power and access to economic well-being' (Tsung and

Cruickshank 2009: 550) while minority languages tend to be 'limited in use and of low social status' (Lin 1997: 196). In recent decades, the rise of English in the PRC (Adamson 2004) has resulted in the phenomenon of trilingual education in minority regions, with the minority language being taught in primary schools in an effort to maintain the students' sense of cultural identity, Chinese being taught for national unity and access to life chances in mainstream society, and English for preparing citizens to cope with the demands of globalization and economic modernization (Adamson and Xia 2011).

This chapter explores the complexities and tensions surrounding language and the identity of Uyghur people in Xinjiang, north-west China. Xinjiang is a vast region with 13 ethnic groups living in mixed communities, mostly in towns and cities, or in remote isolated areas where minority groups, mostly Uyghurs, dominate. Located at the crossroads of the Eurasian continent, Xinjiang was strategically placed on the ancient trading routes from Asia to Europe, known as the famed Silk Road. It was not just goods that were transported and exchanged along the Silk Road towns and cities of ancient Xinjiang. A continuous flow of ideas, cultures, religions and languages between different peoples and continents were also an important part of the exchange between individuals and communities over many centuries. Twenty-four different scripts, used for writing 17 ancient languages, have been unearthed from the Tarim and Turpan basin oasis cities. Further, some of the Turkic manuscripts recovered from Buddhist caves in Dunhuang are written in multiple languages and scripts, indicating the existence of a high degree of linguistic exchanges and multilingual populations, at least in some sections of society (Kamberi 2005).

Historically, the Uyghurs have never been strongly assimilated into the majority Han culture; indeed, there has existed considerable tension, which has occasionally been expressed and repressed in a violent manner, between the two groups over the central and regional governments' political, economic and social policies in Xinjiang. However, to characterize the relationship between Uyghurs and Han as uniformly and mutually hostile would be a misrepresentation of a far more nuanced reality, which this chapter seeks to convey by looking at the interrelationships of the three languages.

The Uyghur language

Uyghur belongs to the south-eastern branch of Turkic languages. Today, the Uyghur language is used by over 10 million people in the Xinjiang Uyghur

Autonomous Region (XUAR) of China (XUAR Census Office 2012: 197) and an estimated further half a million people outside China, mainly in the neighbouring Central Asian countries (Becquelin 2000).

Uyghurs can trace their history to the Uyghur Empire that ruled a vast region from modern day Central Asia to the shores of Pacific Ocean and the Sea of Japan, between 744 AD and 840 AD (Mutii 1982; Rudelson 1997). The Uyghur language evolved through the centuries as the primary spoken and literary language of the Turkic people living in eastern Central Asia. By the time of the Mongol conquest of the region in the thirteenth century, the Uyghurs had developed a sophisticated literary and oral culture and Genghis Khan adopted the Uyghur script as the imperial writing system throughout the expanding Mongol Empire. Many Uyghur literati were recruited to work as court scribes, historians, diplomats, technologist and advisers in the Mongol court and throughout the Empire (Brose 2005). Later, through the Mongols, the Uyghur script was also adopted by Manchus, who ruled China from 1644 to 1911 (Nolan 2002).

After the second half of fourteenth century, Uyghurs adopted a modified version of the Arabic script for their writing and a pan-Central Asian Turkic lingua franca called Chaghatay was used as the literary language. This was in line with Uyghurs' conversion to Islam and closer cultural integration into the wider Muslim Central Asian and Turkic-speaking world. Chaghatay was used until the early twentieth century, when attempts were made to formulate a modern Uyghur language that reflected the emergence of Uyghur identity, as part of the Muslim reform movement in Central Asia and the expansion of Russian power into western Central Asia (Bögü 2002: 1–2).

The modern Uyghur literary language began to evolve in the late nineteenth and the early twentieth centuries (Baran 2007). This coincided with two major historical events. The first was the establishment of a unified and independent Uyghur state in Xinjiang in 1862 centred in Kashgar and its subsequent defeat by the Qing Dynasty in 1877. In 1884, the region was incorporated into the Chinese administrative structure as a formal province of the Qing Empire. Han people from the eastern part of China were encouraged to settle in the region. A Confucian education system was introduced, which favoured the learning of Chinese and memorization of classical works (Millward 2007). The second event was the fall of western Central Asia under Russian rule in the 1860s and the subsequent Russification and later Sovietization of Central Asia. The rise of modern geographical and political boundaries separating the Turkic-speaking Russian Central Asia from Xinjiang made physical and cultural exchanges increasingly difficult (Bregel 1992; Clark and Kamalov 2004; Šilde-Karkliņš 1975).

A poem attributed to Qutluq Shawqi, who was at the forefront of the new educational movement in the early part of twentieth century, entitled 'Mother tongue' is widely quoted by Uyghurs who want to see the preservation of Uyghur mother tongue education and promotion of Uyghur language in society. The short poem was also a hit song for a contemporary Uyghur folk singer, Abdurehim Heyit (Heyit and Shawqi 2012). An English translation of the poem is as follows:

> I salute the people who speak my mother tongue,
> I am willing to pay in gold for the words they speak,
> Wherever my mother tongue is found, be it Africa or America,
> I would go there, whatever the cost and expense,
> Oh, my mother tongue, you are the sacred bequest to us from
>   our great ancestors,
> With you, I desire to share my pride in you in the spiritual world.

Teaching and learning of Chinese by Uyghurs

The relative status of Uyghur and Han languages had been a point of contention between the local Uyghur elite and the Han Chinese ruling class in Xinjiang before the establishment of the PRC in 1949. Two of the 11-point demands brought to peace talks with the Chinese government by the leaders of the Three District Revolution, a revolutionary movement that established an independent multi-ethnic government in northern Xinjiang in 1944, concern the use of Uyghur (referred to in the document as 'the Moslem language', as this is the predominant religion of the Uyghur people). Point 3 demanded that the 'language of the Moslems would be used for all official and social affairs' and Point 4 demands that 'primary schools, middle schools and secondary schools, and the university would all use the Moslem language, and national minority education would be expanded.' The 11-point peace agreement signed between the two sides on 2 January 1946 stated:

- Individuals could use their native written language to produce documents for state and private organizations documents;
- Primary and secondary schools will use the language of the local nationality, but in secondary schools, Chinese will be a required subject. At the university level, Chinese or Moslem language(s) will be used, according to the needs of the course (Benson 1990: 58, 185–6).

This agreement showed for the first time that a conscientious effort was made by both the Three District Revolutionary authorities, which represented the local population, to raise the status of Uyghur language in politics, education and society in Xinjiang and the central government representative to emphasize the importance of learning Chinese by the local population as part of an official agreement. Meanwhile, Chinese-speakers remained as a small minority of the total population concentrated in northern Xinjiang, mainly in urban centres and often in separate quarters from the local population (Clark 2011; Toops 2004).

After Xinjiang was incorporated into the PRC in 1950, the Uyghurs were recognized as one of the 55 minority nationalities in China and, in 1956, Xinjiang was named the XUAR, one of four provinces in the country to be designated as an autonomous region, in recognition of the dominant demographic position of the Uyghur population (Communist Party of China Central Committee Archives Research Office and Communist Party of China XUAR Committee 2010). The Uyghur language was legitimized as an official regional language, along with Mandarin Chinese. Large-scale linguistic surveys were conducted between 1955 and 1957 to establish a standard variety of the language to be used as the official dialect and literary language. The Central dialect, spoken by 90 per cent of the Uyghur population in Xinjiang, was chosen as the basis for the new standard language. The Xinjiang Provincial Language and Scripts Steering Committee was set up in 1950 and was headed by the Provincial Governor, Burhan Shahidi. The Committee was responsible for coordinating the implementation of the national and the regional language policies as well as standardizing Uyghur and other ethnic minority languages by producing standard orthographies, dictionaries and guidance on the official language use in public domains and so on. Unusually high-level regional government and Communist Party officials headed the Committee in subsequent years underlining the importance of its work and high stakes involved in its decisions (XUAR Local Gazettes Editorial Commission and 'Annals of Xinjiang, Language Section' Editorial Board 2000).

Until the twentieth century, the majority of Uyghurs, like the Han and other ethnic groups in China, were monoglot and illiterate. After 1950, two parallel types of education systems were created across Xinjiang, based on the language of instruction, in line with the requirements of the National Minority Regional Autonomy law and policies (Xia 2007). In Uyghur language schools, Uyghur was the medium of instruction for all subjects except Chinese, from primary and secondary school education, as well as at university level for the majority of disciplines. Most Uyghurs came to regard mother-tongue education as their inalienable right guaranteed under the Constitution and other relevant national and regional legislation (Tsung and Cruickshank 2009). The Regional authorities were permitted to produce tailor-made textbooks for Uyghur and other ethnic minority languages (Xia 2007). At universities and professional and technical colleges, classes were divided according to the language of instruction (XUAR 50th Anniversary Organising Committee and XUAR Statistical Bureau 2005).

The Regional government approved a local law in 1988 regulating the use of Uyghur and other ethnic minority languages in the XUAR, giving specific guidance on all major areas where the ethnic minority languages must be used alongside Chinese. The law was aimed at improving and protecting the status and the use of minority languages in public institutions and privately run business and other professional organizations. Inspectors worked along with the local Industries and Commerce Regulatory Authority to monitor the use of languages on shop signs, institutional name placards, official pronouncements and other public documents with the authority to impose fines for any non-compliance (Sugawara 2001). While the actual implementation was far from smooth, it nonetheless symbolized an important recognition for the Uyghur language, and in turn the Uyghur people's status as the titular minority nationality in the XUAR (XUAR Local Gazettes Editorial Commission and 'Annals of Xinjiang, Language Section' Editorial Board 2000). While this initiative has helped to preserve and develop Uyghur cultural traditions, language and literature, as well as ethnic and religious identity, it also conflicted with the ever-increasing pressure to become proficient in Chinese. In 1992, the Regional authorities issued another legal document, entitled 'XUAR Provisional Regulation on the Usage of Chinese', which appear to counterbalance the previous document by stressing the importance of promoting the learning of Chinese by ethnic minorities (XUAR Local Gazettes Editorial Commission and 'Annals of Xinjiang, Language Section' Editorial Board 2000).

In the first decade prior to 1959, most primary school pupils followed the system of learning Uyghur and using it as the medium of instruction. Chinese was not taught till they reached secondary school (Ouyang 2008). In 1959, it was decided by the regional education authorities that Chinese would start from Primary 4. Students who entered tertiary institutions had to take a 1-year pre-sessional course. After 1959, more official documents further enhanced Chinese in primary and secondary school curricula. After the Cultural Revolution in 1977, the regional government stipulated that ethnic minority schools should provide Chinese as the compulsory second language school subject from Year 3 of primary school until the end of secondary school. No foreign language courses would be provided (Sunuodula and Feng 2011).

Policies related to language provision for minority groups issued since 1977 have further stressed the importance of teaching Chinese to minority pupils. Against the backdrop of the restoration of the traditional Uyghur written script and a relatively liberal period for bilingual education after the death in 1976 of the former paramount leader, Mao Zedong, a document issued in 1985 asserted that within 5 years school teachers and administrators in the region were required to use Chinese in all formal domains, such as classrooms and meetings. All secondary school leavers were required to have competence in Chinese. A 2004 document on 'bilingual education' goes further by asserting that Chinese should be made the main or sole language of instruction in primary and secondary school classrooms (Feng and Sunuodula 2009). The most recent document with specific aims for bilingual education for pre-schools, primary and secondary schools issued in 2010 by the XUAR Government specified that bilingual education would develop through three stages. The first stage mandated that, by 2012, 85 per cent of pre-school children would receive bilingual education. The goal of the second stage was to universalize bilingual education in primary and secondary schools by 2015. Ultimately, the third stage aims, by 2020, to enable students after senior secondary school to demonstrate oracy and literacy in Chinese (Chen and Teng 2012). The aim of the last stage is telling, revealing that 'bilingual education' has come to mean the promotion of Chinese through an education system in which Chinese is both taught as a school subject and used as the medium of instruction for other subjects, regardless of the special status of Uyghur as a minority language (Office of the XUAR Bilingual Education Steering Group 2012; Schluessel 2007; Feng 2005).

This conceptualization of 'bilingual education' has posed unprecedented challenges to the position of the Uyghur language in political, economic, social and cultural spheres and for the Uyghurs living in Xinjiang who use Uyghur as their primary language. The most directly affected have been the students and staff at minority language medium schools and other educational institutions. They are now required to become fluent (or near fluent), within a short space of time, in both spoken and written Chinese. The teachers also have had to switch from Uyghur to Chinese in conducting their teaching (Ma 2009). The symbolic effect of this change on Uyghur ethnic, social and cultural identity is just as great as the economic and tangible impacts.

The policy has been rigidly implemented. For example, in Khotan County, where 96.4 per cent of the population is Uyghur, a document from 2004 on the official Khotan Education website states that students must be proficient in Chinese by achieving Level 4 in the Chinese standard proficiency test by the end of compulsory education. Specific levels of proficiency in Chinese are also listed for teachers of minority background who work in schools. The document calls for those who fail to reach those levels within the set timeframe to be replaced or forced out of the teaching profession (Khotan County CCP Committee 2004).

Research and scholarship related to language provision for minority groups in Xinjiang correspond to the tone articulated in the policy documents. Recent publications on bilingual education focus on the importance of Chinese and how Chinese could be effectively promoted in Xinjiang schools. The most representative of the kind is an officially sanctioned collection of essays published by Xinjiang Education Press (Liu 2008). The volume, in Chinese, is titled 'Chinese and Bilingual Education in Xinjiang Primary and Secondary Schools' and includes a collection of 29 essays. All these essays, analyses of policy documents, survey reports, textbook writing and classroom practice, concentrate exclusively on the teaching and learning of Chinese. Many essays have the term 'bilingual' in the title, but the role of minority languages is ignored throughout.

English in Xinjiang

China, like the rest of Asia, has felt the impact of the English language over the past two centuries. The expansion of maritime trade and subsequently colonialism provided the initial contact and, in more recent decades, the role of English as a global language has increased the pressure on China to engage with the language. Engagement was initially restricted as China sought to maintain cultural integrity. When the European traders arrived in the late eighteenth century, Chinese authorities confined them to a small area of Guangzhou in southern China and severely limited the interactions between foreigners and locals. Only a few Chinese businessmen were permitted to trade with their foreign counterparts, assisted by 'linguists', who were despised by their compatriots for acquiring a very basic knowledge of English terms for commodities, numbers, weights and measures (Feng 1863; cited in Teng and Fairbank 1979: 51). As trade and opportunities for employment increased in the territory seized by foreign powers (such as Hong Kong, Shanghai and Tianjin) and missionary activities grew in remoter areas, interest in learning English increased among the Chinese populace. At the same time, state officials called for the strategic study of English – albeit with gritted teeth – as a means to access Western science and technology in order to strengthen China's capacity to resist further territorial and cultural incursions. The first *Tongwenguan*, a college for this very purpose, was established in 1861. The reform agenda of the Self-Strengtheners held sway at the turn of the twentieth century and English became an official subject on the school curriculum from 1903. However, these attempts at modernizing China were not achieved without resistance, often violent, as manifested in anti-foreign movements such as the Boxer Rebellion.

While English was introduced to much of the Chinese hinterland in the nineteenth and early twentieth centuries through the activities of missionaries and merchants spreading out from the treaty ports on the eastern coast of the country, the language entered Xinjiang mainly from the west. The cities of Kashgar and Turpan are located on the ancient Northern Silk Road that connected the former Chinese capital, Chang'an (modern Xi'an) with Europe, Persia and Arabia. The region was also embroiled in the 'Great Game' of geo-political manoeuvring between Britain and Russia, as the former sought to contain the threat to India of the latter's expansion in Central Asia in the late nineteenth century. In the early twentieth century, English teaching was undertaken in Kashgar by Swedish missionaries arriving from the west (not from the treaty ports on the eastern and southern seaboard of China). Although they mainly taught students from the Han majority, the classes included Uyghurs, and local Muslims were inducted as teachers in the school (Fallmann 2003). The new education movements that were initiated in late nineteenth century, and formed the foundation of modern Uyghur education and identity formation, advocated the study of languages such as Russian and Turkish. But, until the 1950s, only a small number of Uyghurs had learnt Chinese, Russian or any other languages (Clark 2011; Fuller and Lipman 2004: 334).

The teaching of English in China went through stormy periods after it was introduced into the formal school curriculum in 1903, as part of the Qing Dynasty's attempt at modernization programme known as the Hundred Days Reform. Teaching was strongest in the cities, where teachers could be trained and access to native speakers was easier. The provision of English in minority areas has very often been piecemeal or non-existent due to the lack of resources. During the 1930s, there was a backlash against English teaching, as it was seen by some academics and politicians as detracting from the development of patriotism, and the Japanese invasion and subsequent civil war in the 1940s further reduced the status of the language in the education system. After the founding of the PRC in 1949, English was only offered sporadically in schools, given the failure of countries such as the United States, Great Britain and Australia to recognize the new nation. Attention was focused on a major campaign to boost standard Chinese, while Russian, the main language of the cooperative partners from the Soviet Union, was preferred as the foreign language. English was boosted by the Sino-Soviet schism in the early 1960s, as there was greater emphasis on China's economic and political engagement with the rest of the world, but the development of English in the country was greatly curtailed by the political upheavals of the Great Proletarian Cultural Revolution, which lasted from 1966 to 1976. At this time, many teachers of the language were vilified, imprisonment or even murdered (Adamson 2004). English only started to recover after the visit to China by the US President, Richard Nixon, which ushered in a period of détente and ping pong diplomacy.

The rise of Deng Xiaoping to the post of paramount leader in 1978 introduced an era of modernization that has resulted in China becoming a major world economy today. In modern China, English is widely used in science and technology, mass media, commerce, tourist industry, academia, formal and informal education systems, postal services, customs, the law and other settings (Gil and Adamson 2011).The role and status of English have accelerated to the extent that:

> A vast national appetite has elevated English to something more than a language: it is not simply a tool but a defining measure of life's potential. China today is divided by class, opportunity, and power, but one of its few unifying beliefs – something shared by waiters, politicians, intellectuals, tycoons – is the power of English. ... English has become an ideology, a force strong enough to remake your résumé, attract a spouse, or catapult you out of a village. (Osnos 2008)

This appetite has spread to Xinjiang in recent years and is reflected in the life stories of some prominent Uyghurs. For example, Kasimjan Abdurehim was the founder of a well-known language centre after leaving school at the age of 12 and becoming a businessman. He learnt English and gained entrance to Xinjiang University. He won numerous awards for his English ability, including third place in the China Central TV Cup University Student English Speaking Contest. In 2010, he was named as the 'Young Entrepreneur of the Year' in Xinjiang. Abdurehim expressed his philosophy as follows:

> In order to create an advanced culture, we need to be equipped with advanced thought, advanced viewpoints and advanced worldview. In order to equip ourselves, we need to have the language. (Abdurehim 2012)

The study

In order to understand how these policy changes and the changes in the wider linguistic landscape are affecting Uyghurs and how Uyghurs perceive these changes, we conducted empirical research in Xinjiang with selected university students and their lecturers. A university in Urumqi, the regional capital and the largest city in the province, was chosen as the research site. This is due to a relatively liberal political atmosphere for research in the city, the concentration of the region's most universities and other higher education institutions and relatively easy physical and transportation access to the city. The university where the research participants were based had an even distribution of student numbers from Uyghur and Han ethnicities.

The students and the lecturers were selected primarily on the basis of their membership in the Uyghur linguistic group, experience of learning and practising Mandarin Chinese and English languages (Lanza 2008). All the student participants received their primary and secondary education at schools where Uyghur language was the language of instruction, with Chinese language as one of the core school subjects, prior to their university education. Most came from predominantly Uyghur populated areas of Xinjiang where there is strong ethnolinguistic vitality (Landry and Bourhis 1997) and much of the verbal and written communication within the speech community (Gumperz 2009) is conducted in Uyghur. They had also completed a 1-year compulsory pre-university Chinese language programme before being allowed to proceed to their specialized subjects at university level, which were solely taught in Mandarin Chinese. At the time of the fieldwork, the vast majority of Uyghurs studying at tertiary-level educational institutions had been educated in their mother tongue at school prior to their university study (Sunuodula and Feng 2011), though the situation has been in flux and changing in recent years in favour of strengthening the position of Mandarin Chinese. Thus the students can be regarded as learners of Mandarin Chinese as a second language (Richards and Schmidt 2010) and English as a third language, rather than trilinguals with a similar level proficiency in all three languages. Despite the overwhelming influence of English language in education and society nationally, the number of Uyghurs who had had the opportunity to study English was very small and it was often the case that this was done through informal and private education. The formal education for Uyghurs at primary and secondary level, unlike many other regions in China, did not include the teaching of a foreign language and, even at the tertiary level the provision appears to be patchy and unsystematic, as reflected in our participant interviews.

The relevant sampling frames or lists of trilinguals at the research site was hard to come by, if they existed at all, making it difficult to identify all of the individuals in the population, which is necessary for a random sampling method. Thus the method of sampling research participants and conducting research interviews has to be flexible to offset the difficulty in identifying the participants as well as selection of interview questions due to the sensitive political situation regarding politics of language. The political sensitivity involved in the investigation into language policy and practice at the research site was one of the major considerations in the research design which influenced the approach we adopted in choosing the participants, the research site and the interview questions. Ten tertiary students were chosen for two rounds of interviews which involved a first round of minimally structured interviews followed by a second round of semi-structured interviews with a focus on emergent themes from the first round. The research design adopted the purposive sampling method, where individuals selected from a group or community are judged suitable by the researcher, on the basis of participation observation of the group or community. This was supplemented by a quota sampling where participants' gender, subject speciality, the level of study and place of origin were used as added dimensions (Lanza 2008; Ritchie and Lewis 2003: 96). The interviews were conducted in Uyghur, the first and primary language of all the research participants for which they expressed a preference as the interview language and in which they felt most comfortable in expressing themselves. It is also the first language of the interviewer (Sunuodula), which gives the advantages of insider access to the research participants' meaning making and establishing trusting partnerships so that the relevant questions can be discussed relatively freely. Our focus is on their perceptions of Chinese and English in relation to Uyghur, their willingness to invest in these second and third languages and the process of social identity negotiation and transformation.

The qualitative research was followed by a quantitative research project, which was carried out between July 2010 and May 2011 at four sites: two senior secondary schools in Uyghur-dominated locations in southern Xinjiang, a junior secondary school class in a Han-dominated city in northern Xinjiang and a class in a boarding school for Uyghurs located in a city in eastern China where the Han make up the absolute majority. The research sites for quantitative investigation were chosen on the basis of linguistic demography, language ecology, socio-economic conditions and access to resources which are relevant to the acquisition of second and third languages.

One of the two schools in southern Xinjiang was originally a Uyghur language medium school and the Uyghur students form the majority. The language of instruction has recently been changed from Uyghur to Mandarin Chinese but the students used Uyghur language as their primary language of communication and reported difficulty in understanding the instruction given in Mandarin Chinese in the classrooms. The school is located in a county-level town where educational resources are scarce and there is a shortage of qualified teaching staff, especially for foreign languages. The second school has always been a Mandarin Chinese medium school and the curriculum followed the nationally set standards. Although Mandarin speakers of Han ethnicity are in the majority, it has seen a big jump in Uyghur student enrolment in recent years. The Uyghur students at this school are bilingual speakers proficient in both Mandarin Chinese and Uyghur. The school is located in a prefectural city where the socio-economic conditions are more favourable and there is a significant international tourist presence and vibrant foreign economic activities. The school has access to greater state funding and had a supply of qualified teaching staff for foreign language instruction. The other two schools are Mandarin Chinese medium schools where special Uyghur boarding classes were set up as part of a government scheme (Chen 2010). The Uyghur-speaking students at these two schools are a small minority, and the linguistic ecology of the places where these two schools are located is dominated by Mandarin Chinese. These two schools have better access to educational resources, including highly qualified teaching staff, compared with the schools located in Uyghur areas of southern Xinjiang. The curriculum standards for the special Uyghur classes are the same as those for Han students and follow the national standard curriculum. A total of 190 students completed the questionnaires. Two teachers and four policy-makers were selected as key informants for further interviews. This chapter presents some of the findings that are reported in greater detail in Adamson and Feng (2009), Sunuodula and Feng (2011) and Sunuodula and Cao (2014).

Perceptions of 'Bilingual' education

Our interview data suggest that many Uyghurs are zealous in their efforts to use and maintain their language and offer considerable resistance to efforts to change the status quo. Uyghur ethnic, cultural and social identity is deeply embedded in Uyghur language and most Uyghurs take pride of their language and cultural traditions:

> I do not worry about the threat to Uyghur language and culture. Uyghur culture and language are well advanced and deeply rooted among the Uyghurs. (Student 1)
>
> Uyghurs possess a well-developed tradition of commerce and trading. This is also very important for preserving the Uyghur identity. (Student 2)
>
> I am confident that Uyghur language will survive in future and my aim of learning other languages is to learn the valuable aspects of other cultures. (Student 1)

Many others, however, spoke of fears for the future of Uyghur in the face of the dominant position of Chinese in education:

> I am very concerned about the overwhelming influence and pressure to learn Chinese. (Student 1)
>
> Some classes are taught in Uyghur but the textbooks and the exams are in Chinese. I am concerned about the future of Uyghur language and culture and worry that they may disappear. (Student 3)

For most people who reside in the countryside where more than 80 per cent of the Uyghur population live, Uyghur is the only language they know and use. Uyghur still is used extensively in private and public domains by Uyghurs in Xinjiang. Some students questioned the government's overwhelming drive to push Chinese as the dominant language at the expense of Uyghur language in education as well as in economic, political and social spheres. They were mainly critical of what they see as the marginalization of their language, the rushed way the measures to promote Chinese were introduced and the disregard for the symbolic and historic value of Uyghur language for the Uyghur ethnic identity and culture:

> Han people see their language as the dominant language. The Han officials in the countryside will always to talk to Uyghur farmers in Chinese, despite knowing that the farmers don't understand Chinese. (Student 4)
>
> Recently, a Tajik benefactor to the University gave a speech to a group of Han students who were in their third year specialising in Uyghur language. The Han students demanded to have a Uyghur-Han translator to translate it. The President of the University reminded the Han students that the Uyghur students face the same problem almost everyday but don't get translators. (Student 5)

Any attempt to weaken the use of the language and its social and political importance is perceived as a threat to Uyghur cultural, ethnic and historic identity. The same student mentioned a sense of defiance:

> Imposing Chinese and culture on Uyghurs will not succeed. Most children and their parents are opposed to having their children taught in Chinese. . . . Some students are resisting learning Chinese. (Student 4)

They were dubious about their prospects:

> Learning and using Chinese has become a norm as most lectures are delivered in that language. We are being told that Uyghur language is not advanced enough and holding us up against economic and social development. We are also being told that is why we should be proficient in Chinese. . . . If they are genuinely helping us to develop and better ourselves, why don't they provide us with the same opportunities to learn as the Han people? We don't get a job for being proficient in Chinese. There are many Uyghur university graduates who have graduated from top universities in the east using Chinese and they are still unemployed. (Student 2)

> There seems to be a trade-off between producing a student with subject knowledge and a student with Chinese fluency as the educational outcome. The current 'bilingual education' policy and practices disregard the natural and scientific educational development. I disagree with the bilingual education practices which only stress the importance of Chinese. (Student 4)

Uyghur students also expressed concern about their lack of knowledge and skills in Chinese and its effect on their educational, economic and social prospects:

> I went to Uyghur school and all subjects except Chinese were taught in Uyghur. I am good at written and reading Chinese but not good in oral and listening skills. (Student 2)

> Uyghurs are the least knowledgeable in Chinese compared with most other minority nationalities in China. (Student 1)

> I learned Chinese with great motivation and enthusiasm at school but that has now faded due to the majority in the class having a poor command of the language. (Student 3)

> There is a conflict between Chinese learning and learning subject knowledge and individual creativity. My Chinese bilingual education started in 2001.

> It was very difficult to understand lectures in Chinese for me and it is still not enjoyable because I don't have sufficient knowledge of the language.... I used to be able to compose poetry and short stories in Uyghur and had a lot of creative imagination when I was at school. My mother tongue is the essential tool for me to think and create and it can never be replaced. I am now becoming a passive learner because I lack proficiency in Chinese and I am not able to think creatively in Chinese. I am losing interest in the subjects as I am not able to understand, digest and internalise the knowledge I have learned using Chinese. (Student 4)

> Chinese is a difficult language to learn. I am required to write my dissertation in Chinese. There is little originality and creativity in it because I don't have deep enough knowledge of Chinese to fully express myself. (Student 5)

> I used to be able to compose poetry and short stories in Uyghur and had a lot of creative imagination when I was at school. My mother tongue is the essential tool for me to think and create and it can never be replaced. I am now becoming a passive learner because I lack proficiency in Chinese and I am not able to think creatively in that language. I am losing interest in the subjects as I am not able to understand, digest and internalize the knowledge I have learned using Chinese. (Student 5)

Findings from the quantitative questionnaire data also point to the fact that the respondents perceive the role of their mother tongue in formal education as very important to them, with 84 per cent expressing support for further strengthening of Uyghur in schools. Nonetheless, there was agreement and recognition among the majority of the students interviewed for the need to learn and become sufficiently proficient in Chinese. They recognized the economic, political and practical value of learning the language:

> Chinese is the official language of China and we must learn it for employment. Learning Uyghur, Chinese and English will provide greater employment opportunities. (Student 2)

> Uyghurs must learn Chinese despite the poor quality of teachers and pressure to learn. Chinese can also help in learning English. Some students who did not reach the required level of Chinese proficiency after the pre-sessional language year have been expelled from the University. (Student 4)

A significant majority of respondents (80 per cent) to the questionnaire supported the strengthening of Chinese language learning in their school curriculum. Based on the interviews and responses to open-ended questions on the student questionnaire, it can be observed that Uyghur students show strong extrinsic orientations towards learning Chinese:

> Chinese is very important for me to find a job.
>
> I want to be a teacher in the future. It is a must that I learn Chinese well.
>
> My parents want me to learn Chinese well.
>
> Chinese is our national language. We have to learn it to communicate with others outside Xinjiang.
>
> I will take the College Entrance Examination in Chinese, so I will need to study it hard.

All four policy-makers interviewed are very supportive of the forceful promotion of Chinese in Xinjiang. They believe that teaching Chinese to Uyghur students will lead them to better employment and greater economic benefit. The Uyghur language is also important, but ranks lower than Chinese. As one official at the Xinjiang Education Department put it:

> It is a choice between development and culture. If Uyghur people hope to raise their incomes and improve their living conditions, they must learn to speak Chinese. It is a basic tool for them to participate in the country's economic development. It is unavoidable that the minority language and culture will be affected to some extent. But they have to make the choice.

Perceptions of English

The majority of interviewees for the qualitative project expressed enthusiasm for the potential employment and educational opportunities, as well as economic benefits, accruing from learning English. As this student explains:

> I am very positive about having the opportunity to be educated in a bilingual (English-Uyghur) or trilingual (English-Uyghur-Chinese) environment. I am currently learning English by myself. English is the world language. Trade and commerce is becoming globalised and computers use English for programming. Many fashion brands and well-known products originate from English-speaking countries and many famous cosmetic brands are also from these countries.... Knowledge of English has also become important for finding employment and being able to use computers. (Student 6)
>
> English is an important language. It is a world language. Uyghurs learn English spontaneously. It is important to know English for learning new and

cutting edge academic knowledge and scholarly exchange. Many Han scholars publish their work in English. English dominates the academic literature published. (Student 6)

For some Uyghur students, learning and using English language is associated not only with cultural or economic benefits, but it is also an ideological and political act:

Uyghurs love their freedom and we are open to the wider world. Uyghurs are more interested in the international news than the Chinese domestic news; we are more inclined to be integrated into the wider world than just being confined to the borders of China. This is one of the reasons why Uyghurs are so interested in and motivated to learn English. Learning English and learning things in English can allow opportunities for the Uyghurs to be integrated into the wider world. (Student 6)

I very much welcome the opportunity to study the subjects in English. This will provide both Han and Uyghurs with the same starting point and equal footing and the Han student will get the taste of how it is like to learn subject knowledge in a foreign language. If a lecture is delivered in English and other factors being equal, Uyghurs can compete with the Han students. In the oral English language classes that I have recently attended, most Uyghur students perform better than their Han counterparts attending the same class, despite the fact that the Hans would have studied English at least seven or eight years longer than the Uyghurs. (Student 5)

The respondents to our questionnaire survey all showed strong willingness to invest in learning English and confidence in themselves to be successful in achieving better results than their Han counterparts, provided that they are given the same opportunities in education. Two thirds of our questionnaire respondents strongly supported the improvement of English language education in their schools and 90 per cent agreed with that proposition, which is the highest level of support for any of the three languages in question.

Discussion

The perceptions of stakeholders set out in this chapter illustrate the intrinsic relationship between language education and politics, especially the politics of identity. For the Uyghurs in Xinjiang, the Uyghur language forms an essential part of their ethnic identity, while Chinese and English offer opportunities for educational, economic and social advancement. However, the current situation does not suggest that a win-win-win form of trilingualism is being fostered in the school system. Indeed, there is a strong perception on the part of many Uyghurs that, despite some supportive policy measures, their language and sense of distinctive identity are regarded as collateral damage in the drive for modernization and engagement with globalization. Out of the three languages (Uyghur, Chinese and English), Chinese reigns supreme. This is evident in the mass media and policy documents as well as in long-standing or recent discourse on bilingual or trilingual education and bilingualism and trilingualism for minority groups. The importance of Chinese is recognized by all stakeholders including parents and students for the economic opportunities it provides, but with considerable reluctance, given the political threats to the sustainability of the Uyghur language and cultural identity. However, the tensions arising from the predominance of Chinese and the increasing settlement of Han in the XUAR are not reflected in attitudes towards English. The latter tend to be more positive, as English is not seen as endangering Uyghur – the relationship between the two languages is viewed as one of peaceful coexistence – and competence in the language is one area in which Uyghurs, given sufficient access to English language learning resources, might compete on a level playing field with the Han.

Why does the language policy for schools fail to promote the Uyghur language? The policymaker who is quoted earlier views the issue as a stark choice between economic modernization and backwardness. There may also be a superiority complex on the part of some Han officials when dealing with Uyghurs, as well as some political concerns that learning the language might inflame Uyghur passions and encourage the separatists to escalate their campaign against the Chinese state. There is a risk to this approach of creating a sense that assimilation is the only option, which reduces the chances of a more harmonious accommodation of the Uyghur people within the nation state that a promotion of a stronger model of trilingual education might provide.

Acknowledgements

We are grateful to Dr Frederik Fallmann for sharing his expertise with us. The research for this chapter was funded by the Universities' China Committee in London (UCCL) and the Research Grants Council of Hong Kong (General Research Fund 840012). Views expressed are those of the authors.

References

Abdurehim, K. (7 April 2012), Madiniyat Bostani. No. 243. *Interview with Kasim Abdurehim*. Urumqi: Xinjiang TV5. Retrieved 2 December 2013 from http://v.youku.com/v_show/id_XMzc2OTEwNzIw.html. (In Uyghur.)

Adamson, B. (2004), *China's English: A History of English in Chinese education*. Hong Kong: Hong Kong University Press.

Adamson, B. and Feng, A. (2009), 'A comparison of trilingual education policies for ethnic minorities in China'. *Compare* 39(3): 321–33.

Adamson, B. and Xia, B. (2011), 'A case study of the College English Test and ethnic minority university students in China: Negotiating the final hurdle'. *Journal of Multilingual Education* 1(1).

Baran, L. (2007), 'Past and future of contemporary Uyghur literature'. *Bilig [Knowledge]* 42: 191–211. (In Turkish.)

Becquelin, N. (2000), 'Xinjiang in the nineties'. *The China Journal* 44: 65–90.

Benson, L. (1990), *The Ili Rebellion: The Moslem Challenge to Chinese Authority in Xinjiang, 1944-1949*. Armonk, NY: M. E. Sharpe.

Bögü, A. A. (2002), *Chagatai Uyghur language*. Urumqi: Xinjiang University Press. (In Uyghur.)

Bregel, Y. (1992), 'Central Asia in the 12th-13th/18th-19th centuries', *Encyclopaedia Iranica*. Costa Mesa, CA: Mazda Publishers. Retrieved 2 December 2013 from http://www.iranicaonline.org/articles/central-asia-vii.

Brose, M. C. (2005), 'Uyghur technologists of writing and literacy in Mongol China'. *T'oung Pao* 91(4/5): 396–435.

Chen, Y. (2010), 'Boarding school for Uyghur students: Speaking Uyghur as a bonding social capital'. *Diaspora, Indigenous, and Minority Education* 4(1): 4–16, doi:10.1080/15595690903442231.

Chen, X. J. and Teng, X. (2012), 'An investigation into the situation of bilingual education in Kashghar and Hotan in Xinjiang'. *Journal of Xinjiang Education Institute* 28(1): 10–15. (In Chinese.)

Clark, W. (2011), 'Ibrahim's story'. *Asian Ethnicity* 12(2): 203–19.

Clark, W. and Kamalov, A. (2004), 'Uighur migration across Central Asian frontiers'. *Central Asian Survey* 23(2): 167–82.

Communist Party of China Central Committee Archives Research Office and Communist Party of China XUAR Committee (2010), *Selected Documents on Xinjiang Affairs: 1949-2010*. Beijing: Central Committee Archives Publishing House. (In Chinese.)

Fallmann, F. (2003), 'Swedish missionaries, modernization and cultural exchange in China: The Mission Covenant Church of Sweden in Hubei and Xinjiang'. *Christianity and Chinese Culture*. Vol. 5. Wuhan: Hubei Education Press, pp. 335–53.

Feng, A. W. (2005), 'Bilingualism for the minor or the major? An evaluative analysis of parallel conceptions in China'. *International Journal of Bilingual Education and Bilingualism* 8(6): 529–51.

Feng, A. W. and Sunuodula, M. (2009), 'Analysing minority language education policy process in China in its entirety'. *International Journal of Bilingual Education and Bilingualism* 12(6): 685–704.

Fuller, G. E. and Lipman, J. N. (2004), 'Islam in Xinjiang', in S. F. Starr (eds), *Xinjiang: China's Muslim Borderland*. Armonk, NY; London: M.E. Sharpe, pp. 320–52.

Gil, J. and Adamson, B. (2011), 'The English language in China: A sociolinguistic profile', in A. Feng (ed.), *English Language Education across Greater China*. Clevedon, UK: Multilingual Matters.

Gumperz, J. J. (2009), 'Speech community', in A. Duranti (ed.), *Linguistic Anthropology: A Reader*. Malden, MA: Wiley-Blackwell, pp. 66–73.

Heyit, A. and Shawqi, Q. (2012), *Ana til [Mother tongue]*. Retrieved 2 December 2013 from http://www.youtube.com/watch?v=P3kP-hkknbw. (In Uyghur.)

Kamberi, D. (2005), *Uyghurs and Uyghur Identity*. Philadelphia, PA: Dept. of East Asian Languages and Civilizations, University of Pennsylvania. Retrieved 2 December 2013 from http://www.sino-platonic.org/complete/spp150_uyghurs.pdf.

Khotan County CCP Committee and Khotan People's Government (2004), *Suggestions for Implementing the Xinjiang Autonomous Region CCP Committee and People's Government's Document 'Concerning the Decision to Vigorously Promote "Bilingual" Education Work*. Retrieved 12 November 2007 from http://www.htedu.gov.cn/Article/ShowArticle.asp?ArticleID=237. (In Chinese.)

Landry, R. and Bourhis, R. Y. (1997), 'Linguistic landscape and ethnolinguistic vitality: An empirical study'. *Journal of Language and Social Psychology* 16(1): 23–49, doi:10.1177/0261927X970161002.

Lanza, E. (2008), 'Selecting individuals, groups, and sites', in L. Wei and M. G. Moyer (eds), *The Blackwell Guide to Research Methods in Bilingualism and Multilingualism*. Malden, MA: Blackwell Publishing, pp. 73–87.

Lin, J. (1997), 'Policies and practices of bilingual education for the minorities in China'. *Journal of Multilingual and Multicultural Development* 18(3): 193–205.

Liu, J. (ed.) (2008), *Chinese and Bilingual Education in Xinjiang Primary and Secondary Schools*. Urumqi: Xinjiang Education Press. (In Chinese.)

Ma, R. (2009), 'The development of minority education and the practice of bilingual education in Xinjiang Uyghur Autonomous Region'. *Frontiers of Education in China* 4(2): 188–251.

Millward, J. (2007), *Eurasian Crossroads: A History of Xinjiang*. New York: Columbia University Press.

Mutii, I. (1982), 'Three important ethnic groups in Central Asia and their language', in *Collection of Essays on Xinjiang History*. Urumqi: Xinjiang People's Press, pp. 63–84. (In Chinese.)

National Bureau of Statistics of China (2011), *Tabulation on the 2010 Population Census of the People's Republic of China*. Retrieved 2 December 2013 from http://www.stats.gov.cn/english/statisticaldata/censusdata/rkpc2010/indexce.htm.

Nolan, C. J. (2002), 'Qing (Ch'ing, or Manchu) Dynasty (1644–1912)', *Greenwood Encyclopedia of International Relations*. Santa Barbara, CA: ABC-CLIO. Retrieved 2 December 2013 from http://www.credoreference.com/entry/abcintrel/qing_ch_ing_or_manchu_dynasty_1644_1912.

Office of the Xinjiang Uyghur Autonomous Region Bilingual Education Steering Group (ed.) (2012), *Xinjiang Ethnic Minority Bilingual Education Policy Explained*. Urumqi: Xinjiang People's Press. (In Chinese.)

Osnos, E. (2008), 'Crazy English: The national scramble to learn a new language before the Olympics'. *New Yorker*, 28 April 2008. Retrieved 22 December 2008 from http://www.newyorker.com/magazine/2008/04/28/crazy-english.

Ouyang, Z. (2008), 'An overview of Xinjiang Chinese and bilingual education policies and regulations since the founding of PRC', in J. Liu (ed.), *Chinese and Bilingual Education in Xinjiang Primary and Secondary Schools*. Urumqi: Xinjiang Education Press, pp. 3–10. (In Chinese.)

Richards, J. C. and Schmidt, R. (2010), *Longman Dictionary of Language Teaching and Applied Linguistics*. 4th edn. Harlow: Longman.

Ritchie, J. and Lewis, J. (eds) (2003), *Qualitative Research Practice: A Guide for Social Science Students and Researchers*. London: Thousand Oaks; Calif: Sage Publications.

Rudelson, J. J. (1997), *Oasis Identities: Uyghur Nationalism along China's Silk Road*. New York: Columbia University Press.

Schluessel, E. T. (2007), '"Bilingual" education and discontent in Xinjiang'. *Central Asian Survey* 26(2): 251–77.

Šilde-Karkliņš, R. (1975), 'The Uighurs between China and the USSR'. *Canadian Slavonic Papers/Revue Canadienne Des Slavistes* 17(2/3): 341–65.

Sugawara, J. (2001), 'Scripts and printing in Xinjiang Uyghur Autonomous Region of China: History and present of publishing culture, a case study of Uyghur language', *Research report*. Tokyo: Tokyo University for Foreign Studies Institute of Asian and African Languages and Cultures. Retrieved 2 December 2013 from http://www.aa.tufs.ac.jp/~tjun/data/gicas/xjcpp.pdf. (In Japanese.)

Sunuodula, M. and Cao, Y. (2014), 'Language learning and empowerment: Languages in education for Uyghurs in Xinjiang', in A. W. Feng and B. Adamson (eds), *Trilingualism in Education in China: Models and Challenges*. Dordrecht: Springer.

Sunuodula, M. and Feng, A. W. (2011), 'English language education for the linguistic minorities: The case of Uyghurs', in A. W. Feng (ed.), *English Language Education across Greater China*. Bristol, UK: Multilingual Matters, pp. 260–83.

Teng, S. Y. and Fairbank, J. K. (1979), *China's Response to the West: A Documentary Survey, 1839-1923*. Cambridge, MA: Harvard University Press.

Toops, S. W. (2004), 'Demography of Xinjiang', in S. F. Starr (ed.), *Xinjiang: China's Muslim Borderland*. Armonk, N.Y.; London: M.E. Sharpe, pp. 241–63.

Tsung, L. T. H. and Cruickshank, K. (2009), 'Mother tongue and bilingual minority education in China'. *International Journal of Bilingual Education and Bilingualism* 12(5): 549–63.

Xia, S. (2007), *Education for China's Ethnic Minorities*. Beijing: Wuzhou Dissemination Press. (In Chinese.)

XUAR Census Office (2012), *XUAR 2010 Census Material*. Vol. 1. Beijing: China Statistical Press. (In Chinese.)

XUAR Local Gazettes Editorial Commission and 'Annals of Xinjiang, Language Section' Editorial Board (2000), *Annals of Xinjiang, Languages Section*. Vol. 76. Urumqi: Xinjiang People's Press. (In Chinese.)

XUAR 50th Anniversary Organising Committee and XUAR Statistical Bureau (2005), *Fifty Years of Xinjiang, 1955–2005*. Vol. 1. Beijing: China Statistical Press. (In Chinese.)

6

'Queensland for Ever & Augus un ballybug go braugh': The Expression of Identity in Nineteenth-Century Irish Emigrant Letters

Marije van Hattum

> ### Editor's Introduction
>
> Marije van Hattum investigates cultural reality and identity contained within language dialects in the Irish diaspora to Australia in the nineteenth century. She shows how Irish emigrants used their native dialect in letters written home and how this indexed their former identity. She shows how the old and new dialects and identities can co-exist within their current language use and reflect a dual identity of Irish Australian.

Introduction

It may not be necessary to have an extensive knowledge of the background of the writer of the words in the title of this chapter, 'Queensland for Ever & Augus un ballybug go braugh [and Ballybug for ever]', in order to identify this person as an Irish emigrant in Australia. Language use is unique to every individual and works like a fingerprint in reflecting our personal identity. At the same time, certain aspects of our language use allow us to link ourselves to certain social groups and thus serve to both create and reflect a social identity (Llamas and Watt 2010). A person's vocabulary, grammar and pronunciation are indexical of their identity, and thus by analysing, for example, the grammar of instances of an individual's language, we can learn much about their identity. Our identity, and thus our language, is shaped by our social context and previous experiences. The effects of migration on the language use of individuals and how the linguistic behaviour of first-generation migrants can signal identity is the main focus of this chapter.

The Modern English period (ca. 1500–1900) is characterized by a substantial increase in regional mobility as a result of technical advancement and of the social, political and cultural changes, both in terms of large-scale urbanization within Britain and in terms of colonization. Internal and external migrations continuously shape the identities and languages of nations, societies and of individuals. An example of how migration has shaped the English language can be found in the borrowing of foreign terms. The colonization of North America has introduced several new lexical items to the English language, such as *moose* and *raccoon*. In present-day English these words are commonly used in most varieties of English and are thus not associated with any particular identity. However, the use of these two lexical items in the early seventeenth century would have signalled the identity of someone who lived in North America.

Emigrants to the New World frequently found themselves in direct contact with speakers of many varieties of English, and where in many cases they had previously been members of a fairly homogeneous social group using a similar dialect to the other members of their group, they now found themselves as part of a social group where everyone spoke a different variety of English, or in some cases even a different language. Theoretical frameworks such as New-Dialect Formation (NDF) (Trudgill 2004) and Schneider's dynamic model for the evolution of World Englishes (Schneider 2003) have given an extensive account of how new, relatively homogeneous varieties of English have developed in former British colonies. However, they have not provided much empirical evidence of what happens in the initial stages of an individual's language use when settling in a colony in the New World. Indeed, this is quite a difficult task, as most of the processes that allow for new, homogeneous varieties of English to arise take place in face-to-face interaction, of which we of course have no testimony. Nevertheless, this chapter will show that, though the emigrant letters under investigation mainly show signs indexical of their former identity, evidence for early stages of the development of a new idiolect and a new identity can be found in the writings of first-generation immigrants.

I will start by providing a brief overview of theories concerned with the expression of identity by means of linguistic forms in Section 2, followed by an account of theories concerning the development of new varieties of English in

Section 2.1. In Section 3, I will provide an analysis of emigrant letters written by three first-generation emigrants. I will show how these letters mainly show signs of their former linguistic identity, but that some minor traces of their new identities can likewise be observed. In Section 4 the results of my analysis will be discussed in terms of the proposed research statement that evidence for the development of a new linguistic identity can be found in the writings of first-generation Irish migrants in Australia in the nineteenth century.

Locating language in identity

According to Llamas and Watt (2010: 1), '[l]anguage not only reflects who we are, but in some sense it *is* who we are, and its use defines us both directly and indirectly'. The way in which speakers reflect and construct their identity has been widely researched over the last couple of decades. As language users, our lifelong socialization has given us the tools to instinctively interpret a person's background by analysing their speech. Our speech marks us as belonging to a particular nation, living within a certain region within that nation, having received a certain level of education, etc. (Joseph 2010).

Identity exists on several different levels: national, social and personal. According to Joseph (2010), there exists a tendency for groups of people who live together in adjoining territory and who perceive themselves as sharing a common interest to develop a similar way of speaking that distinguishes them from other groups which live in close proximity and have different, sometimes even rival, interests. The development of these national identities, or any identity for that matter, largely depends on defining the boundaries of 'us' versus 'them' (Edwards 2009). The common interests within a nation and the shared way of speaking tend to create a cultural unity, a national identity (Joseph 2010).

In the same way that common interests can create a national identity, the loss of common interests can dissolve a national identity. There are many factors that can cause a once unified nation to break up, such as war, religion and natural disasters. The factor of particular interest to this chapter is migration. In Ireland, oppression, religion and famine caused millions of Irish to migrate to the New World, particularly during the nineteenth century. Where once their national identity was without a doubt *Irish*, these migrants now find themselves in a position where they have to rediscover their identity and the social groups to which they now belong.

Social identity, then, is defined by Tajfel (1978: 63) as 'that part of an individual's self-concept which derives from his knowledge of his membership of a social group (or groups) together with the value and emotional significance attached to that membership'. This definition highlights that social identity relates to an individual, and not to the social group the individual belongs to. The use of the term *self-concept* suggests that delineation of group-membership is based on the perception of the individual. In other words, we belong to certain social groups because we think we do. As with national identity, there is a tendency for social groups to develop a similar way of speaking that separates 'us' from 'them'.

I argued above that nations and social groups develop a similar way of speaking which marks speakers as members of that nation or social group. The pronunciation of the word *bath* as either /bæθ/ or /bɑːθ/ allows most British people to identify the speaker as respectively northern or southern. In addition, we tend to associate the latter pronunciation with a more 'posh' accent. Linguistic anthropologists such as Ochs (1992) and Silverstein (2003) have proposed that the relationship between linguistic forms (e.g. pronunciation, grammatical structures or vocabulary) and identity is indexical, and that in the case of the *bath* example above the pronunciation indexes the speaker's identity (Johnstone 2010).

The notion of indexicality goes back to the semiotic theories proposed by Charles S. Peirce (1839–1914). Semiotic theory proposes that we generate meaning through the creation and interpretation of signs, which can take the form of images, sounds, smells, flavour, but also of words (Chandler 2007). Peirce identifies three different types of signs: symbolic, iconic and indexical.

Symbolic signs are signs that we associate with what the sign refers to, the signified. However, symbolic signs are generally arbitrary in the sense that the nature of the sign itself has no connection with the signified, other than the fact that we have subconsciously agreed that there is a connection. The word *cat*, for example, is a symbolic sign, as the individual letters c-a-t have no connection with what a cat actually is. The letter forms of the word *cat* do not tell us that it has fur, that it usually has four legs and a tail and so on. The fact that words are generally symbolic signs of their signified can further be illustrated by the fact that the word for the referent 'cat' is *billi* in Hindi. Thus, among speakers of Hindi it has been subconsciously agreed that *billi* refers to the same referent as the word *cat* does in English.

Iconic signs tend to be direct representations of the signified. Thus, a picture or a drawing of a cat gives us information on the nature of the cat. It can tell us that it has fur, whiskers, two pointy ears and so on. A picture of a cat is thus an iconic sign.

For their part, indexical signs tend to have a concrete and causal relationship to the signified. When we see smoke, we know there must be a fire, even if we cannot see the fire itself. Thus, the sign *smoke* is indexical of fire, as it has a causal relationship with fire. In much the same way, the pronunciation of *bath* as /bɑːθ/ is indexical of southern English or education in a posh school (Joseph 2010).

Silverstein (2003) differentiates between first-order and second-order indexicality. First-order indexicality consists of markers of relatively objective or 'value-free' associations, such as geographical identity. Second-order indexicality consists of markers which carry ideologically loaded information, such as prestige and elitism. If we return to the example of the pronunciation of *bath*, the signification of the /bɑːθ/ pronunciation as southern English can be called first order and the signification as having been to an elite school is second order. It is important to keep in mind, though, that not only do these indexical signs evoke a certain identity in hearers, but they can also be used to construct an identity by the speakers. Thus, indexical forms 'both evoke and construct identities, and they always potentially do both' (Johnstone 2010: 31).

As mentioned above, our previous life experiences have given us the information we need to be able to link indexical meanings to indexical forms, but how do these meanings get attached to certain forms? In other words, how do we know that /bɑːθ/ is indexical of southern English and elitism? According to Johnstone (2010: 32), the answer is quite simple: 'people learn to hear linguistic variants as having indexical meaning by being told that they do, and they continue to share ideas about indexical meaning as long as they keep telling each other about them'. The title of an online article in *The Guardian* asked the question whether 'speaking like an Aussie make[s] you sound insecure?' (McClintock and Earl 2014). Speakers of Australian English have a tendency to raise their intonation upwards at the end of a sentence, and the article tells us that it makes every sentence sound like a question. The Guardian reports a survey which claims that the informants believed this marker to be indexical of insecurity and emotional weakness. Thus, telling their readers about the indexical relationship between this linguistic form and the first-order index of Australian English and the second-order index of insecurity reinforces that relationship and perhaps even introduces this relationship to some people who were not previously aware of it.

If our previous life experiences allow us to evoke and construct identities through linguistic forms, then we can expect life-changing events such as migration to be reflected on our linguistic forms. The next section will explore the outcomes of migration and colonization in terms of language and identity.

Identity and migration

As a result of colonization, the English language has been transported to regions where this language was not previously spoken, either in the location in question or nearby. Trudgill refers to these situations as *tabula rasa* situations (Trudgill 2004: 26). The speakers who migrated to the New World, and who thus introduced the English language in these locations, were not a homogeneous group. The settlers often consisted of speakers from various regional, social and ethnic backgrounds. In Australia, for example, though the majority of speakers were convicts from south-east England, there were also sizeable groups of speakers of other dialects, including a large number of Irish convicts. In addition, internal migration towards the London area meant that even though the earliest settlers might have been living in London before they were transported, they might not have spoken a London dialect of English. Thus, the varieties of English that developed in the newly established colonies were not simply transported variants of previously existing dialects of English. Through processes of dialect mixing, levelling and actuation completely new dialects were formed. One of the most influential frameworks for the development of these post-colonial varieties of English is called NDF (Trudgill 2004).

According to Trudgill (2004), the development of new dialects in tabula rasa contexts generally consists of three stages, which roughly correspond to three successive generations of speakers, as summarized in Table 6.1 below.

During the first stage, speakers of different dialects accommodate towards each other in face-to-face interaction. When speakers of different dialects come in contact with one another, they tend to reduce the amount of stereotypical features of their dialects in order to increase intelligibility. In addition, if the contact is extensive both in terms of intensity and duration, speakers will start to adopt features of the dialects they hear around them. Trudgill (2004) refers to this process as rudimentary levelling. Interdialect development, which also takes place in Stage I, involves the development of new forms which were not present in the input dialects as a result of misanalysis and partial accommodation.

Table 6.1 Three stage of NDF (Dollinger 2008; after Trudgill 2004)

Stage I	Rudimentary levelling	+	Interdialect development
Stage II	Extreme variability	+	Apparent levelling
Stage III	Choice of major forms	+	Reallocation

Second-generation migrants tend to select linguistic forms from different dialects to be part of their own idiolect, which results in extreme variability in Stage II. The total number of variants available to them from listening to first-generation migrants will be somewhat reduced as the second generation will not select those forms that appear too infrequently to be noticed (Gordon 2005). Thus, contrary to the levelling which takes place in Stage I, apparent levelling is subconscious, whereas rudimentary levelling tends to be a conscious process.

Third-generation migrants will develop a focused and socially stable variety in Stage III by reducing the amount of variation to usually one variant per function. This means that more forms will be levelled out, but in some cases more than one variant will become part of the new variety through the process of reallocation. During this process the two forms which previously existed in free variation will now become either socially or even linguistically conditioned. An example of reallocation in the English language is the redistribution of the words *shirt* and *skirt* during the early Middle English period. *Shirt* was the English form and *skirt* was the Old Norse form resulting from the Scandinavian invasions in the late Old English period, but both had the meaning of 'an undergarment for the upper part of the body' in Middle English (OED 2014, s.v. *shirt*, n.). In the fifteenth century the Old Norse form has been reallocated to mean 'the lower part of a woman's dress or gown' (OED 2014, s.v. *skirt*, n.). Trudgill (2004) claims that the determining factor in the selection of forms in Stage III is the principle of majority, but others have suggested that prestige and identity play a role as well (for a discussion see *Language in Society* 37: 2).[1]

The present chapter concerns itself with first-generation migrants, and thus Stage I is of central importance to understanding the expressions of identity in the language of the writers of the letters under discussion. The early phase of the development of a new linguistic identity tends to be characterized by face-to-face accommodation between speakers of different dialects of English. The levelling of native features and the acquisition of non-native features are linguistic signs of accommodation towards a new social identity. This new social identity does not necessarily supplant any older identities, but will rather co-exist alongside them.

As accommodation takes place in face-to-face interaction, the expectation is that the letters of the migrants will largely show forms that are indexical of their 'old' Irish identity and very few signs of the development of a 'new' linguistic identity. Ideally, we would like to analyse face-to-face interaction of these first-generation migrants in Australia, but since the recording of human voices was not yet common place in the nineteenth century, this is impossible. In the absence of spoken data, this chapter makes use of personal letters written by migrants to their families and friends back home. The authors of these letters were often minimally schooled and probably did not write on many other occasions. As they are written mainly between family members and close friends, they are usually written with less self-consciousness than other types of letters (Montgomery 1995), and generally contain instances of informal, intimate and relatively unmonitored language use (Fritz 2007). Fritz (2007) claims that emigrant letters show variable usage between native and acquired linguistic forms from other varieties of English, but Fitzpatrick (1994) notes that emigrants sometimes avoided these non-native features in order to strengthen the weakening link with home. In the following section I will try to demonstrate that, though limited, linguistic forms that are indexical of the emigrant's newly emerging identities as Irish Australians can sometimes be found in these letters.

Locating identity in first-generation emigrant letters

In the nineteenth century, almost eight million Irish people left their native homeland in search of better lives in the New World as a result of factors such as economic depression and famine. Roughly a third of a million Irish migrated to Australia between 1840 and 1914, which seems a small number in comparison to the migration to Britain and the United States. However, though Australia might not have been the most popular destination for the Irish, Ireland was a major source of immigrant influx in Australia. The majority of Irish migrants were dependent on government assistance to pay the fare. According to Fitzpatrick (1994: 10–11), 'Victorian returns for 1852–54 indicate that, even in the first heady rush for gold, only a quarter of Irish arrivals were unassisted compared with three-quarters of those from Britain.' This suggests that, generally, the social standing of the Irish was lower than that of other British settlers. In addition, Hickey (2007) suggests that rural migrants would have spoken an identifiable contact variety of Irish English which would have been avoided by the rest of the English-speaking population of Australia and by second- and third-generation Irish migrants. This would have probably increased the pressure in first-generation speakers to accommodate towards other dialects of English in face-to-face interactions. It also explains why, despite the considerable representation of the Irish among settlers in Australia, so very few linguistic forms in Australian English can be traced back to Irish English. The following sections will explore the dialect forms that were introduced by the Irish to Australia, and it will examine the way in which these and non-native forms are used to reflect and construct the identities of first-generation migrants in Australia. The letters that have been examined for this purpose were written by three different authors: John McCance from county Down, Biddy Burke from county Galway, and Michael Normile from county Clare. The letters and all background information relating to these three authors have been taken from Fitzpatrick (1994).[2]

John McCance (1819–1907)

John McCance and his family migrated to Australia in 1853 and initially settled in Geeling, approximately 75 kilometres south-west of Melbourne, before heading to the gold fields around Castlemaine approximately 120 kilometres north-west of Melbourne in 1856. Gold was first discovered here in 1851 and shortly thereafter, an influx of adventurers had settled in the area and established a small town. This means that the process of NDF in this particular area of Australia had only started a couple of years before the arrival of the McCances, and the English speakers in the area had not yet had the opportunity to develop a uniform dialect.

The letters under analysis were written between 1858 and 1862 to Mr William Orr in Grey Abby county Down. According to Fitzpatrick (1994) William Orr was superior to John McCance, both from a social and an educational point of view. This resulted in slightly more carefully constructed language than can be found in the other emigrant letters. Nevertheless, John's letters are full of linguistic forms which are indexical of Irish English, as we will see.

Let's take example (1) to start with, which shows the use of a third-person singular verb inflection with a plural subject if that subject is not a personal pronoun such as *we*. This linguistic form is very common in vernacular Irish English, but the form can be found in many dialects of English, in particular in Northern England and Scotland (Filppula 1999: 150–9). Thus, this form in isolation is not indexical of Irish English. However, example (1) illustrates another feature commonly found in Irish English, the 'indefinite anterior perfect'.

The verb group *received* is used here to refer to a state of affairs which took place at an unspecified point in a period leading up to the moment of speaking. In present-day Standard English the verb group *have received* would be used. According to Filppula (1999), this perfect frequently occurs with the adverb *ever*, as is the case here. The construction can also be found in earlier forms of English, American English and conservative dialects of British English, but the position of the indefinite anterior perfect is less prominent in these other dialects (Filppula 1999: 91–106).

(1) I could not get away untill his little affairs **was** settled . . . this was their first money we ever received (John McCance 1862)

'I could not get away until his little affairs had been settled . . . this was the first money we have ever received.'

McCance also frequently makes use of a perfect construction with the auxiliary verb *be* instead of StE *have*, as in example (2). The 'be-perfect' is commonly used in Irish English to express the completion of a dynamic activity at the time of speech. This construction appears frequently with 'mutative' verbs such as *leave*, *change*, *die* and *go*, as is the case here (Kallen 1989: 18–19). This linguistic form is said to be rare in other dialects of English, though it was quite common in the early Modern English period.

(2) Boyces Doughters **is dead** since they come hear (John McCance 1861)

'Boyce's Daughters have died since they came here'

Example (2) illustrates another linguistic form that is commonly found in Irish English. According to Hickey (2007), the amount of possible verb forms is reduced in colloquial forms of Irish English. An Irish English speaker might use the form *come* in an instance that would require the preterite *came* in StE, as in example (2). Other examples which can also be found frequently in the writing of John McCance are *seen* for StE *saw*, *beat* for StE *beaten*, the past participle *proved* for StE *proven*, and *took* for StE *taken*. This feature can be found in many dialects of English, but in combination with the other features mentioned in this section serves as indexical marker of Irish English.

So far I have mainly discussed linguistic forms in John McCance's writing that can also be found in other varieties of English, but he also uses some forms that are more unique to Irish English, such as the use of unbound reflexive pronouns. In StE reflexive pronouns are generally governed by an antecedent, but in Irish English reflexive pronouns can appear without an antecedent, as in example (3). This linguistic form can be ascribed to transfer from the Irish language which shows a similar pattern for the word *féin*, which can be used in Irish in reflexive contexts but also in emphatic or polite contexts. (Filppula 1999; Hickey 2007)

(3) I will write to **himself** by it (John McCance 1862)
'I will write him by it [the next mail]'

The previous discussion has demonstrated that John McCance's language is largely indexical of his Irish identity, and many more linguistic forms can be found in the letters to illustrate this point. However, there seem to be no morphological or grammatical forms that are indexical of a changing identity. There are, however, some instances of vocabulary in his letters that are indexical of Australia. In a description of the animals he has come across in Australia, John McCance mentions a *kangaroo*, an *oppossum*[sic] and a *kangaroorat*. In present-day English these words might not seem so exotic or indeed be indexical of someone who lives in Australia, but in the 1850s they were. The first quotation in the Oxford English Dictionary (OED) for *kangaroo* can be dated to 1773 (OED, s.v. *kangaroo*, n.), the first quotation for *opossum* referring to the animal from Australia is from a 1777 text (OED, s.v. *opossum*, n.) and the first quotation for a *kangaroo-rat* comes from 1788 (OED, s.v. *kangaroo-rat*, n.). This shows that these lexical items had only been part of the English language for about a 100 years before John McCance penned them down, and it is unlikely that his addressees made use of these words frequently, if they had ever come across them at all. Even more indexical is McCance's use of the words *bush* and *station*. Though these words have been part of the English language for a long time, they acquired a new meaning in Australia. The word *bush* in John McCance's letter refers to 'the uncleared or untilled districts in the former British Colonies which are still in a state of nature, or largely so, even though not wooded' (OED, s.v. *bush*, n. meaning 9). This particular meaning of the word *bush* is not recorded in the OED until 1826, and McCance's use of this term thus signals his newly developing Australian identity. A similar case can be made for *station* with the meaning 'large cattle or sheep farm', which is recorded in the OED for the first time in 1820 (OED, s.v. *station*, n., meaning 8). This case is especially interesting, as McCance could have also used the word *farm* which is supralocal. Thus, by using the Australian word *station*, rather than the neutral word *farm*, he is indexing the Australian part of his identity.

Biddy Burke (b. 1859)

Bridget 'Biddy' Burke and her brother Patrick migrated to Australia from Balrobuck beg, a small-town land approximately 10 miles north of Galway. The Galway area was still largely Irish speaking around this time and, though Biddy wrote her letters in English, she was bilingual. She arrived in Brisbane in 1880 and took up a position there as a domestic servant. Brisbane was founded in 1824 as a penal colony, but it was not until 1842 that the town allowed free settlers. Thus, at the time that Biddy arrived, the English language spoken in Brisbane would have been far from a focused variety, and Biddy would have been exposed to extreme variability.

The letters under investigation were written to Biddy's parents between 1882 and 1884. Though the content of the letters is full of signs indexical of her mixed Irish Australian identity, very few linguistic clues of this new identity can be found. The linguistic forms are largely indexical of the high-contact variety spoken in Galway. This is not entirely unexpected considering the letters were all written within 4 years of her migration to Australia.

Biddy's letters contain many of the forms found indexical of Irish English in John McCance's letters, such as third-person singular verb inflection with plural subjects (e.g. 4), the indefinite anterior perfect (e.g. 5), the reduction of verb forms (e.g. 6) and the unbound use of reflexive pronouns (e.g. 7).

(4) His wife & children **is** all right (Biddy Burke 1882)
'His wife & children are alright'

(5) also **did** Cannopy **die** yet (Biddy Burke 1882)
'also has Cannopy died yet'

(6) After a lonely Christmas I received your letter yesterday the 1st of Feb which **give** me a start to heare that my father is not well (Biddy Burke 1882)
'After a lonely Christmas I received your letter yesterday the 1st of Feb and it gave me a start to hear that my father is not well'

(7) **Myself** and Patt really we had a grand Christmas of it (Biddy Burke 1884)
'Patt and I had a good Christmas'

There are also a large number of features which are indexical of high-contact varieties which arise out of a situation of what is called 'imperfect learning'.[3] In example (8) we see the absence of a possessive marker in the noun phrase. The juxtaposition of possessors *Thomas Killela & Patt Callop* next to the possessed *death* serves to function as a marker of possession, but there is no formal possessive marker. Example (9) shows an example of the absence of the auxiliary verb *be* in a progressive construction and in example (10) copula *be* is absent before an adjective phrase. All these features would single Biddy out as a speaker of a high-contact variety of Irish English.

(8) and I am so sorrow for **Thomas Killela & Patt Callop death**. (Biddy Burke 1882)

'I am sorry to hear of Thomas Killela & Patt Callop's death'

(9) Dear Winney let me know how all my Cousins **doing** (Biddy Burke 1882)

'Dear Winney let me know how all my cousins are doing'

(10) I hope it **all right** (Biddy Burke 1882)

'I hope it is alright'

Again, the language of Biddy shows many more forms that are indexical of her Irish identity than can be discussed here, but the letters also show some signs of her emerging Australian identity. Like John McCance, Biddy uses the word *bush* several times to refer to 'uncleared or untilled districts'. As argued above, the use of the word *bush* in this way would immediately signal an Australian identity. However, the clearest sign of Biddy's mixed Irish Australian identity are the words in the title of this chapter. In the letter written on the 19 June 1882, Biddy signs off using the phrase in example (11). The code-switching between English and Irish, especially considering the meaning of the phrase, is a clear linguistic marker of an Irish Australian identity.

(11) Queensland for Ever & Augus un ballybug go braugh.

'Queensland for Ever & and the small town for ever'

Michael Normile (1832–80)

The final letters under investigation were written by Michael Normile junior from Derry, county Clare. Michael and his sister Bridget left for Australia in 1854 and initially settled in Lochinvar, New South Wales before moving to West Maitland. West Maitland was founded in 1820 and was thus a relatively new town when Michael Normile settled there. Again, this suggests that Michael Normile was not exposed to a uniform variety of English to which he had to accommodate, but he was exposed to many different dialects of English.

The letters were written to his father Michael Normile senior across a time-span of 13 years, from 1854 to 1865. The Normile letters are perhaps the most interesting collection under investigation here, as for the first time we can see signs of dialect levelling and linguistic accommodation. The letters of Michael Normile are full of indexical markers that point towards an Irish identity, including many of the forms discussed for John McCance and Biddy Burke, such as third-person singular verb marking with plural subjects (e.g. 12), reduced number of verb forms (e.g. 13) and the indefinite anterior perfect (e.g. 14).

(12)   All the crops **pays** very well (Michael Normile 1855)
       'All the crops pay very well'

(13)   I **seen** this last Summer 4 months without a drop of rain (Michael Normile 1855)
       'this last summer I saw 4 months without a drop of rain'

(14)   Let me know **did** Mr James Shannon **get married** as yet. (Michael Normile 1855)
       'Let me know if Mr James Shannon has gotten married yet'

Thus, as with the McCance and Burke letters, the majority of the linguistic forms in the Normile letters are indexical of Irish identity. However, as these letters have been written across a time span of 13 years, I contrasted the amount of non-standard and standard forms between the first couple of letters and the last couple of letters. One of the linguistic forms which draw our attention is the use of non-standard perfect constructions against the use of the standard perfect. In the early letters, Michael Normile is consistent in using non-standard perfect constructions, such as the indefinite anterior perfect illustrated in example (13) above. However, in his later letters, Michael contrasts the use of non-standard perfects with the use of the StE *have*-perfect, as can be seen in example (15) below.

(15)   I **have been** a bad son to you dear Father but I could not help it (Michael Normile 1863)

Another feature that shows a similar pattern is the use of inverted word order in indirect questions, as in example (14) above and examples (16) and (17) below. The final paragraph of most of Normile's letters is devoted to enquiring about his family, neighbours and friends back home. In the first couple of letters he wrote to his father, he consistently used an inverted word order after an introductory phrase such as *let me know*. Bliss (1984) makes a distinction between simple and complex indirect questions (e.g. 16 and 17, respectively). In StE, simple indirect question would be preceded by *if* or *whether*, whereas complex indirect questions are introduced by a wh-word such as *how, why* or *where*. Regardless of whether the indirect question is simple or complex, the word order of the question is subject + verb, meaning there is no inversion. We can see from the examples below that in simple indirect questions (e.g. 16) the conjunction *if* is missing and that both examples show a verb + subject word order, that is they both show inversion. Bliss (1984) and Filppula (1999) argue for influence from Irish in the development of this construction in Irish English.

(16) Let me know **had Johny Lenane** the garden this last year (Michael Normile 1854)

'Let me know if Johny Lenane had the garden this last year'

(17) Let me know how **is Martin McDonell Senr** (Michael Normile 1854)

'Let me know how Martin McDonell Senr is'

In Normile's later letters, he still devotes quite some words to enquiring after what is happening at home, but in contrast to his earlier letters, he is starting to use the StE form without inversion alongside the IrE form with inversion, as can be seen in examples (18) and (19). Thus, it seems that, probably as a result of levelling, Michael Normile has introduced the use of certain StE forms in his later letters, whereas his earlier letters were consistent in the use of non-standard forms which were indexical or Irish English. It is important to note that the Irish English forms occurred alongside the StE forms in the later letters and were thus not completely levelled out, as is expected from what we know about levelling and linguistic accommodation.

(18) Let me know how **Mr Shannon is** situated (Michael Normile 1863)

(19) Let me know where **Mr Shannon lives** (Michael Normile 1865)

Conclusion

The aim of the present chapter was to investigate the written language of first-generation Irish immigrants in Australia in the nineteenth century, in order to see whether signs of their changing identity could be found in their writings. The expectation was that few linguistic signs of a newly emerging Australian identity would be found in the letters, since linguistic accommodation tends to take place spontaneously in face-to-face interaction and not in writing. Indeed, the writings of John McCance in the late 1850s and early 1860s showed little signs of an Australian identity. The only evidence of his new identity could be found in the adoption of certain loanwords, such as *kangaroo*, and the use of existing English words which had recently acquired new meanings in Australia, such as *bush* or *station*. Biddy Burke's letters, written between 1882 and 1884, were also largely indexical of the high-contact variety spoken in her home county, though she also used some Australian terms such as *bush*. Biddy's code-switching between English and Irish in the phrase *Queensland for ever & augus un ballybug go braugh*, however, was a clear indexical sign of her newly emerging Irish Australian identity. The letters of Michael Normile showed some small traces of linguistic accommodation. Apart from some loanwords, his writings were also largely indexical of Irish English, but the letters gradually started to show signs of increased variability. Whereas his early letters made exclusive use of the Irish English perfects, such as the indefinite anterior perfect, his later writings started to include uses of the StE *have*-perfect alongside the Irish English perfects. A similar pattern was found in his formation of indirect questions, which in the early letters made exclusive use of the Irish English forms, but in his later letters showed variation with the StE pattern.

To conclude, it seems that investigating the written language of first-generation Irish migrants in Australia can provide valuable insights into the development of colonial identities and the early development of post-colonial varieties of English. A contrastive investigation of letters written to the 'old' social group in the homeland and letters written to the 'new' social group in the colony was beyond the scope of this chapter, but would certainly yield further insights into the accommodation and levelling processes in the language of first-generation migrants during the early development of post-colonial varieties of English.

Notes

1. As my chapter focuses on linguistic accommodation among first-generation migrants, this discussion is beyond the scope of the present paper.
2. I would like to express my gratitude towards Professor David Fitzpatrick for providing me with electronic versions of these letters and for allowing me to use them for linguistic research.
3. For a more detailed account of imperfect learning and the development of high-contact varieties see, for example, Thomason and Kaufman (1991) and Thomason (2001).

References

Bliss, A. J. (1984), 'English in the south of Ireland', in P. Trudgill (ed.), *Language in the British Isles*. Cambridge: Cambridge University Press, pp. 131–51.

Chandler, D. (2007), *Semiotics for Beginners*. London: Routledge.

Dollinger, S. (2008), *New-dialect Formation in Canada: Evidence from the English Modal Auxiliaries*. Amsterdam and Philadelphia: John Benjamins.

Edwards, J. (2009), *Language and Identity*. Cambridge: Cambridge University Press.

Filppula, M. (1999), *The Grammar of Irish English: Language in Hibernian Style*. London: Routledge.

Fitzpatrick, D. (1994), *Oceans of Consolation: Personal Accounts of Irish Migration to Australia*. Cork: Cork University Press.

Fritz, C. (2007), *From English in Australia to Australian English – 1788-1900*. Frankfurt am Main: Peter Lang.

Gordon, M. J. (2005), 'Review of New-dialect formation: The inevitability of colonial Englishes, ed. Peter Trudgill'. *Journal of Sociolinguistics* 9(1): 146–50.

Hickey, R. (2007), *Irish English: History and Present-day Forms*. Cambridge: Cambridge University Press.

Johnstone, B. (2010), 'Locating language in identity', in C. Llamas and D. Watt (eds), *Language and Identities*. Edinburgh: Edinburgh University Press, pp. 29–36.

Joseph, J. E. (2010), 'Identity', in C. Llamas and D. Watt (eds), *Language and Identities*. Edinburgh: Edinburgh University Press, pp. 9–17.

Kallen, J. L. (1989), 'Tense and Aspect Categories in Irish English'. *English World-Wide* 10: 1–39.

Llamas, C. and Watt, D. (2010), *Language and Identities*. Edinburgh: Edinburgh University Press.

McClintock, A. and Earl, R. (2014), 'Does speaking like an Aussie make you sound insecure?', *The Guardian*, 14 January, http://www.theguardian.com/commentisfree/2014/jan/14/speaking-like-an-aussie-insecure-australian-upward-inflection.

Montgomery, M. (1995), 'The linguistic value of Ulster emigrant letters'. *Ulster Folklife* 41: 26–41.

Ochs, E. (1992), 'Indexing gender', in A. Durant and C. Goodwin (eds), *Rethinking Context: Language as an Interactive Phenomenon*. New York: Cambridge University Press, pp. 146–69.

OED online (January 2014), *The Oxford English Dictionary*. Oxford: Oxford University Press. www.oed.com (last accessed on 20 February 2014).

Schneider, E. W. (2003), 'The dynamics of new Englishes: From identity construction to dialect birth'. *Language* 79(2): 233–81.

Silverstein, M. (2003), 'Indexical order and the dialectics of sociolinguistic life'. *Language and Communication* 23: 193–229.

Tajfel, H. (1978), 'Social categorization, social identity and social comparison', in H. Tajfel (ed.), *Differentiation Between Social Groups: Studies in the Social Psychology of Intergroup Relations*. London: Academic Press, pp. 61–76.

Thomason, S. G. (2001), *Language Contact. An Introduction*. Edinburgh: Edinburgh University Press.

Thomason, S. G. and Kaufman, T. (1991), *Language Contact, Creolization, and Genetic Linguistics*. Berkeley: University of California Press.

Trudgill, P. (2004), *New-dialect Formation: The Inevitability of Colonial Englishes*. Edinburgh: Edinburgh University Press.

7

Indigenous Languages, Cultures and Communities in the Amazon: Strengthening Identities

Alex Guilherme

> ### Editor's Introduction
>
> Alex Guilherme explores the return to a former indigenous identity by Amazonian communities in Brazil. Much like in previous chapters Alex acknowledges that language indexes identity. This chapter, however, calls to mind the peril in which minority languages find themselves. Much in the same way as the Uyghur population of Chapter 5, languages in the Amazonian areas are not only minority but also marginalized. Furthermore the dramatic situation here is that they are at risk of demise and eventual death with the concomitant death of culture. Alex details government projects to reverse this trend and revitalize languages and cultures in these areas.

Prologue

In the *Philosophical Investigations* Wittgenstein drew our attention to the importance of 'language' when he stated that 'the speaking of language is part of an activity, or a form of life' (*PI* 23). That is, a language implies a 'complex form of life' which is revealed through the way speakers think, live and act and therefore it defines their very 'identity'. However, 'language death' is an undeniable phenomenon of our modern times as languages have started to disappear at an alarming rate, and this has prompted linguists, anthropologists, philosophers and educationists to engage with this issue at various levels in an attempt to understand it. In this chapter I refer to some interesting and innovative educational projects in the Amazon region of Brazil, which are revitalizing local languages, cultures and communities. I will argue that these educational ventures might be viewed as useful templates for other countries and peoples seeking to reverse or avoid 'language' death and strengthen their own 'forms of life' and 'identities'.

Introduction: Language death, culture death

In his seminal article, 'Language Death and Disappearance: Causes and Circumstances', Wurm (1991: 1) notes:

> Many languages have disappeared without being known to us in any great detail, with only some fragmentary materials in them – written or noted down by speakers or observers of them hundreds or even thousands of years ago – at our disposal to give us some idea as to what those languages were like. Others have disappeared without even that scanty information about their nature being available to us; only their names are known from historical records, or perhaps some remarks were written down by someone many years ago and were preserved over the ages to tell us something about some special features of such a language or such languages and who and what kind of people their speakers were. Many other languages, certainly a much larger number than the dead languages about which we know something, have disappeared without our knowing anything of or about them.

This state of affairs becomes even more worrying if we consider that more than half of the world's languages have become extinct in the past 500 years, and it is now estimated that only half of the current 6,000 spoken languages will be alive by the end of this century (cf. UNESCO 2012a); however, some pessimistic theorists argue that only 10 per cent of the current spoken languages (i.e. about 600 languages) have a reasonably good chance of surviving in the long run (cf. Janse 2003: X).

A number of linguistic factors such as the death of all speakers, changes in the ecology of the language (i.e. speakers leave their communities and marry into other linguistic groups) and cultural contact and clash (i.e. in which case a language is 'substituted' by another) (cf. Wurm 1991) are involved in the process of language death, but non-linguistic factors, such as lack of economic opportunities, rapid economic transformations and sociopolitical circumstances (e.g. discrimination, repression and official language policies), are also involved (Janse 2003: IX–XVII). Certainly, all these factors are interrelated in many instances, but it has also been contended that the current process of globalization is partly responsible for the increase of 'language death' because it undermines local cultures throughout the world in its pursuit for standardization and uniformity, which are understood to be more cost-efficient and market-friendly than 'difference and diversity'. As a consequence of this, the dominant Western culture is imposing itself throughout the world and weakening local languages and cultures in the process (cf. Shiva 1993).

This process of mass language extinction has accelerated considerably recently prompting many linguists and anthropologists as well as philosophers and educationists to engage at various levels with this issue. For instance, Fanon (1967: 17), a major political theorist and prominent figure in the process of decolonization in Africa, noted the important connection between language and culture in *Black Skin, White Masks* when he said that 'to speak means to be in a position to use a certain syntax, to grasp the morphology of this or that language, but it means above all to *assume a culture*, to support the weight of a civilization' [my emphasis]; that is, to speak a language is to be part of a 'way of life' and as such it is part and parcel of one's very 'identity'. So much so that Fanon argued that part of the process of decolonization consisted in replacing local school systems based on the *metropole*'s culture, traditions and language, with one focusing on the local one so to reverse (or at least try to) the acculturation and loss of identity of subjugated peoples.

Perhaps, more enlightening for our appreciation of the seriousness of the 'language death' phenomenon and its connection to 'identity' is Wittgenstein's detailed and still extremely influential work on philosophy of language. In the *Philosophical Investigations*, Wittgenstein starts his discussion on language with the following quote from Augustine's *Confessions*, a text written in the fourth-century CE; I quote:

> When they (my elders) named some object, and accordingly moved towards something, I saw this and I grasped that the thing was called by the sound they uttered when they meant to point it out. Their intention was shown by their bodily movements, as it were the natural language of all peoples: the expression of the face, the play of the eyes, the movement of other parts of the body, and the tone of voice which expresses our state of mind in seeking, having, rejecting, or avoiding something. Thus, as I heard words repeatedly used in their proper

places in various sentences, I gradually learnt to understand what objects they signified; and after I had trained my mouth to form these signs, I used them to express my own desires. (*PI* 1)

It might appear strange that Wittgenstein chose Augustine's work and views as his start point for his discussion on language, and therefore this needs clarification. Wittgenstein makes use of this quote to criticize a commonly held philosophical position that language is merely a system of signs in which 'every word has a meaning' and 'individual words in language name objects' (*PI* 1). The philosophical problem identified by Wittgenstein in Augustine (and which bears correlations with the view expressed by modern theorists, such as Frege) is that we should not think of language just in terms of how it functions and that there is much more to it than that.

Wittgenstein goes on to suggest that 'the speaking of language is part of an activity, or *a form of life*' [my emphasis] characterized by 'language-games' encompassing 'giving orders, and obeying them; describing the appearance of an object, or giving its measurements; constructing an object from a description (a drawing); reporting an event; speculating about an event; forming and testing a hypothesis; presenting the results of an experiment in tables and diagrams; making up a story, and reading it; play-acting; singing catches; guessing riddles; making a joke, telling it; solving a problem in practical arithmetic; translating from one language to another; asking, thanking, cursing, greeting, praying' (*PI* 23). Obviously, this list is not exhausted by Wittgenstein's suggestions, but it demonstrates that Augustine's understanding (like that of others) who have philosophized about language is impoverished exactly because it characterizes 'language' through its functions and suggests that we learn language like 'a stranger in a foreign country'; that is, someone who 'does not yet understand the language of the inhabitants of this strange country, but . . . is already the master of the linguistic techniques that comprise the practical ability to use language: "as if it already had a language, only not this one. Or again, as if the child could already *think* only not yet speak . . . (*PI* 32)"' (McGinn 1997: 65). As such, those reductionist accounts of language do not capture the essence, complexities and richness of 'language'.

Thus, for Wittgenstein, to speak a language implies a 'complex form of life that is revealed in the way speakers live and act, both in their past history and in their current and their future ways of acting and responding' (McGinn 1997: 93). To truly understand Wittgenstein's notion of a 'form of life', we have to refer to the social behaviour involved in the use of 'particular linguistic concepts' (cf. Nielsen 2008: 77; Malcolm 1954: 550; Rhees 1954: 69). One practical example of this has been noted by Harrison (2007: 206) who explains that 'the complexities surrounding how to say "go" in Tuvan' and that 'without [an] awareness of how speakers attend to the ground underfoot and to river current, it is hard to imagine even understanding that this system exists, let alone how it works. This small portion of Tuvan grammar depends on the human body's interaction with the local environment, as interpreted through Tuvan cultural norms'. This is but an example, and other can be easily found.

It is important to note here that Wittgenstein does not make use of the idea of 'form of life' in a biological or non-historical sense; rather, he applies it to historical groups who form communities sharing and connected through very complex language-based cultural practices. Hence, 'coming to share, or understand, the form of life of a group of individual human beings means mastering, or coming to understand, the intricate language-games that are essential to its characteristic practices' (McGinn 1997: 51). It is therefore arguable that 'speaking a language', specially one's mother tongue, is directly and intrinsically connected to one's 'identity' because 'language' is that which grants us membership of a 'cultural community', and as such, the disappearance of a language also implies the vanishing of a 'cultural community'. This is epitomized by the following passage by Crystal (2007: 1):

> Take this instance, reported by Bruce Connell in the pages of the newsletter of the UK foundation for Endangered Languages (FEL), under the heading 'Obtuaries':
>
> During fieldwork in the Mambila region of Cameroon's Adamawa province in 1994-1995, I came across a number of moribund languages. . . . For one of these languages, Kasabe . . . only one remaining speaker, Bogon, was found. . . . In November 1996 I returned to the Mambila region, with part of my agenda being to collect further data on Kasabe. Bogon, however, died on 5th Nov. 1995, taking Kasabe with him . . .
>
> There you have it. . . . On 4 November 1995 Kasabe existed; on 5 November, it did not.

In this chapter I refer to some innovative educational ventures seeking to revitalize local *languages*, *cultures* and *communities* in the Amazon region of Brazil and I analyse these projects in the light of some of Paulo Freire's ideas, particularly his views on conscientisação, praxis and contextualization. I finish by arguing that these ventures might be viewed as useful templates for other countries and peoples seeking to reverse or avoid 'language death', because they aid fragile communities to gain a new impetus as 'forms of life', and in doing so they are able to reassert their own 'identities'.

Education in the Amazon region of Brazil: The historical context

The Amazon region of Brazil is vast and encompasses some 5 million km² (i.e. 61 per cent of the Brazilian territory) and possesses at least 10 per cent of the biodiversity of the planet (FAO 2006a). When the Portuguese arrived in Brazil in 1,500 CE there were around 1,300 languages spoken in the current territory of Brazil. After centuries of extermination, diseases and integrationist policies, a number of native languages have either disappeared or are facing the danger of extinction. The UNESCO *Atlas of the World's Languages in Danger* states that there are currently 190 languages spoken in the Brazilian territory (only India (197 languages) and the United States (191 languages) have more spoken languages); however, 12 of these have become extinct in recent years (i.e. Amanayé; Arapáso; Huitoto; Krenjê; Máku; Múra; Nukiní; Torá; Umutina; Urupá; Xakriabá; Yuruti) and a number of others face various degrees of danger from vulnerable to critically endangered (cf. UNESCO 2012b). Most of these languages are grouped into three distinct families, namely Tupi, Macro-Jê and Aruak; however, some languages, such as Karib, Pano, Maku, Yanoama, seem not to belong to these families and researchers have been unable to classify them (Rodrigues 1986).

These languages, cultures and communities, these 'forms of life', can never be brought back, representing an enormous loss for humanity. In addition to this, the continuous weakening of many native communities through integrationist policies is a phenomenon that showed no signs of slowing down; rather, it appeared to be accelerating until very recently. The situation in Brazil is an example of what has happened, and still happens, across the world; for instance: Australia practised similar 'integrationist' policies until the 1960s and 1970s (e.g. 'the Stolen Children' issue; cf. 'Stolen Children' Report 1997); the United States sought the 'Americanization of Native Americans' during the 1790–1920 period (cf. Hoxie 1984); Canada sought 'assimilation' of native Indians through schooling from the 1840s to the 1990s (cf. Milloy 1999) – many other examples of these practices can be found throughout the world. However, very recently some interesting educational ventures have emerged in the Alto Rio Negro area of the Amazon Region, which appear to be overturning this situation and giving a new impetus to native languages, cultures and communities.

There are a number of ethnic groups in Brazil constituting true microsocieties totalling no more than 821 thousand individuals, or 0.4 per cent of the Brazilian population (IBGE 2013). Only five of these ethnic groups possess populations between 15,000 and 30,000, and 77 per cent has a population of less than a thousand individuals (Kahn 1997: 49). The Alto Rio Negro is an area border between Brazil and Colombia of very difficult access covering some 106 thousand km² (roughly the size of England) and inhabited by some 30,000 individuals of 22 different ethnic groups. These 22 groups are part of that which is called in Brazil, 'contacted groups'. This is so because since the 1960s the Brazilian government, under the influence of the Villas Boas brothers, has a policy of non-interference with 'isolated groups'. The Brazilian National Indian Foundation (FUNAI) states that there are reports of 82 'isolated groups', of which 32 were confirmed (FUNAI 2012). It is interesting to note that once these 'isolated groups' are identified the area inhabited by them is demarcated and it becomes a federal offence to contact or interfere with them; however, these groups are free to contact the 'white man' if they wish to do so. The Villas Boas brothers argued that these microsocieties are so fragile that any forced contact would effectively kill individuals, communities and cultures (cf. Vilas Boas 1990). Incidentally, when reserves are created to protect 'isolated groups', they also protect the environment and biodiversity of the area.

The educational provision for those 'contacted groups' in the area of Alto Rio Negro was entirely at the hands of religious missionaries until a few years ago. This started in the seventeenth century with the Jesuits, Franciscans and Carmelites, who arrived in the region and provided formal schooling for the natives in a unsystematic manner (Lasmar 2009: 14). However, in 1914 the Salesians moved into the region, establishing permanent missions and schools, offering mainly primary education. At the same time, the Brazilian government started to provide direct support to these missions, since it understood that they helped to secure the northern frontiers and 'integrated' the natives into Brazilian society.

The Salesian educational ethos follows the precepts set by its founder, Don Bosco (1815–88). When Don Bosco arrived in Turin in 1841 he was faced with difficult social realities. The city of Turin was undergoing fast changes brought about by industrialization, commerce and migration. This situation caused many to live in very precarious housing, poor hygiene, morally dubious settings and lack of access to education. This led Don Bosco to design a 'preventive system of education', which is based on religion, reason and kindness. It consists in making individuals aware of rules and then watching carefully over them so that they can be given guidance at the minor sign of lacking moral fibre. This system does not employ aggressive physical or psychological reprimands because it understands that these might stop bad behaviour but are of no help in improving the character of subjects. It was envisaged that this system would forge *good Christians and honest citizens*, and Camargo and Albuquerque (2006: 448) note that it spread rapidly throughout the West and Westernized World because its three fundamental pillars (i.e. reason, religion and kindness) coincided with the ideals of the time.

When the Salesians moved into the Amazon region of Brazil, they took this 'system' with them and used it to *catechise* and *educate* the natives. The aim was to make of these native peoples *good Catholics and trustworthy Brazilian citizens* who would swear allegiance to both Church and State – something that is in accord with Don Bosco's dictum '*good Christians and honest citizens*'. This played on the strict integrationist policies of the Brazilian government, who envisaged a country without natives, where all would be Brazilians and integrated to the 'white man's' society by the year 2000, and the catechesis and education of these natives was instrumental to achieve these goals (Sumiya 2005: 118–19) – this implies a fundamental change of the natives' 'identities', and I will return to this point below. Thus, this particular religious and educational venture was used to control individuals, body and soul, forcing them into accepting Church and State without questioning, and as such these educational initiatives can be said to be that which Foucault (1979) referred to in his seminal work *Discipline and Punishment* as 'institutions of power' *(institutions de séquestre) (Albuquerque 2007: 9)*. A few years later, in his essay 'The Subject and Power' he commented specifically on 'educational institutions' and said:

> Never... in the history of human societies... has there been such a tricky combination in the same political structures of individualization techniques and of totalization procedures. This is due to the fact that the modern Western state has integrated in a new political shape an old power technique which originated in Christian institutions.... Take, for example, an educational institution: the disposal of its space, the meticulous regulations which govern its internal life, the different activities which are organized there, the diverse persons who live there or meet one another, each with his own function, his well-defined

character – all these things constitute a block of capacity-communication-power. The activity which ensures apprenticeship and the acquisition of aptitudes or types of behavior is developed there by means of a whole ensemble of regulated communications (lessons, questions and answers, orders, exhortations, coded signs of obedience, differentiation marks of the 'value' of each person and of the levels of knowledge) and by the means of a whole series of power processes (enclosure, surveillance, reward and punishment, the pyramidal hierarchy). (Foucault 1982: 782; 787)

It could be said that the Salesians did not realize their instrumental role in controlling the peoples in this area of the Amazon region, that they had become 'institutions of power', because the oppressor does not always realize his own condition and when he becomes aware of it he might assume an even more paternalistic attitude. As Freire (1972: 27) says:

Discovering himself to be an oppressor may cause considerable anguish, but it does not necessarily lead to solidarity to the oppressed. Rationalizing his guilt through paternalistic treatment of the oppressed, all the while holding them fast in a position of dependence . . . [my emphasis]

Yet, when the Salesians arrived in the region they saw the native populations with European eyes, just as their predecessors had done. For instance, one of the missionary priests writes in his diary that the indian is 'like an animal . . . who did not have beds to sleep . . . who spend the night between dogs; grabbed roots and nibbled it like rats' [my translation] (cf. Giaconne 1949 in Albuquerque 2007: 15). However, one way of looking at the Salesian motivation to move into the region is to consider that they presumed that the native (now a *savage*) has an urgency of needs, both moral and material, which must be met through catechesis and education. Another way to understand their interest in the region is to consider that they thought of the native populations as *Christians at heart* and that their catechism and education are a way of returning them to the one true religion (just as the Jesuits would have done). Whatever their reasons and motivations were, the main implication is that the natives need to be 'civilized' so to become faithful to Church and State, losing their original 'identities' and assuming another, 'whiter', in the process.

That said, the establishment of Salesian missions in the Amazon region of Brazil presents us with a paradoxal situation. On the one hand, they protected the natives from the 'white men' who wanted to use them as 'labourers' or 'exterminate them for their land'; on the other hand, they imposed themselves upon these communities so to turn them into 'good Christians and citizens', and as a consequence of this, they adopted a very critical attitude towards the native culture and expressed an aversion for certain cultural practices (e.g. male initiations), which are fundamental for the 'identity' of these native communities (Lasmar 2009: 14; Sumiya 2005: 119). This negative attitude towards local customs was certainly not something particular to the Salesians or to their work in the region, but something quite common in early missionary work across the world, and this has led to a huge loss of some invaluable cultural heritage (i.e. their myths, concepts, religion, as well as their knowledge about the local environment, its food and medicinal resources), and arguably, to a crisis in native communities' 'identities'.

Nevertheless, with the Salesian missions those native groups gained access to fundamental primary education, which was provided by some 160 local schools, as well as to secondary schools in the larger centres (such as Pari-Cachoeira, Taracuá and Iauaretê), and as a result of this, these native communities display one of the highest levels of alphabetization in Brazil (cf. Kahn 1997: 57). But because they were very critical of traditional cultural practices (e.g. hunting; fishing), it produced an idle 'qualified workforce' apt and keen to work on an urban setting and disinterested and disconnected from its own community, its own 'form of life'. As Rezende (2004: 9) says:

> Our grandparents sought to bring us up as good Indians ... so that their children and grandchildren were capable to respect their family, their ethnic brothers and sisters as well as those of other ethnic background. They taught their children how to work (e.g. agriculture, hunting, fishing, handcrafts, etc.) because it was only in this way that one could judge if someone was prepared for life. This was a different model of education and one can refer to it as 'the education for a native life'. However, the current schooling system prepares the young for a way of life alien to their lives in the native community and when they finish their studies they still have to return to a life for which they were not prepared (e.g. agriculture, hunting, fishing, handcrafts, etc.). [my translation]

This led many members of these native groups to live in shantytowns around Manaus (i.e. the capital city of the Brazilian state of Amazonas, and a city with some 2 million inhabitants) or around the missions in São Gabriel da Cachoeira or Iauaretê living off handouts from the community (cf. Kahn 1997: 57; Brandhuber 1999). That is, many individuals and families end up living in dire poverty in urban areas while weakening the social fabric and number of inhabitants of their own traditional communities.

This state of affairs hides a peculiar facet of Brazilian society. There appears to be an understanding that natives 'stop being Indians' and 'become more like the white man' when they move into urban areas and speak Portuguese. However, their very presence has generated prejudice and other negative attitudes in many city dwellers who display openly the following kind of discourse: 'the native is a savage'; 'the native is lazy'; 'the native is not Brazilian'. This sort of discourse has much in common with the early explorers and missionaries' attitudes towards native communities, which suggests that they have become ingrained and are still being perpetuated within Brazilian society. The point here is that the native might speak Portuguese, wear clothes, use a mobile phone, but he is still rejected in the urban space by the wider society. This situation is not particular to Brazil and can be identified in several countries throughout the world (e.g. Australia; Canada; USA). It is arguable that behind this situation lies a lack of mutual understanding, and finding ways of correcting this is an imperative for the good-functioning of society (e.g. the native seems not to understand that the sidewalks are meant for pedestrian traffic and uses it as a waiting or meeting stop; or as somewhere to store merchandise waiting to be shipped to their local communities) (cf. Borges 2011). I would suggest that this lack of understanding can be rectified through education; for instance: (i) in formal education, the national curriculum should put an emphasis on cultural aspects so to encourage a better understanding of native cultures; (ii) non-formal education could also be used so to bring these communities (i.e. 'jungle dwellers' and 'city dwellers') together and help them to gain a better understanding of each other; (iii) informal education, perhaps through making correct information about these communities more easy available (e.g. through the media, such as television documentaries and newspaper articles) – the ease with which non-formal education ventures can be set up is very often overlooked by individuals and authorities.

To conclude this section. It is extremely important to note that the Portuguese language was *imposed* on those native groups, and this was a condition for considering them *civilized* and a requirement for learning other disciplines, such as mathematics, literature and history. As such, all native languages were systematically forbidden by the Salesians, and when they caught children speaking local languages, the children were disciplined and reproved, and 'encouraged' to stop using them as this was the only way for them to cease being natives and become true Brazilians (Albuquerque 2009: 2–3). This is a prime example of a dominant culture imposing itself on another, leading to a very negative impact on local languages, cultures and communities, and ultimately on those people's very 'identities'.

Paulo Freire: *Conscientização, Praxis* and contextualism

Paulo Freire, the prominent Brazilian educationist, understands that education can either liberate or oppress people; the former is 'dialogical education', the latter is 'banking education'. This leads him to defend the view that no educational system is ever 'neutral' and they can either 'liberate' or 'domesticate' people (cf. Archer 2007: 10; Freire 1972: 41–2) through the way they are organized, the choice of content and kind of power-relations established between educator and students.

Freire (1972: 45–7) argues that 'banking' education is:

> an act of depositing, in which the students are the depositories and the teacher the depositor . . . [and] the scope of action allowed to the students extends only as far as receiving, filling, and storing the deposits . . . and [consequently] the more students work at storing the deposits entrusted on them, the less they develop the critical consciousness which would result from their intervention in the world as transformers of that world . . . they accept the passive role imposed on them.

'Banking' education is a type of 'domestication' imposed upon the masses by the oppressive elites, who seek to maintain their positions. Through this kind of education, subjects learn to fit into the system that subjugates them and to not question their oppressed situation.

In contrast to 'banking education is "dialogical education"'. This kind of education leads to *conscientization* (i.e. from the Portuguese *conscientização*) and *praxis*. The concept of *conscientização* is a complex one, and it is not always captured by the English word conscientization (in the sense of being a form of *'awareness'* that does not implicate 'action'). In Portuguese it means the continuous, critical and dialogical insertion of individuals into their historical context while truly believing in the transformative powers of human agency and a commitment to confronting and trying to overcome the 'limiting and oppressive situations' faced by them (Freire 1972: 71–2). For this to take place the subject must become 'conscious' of the problems faced by his or her existential condition while realizing that they are the outcome of society's structures of power. It is only in this ways that subjects can achieve a global discernment of the structural injustices embeddded in the very fabric of their societies. However, if the subject understands his or her problems as something personal, he or she will sense them as something 'natural'. This is something that is perhaps more easily perceivable in neo-liberal societies because: 'the fatalistic, discouraging ideology which drives the liberal discourse stalking the world. In the name of postmodernism it seeks to persuade us that we can do nothing to change the social situation which, once seen as historical and cultural, is now becoming "almost the natural state"' (Hurtado 2007: 52).

Praxis is something directly connected to *conscientização*. This means that once the subject becomes 'conscious', he or she will perform 'informed actions' (i.e. *praxis*) so to alter his or her situation and exact the structural injustices of his or her society. Therefore, *conscientização* leads to praxis. Without *conscientização* the subject will have a 'fear of freedom' (cf. Freire 1972: 23), and will not contemplate the possibility of being autonomous and of 'other alternatives' to the status quo. Without *conscientização*, the subject can only engage in a form of 'activism', which does not offer proper alternatives on how to deal with society's structural injustices.

For Freire, *conscientização* and praxis can only happen if subjects are able to read and write, and this is one of the main reasons why he was so involved with projects focusing on the eradication of illiteracy (e.g. Brazil; Chile; Guinea-Bissau). According to his views, these ventures are 'political' because when one is denied the capacity to read and write, one is also denied one's right to express one's views and to access information pertinent to one's condition. Hence, when one knows how to read and write, one can participate politically and culturally in one's society.

Contextualism is another important Freirian idea. For him, no one is an empty vessel waiting to be 'educated' because everyone possess knowledge (e.g. of traditions; of the local environment) and a life history, which must be taken into account. As such, 'the illiterate are illiterate only insofar as writing is concerned, they are not illiterate with respect to oral traditions or life learning experiences ... reading the world precedes reading the word' (Boff 2011: 135). This means that the educational process must be *contextualized*, and that 'schools ought to include discussions and reflections about the kinds of knowledge and training' the community already has (cf. Azevedo 2009: 16). The importance of this becomes very clear if we consider Freire's literacy method. This method requires only 30 contact hours and employs a range of so-called 17 'generative words' (i.e. words that are meaningful to the student's social *context*), which are used as a focal point for discussing issues that are pertinent to the community of learners (e.g. problems faced by the community) (cf. Sumiya 2005a). It is arguable that this method is not paternalistic because it does not start with pre-set values and perspectives of reality and tries to impose them on the local population (e.g. a literacy book inhabited by 'white men' and used by 'black

African communities'). And this has the effect of improving the self-esteem of the local community and of allowing it to interact culturally, economically and socially on a more equal footing with other communities and societies (NB. this is something Fanon argued very eloquently in his writings; cf. Fanon 1963, 1967; Morgan and Guilherme 2013).

Freire's educational philosophy has become the foundation of some new educational ventures involving native indians in Brazil and I turn my attention to these now.

New developments in native education in Brazil

In 1964 the Brazilian military ousted the democratically elected government in a military coup d'état that lasted until 1985. In 1988 Brazil proclaimed a new constitution as the country took its first steps towards re-democratization. This constitution replaced old integrationist policies towards native indians with ones forged on respect for their ethnicity and that recognized the importance of cultural diversity; moreover, it secured the right to a differentiated educational system if native communities so choose. It was only 10 years later, in 1998, that Brazilian educationists and officials from the Ministry of Education started to develop new national policies for indigenous education, and in 2004 a report was distributed to all native communities throughout Brazil, which was the catalyst of major changes in indigenous education in the Alto Rio Negro area of the Amazon region of Brazil (cf. Azevedo 2009: 16–19).

As I mentioned before, until recently the educational provision in the area was entirely provided by the Salesian missions that had been established at the beginning of the twentieth century. However, it is arguable that these ventures are a classical instance of that which Freire calls 'banking education'. This is the case because the Salesian's primary motivator was to 'civilize' the natives and to turn them into *good Christians and honest citizens*, faithful to the Church and State. 'To civilize' in this case means to 'domesticate' because it aims at forcing subjects to fit into the very system that dominates them, and this is only achievable through 'banking education' since it *teaches* individuals not to question and to accept their situation.

It is further arguable that the Salesians committed a serious error when they assumed that the culture and languages spoken by those natives were *less valuable* and important than the 'white man's culture' and the Portuguese language. Those communities were illiterate only insofar as reading and writing is concerned, but they still had a language and a culture rich in oral traditions; that is, as Boff (2011: 135) says: 'they didn't read the word, but they read the world'. As such, the Salesian's attitude towards those native communities was both patronizing and oppressive (though well intentioned) because: (i) it understood that the native indians were *empty vessels*, to be filled with the 'white man's knowledge' by means of the Portuguese language; and (ii) it repressed cultural practices judged to be inconsistent with the 'white man's culture' (e.g. speaking in the native language; traditional ceremonies and dances). This had a major negative impact on those native groups' 'identities' leading to the weakening of local languages, cultures and communities; it was a sort of *psychological violence* that caused those native groups to start seeing themselves as *inferior* to the 'white man'. The result of this was the disappearance or the endangerment of many groups, and as I mentioned previously, Fanon discussed the implications of this kind of *psychological violence* (as well as of *physical violence* and *structural violence*) to a great extent in his writings (cf. Fanon 1963, 1967).

The Salesian's use of Don Bosco's 'preventive system' in these native communities is also something problematic because it had been designed to deal primarily with street kids in the large urban and industrialized areas of Europe. Hence, its use in very small communities that are economically founded on hunting, fishing and agriculture of subsistence, such as those in the Amazon region, is a case of de-*contextualization* and it caused individuals to be inapt to live in their own communities because it suppressed their 'way of life' and affected their 'identity'. However, the literacy skills provided by the Salesians to those indigenous groups, Freire would have said, provided them with the very tools to start understanding their situation (*conscientização*) and to engage in trying to resolve the injustices affecting them (*praxis*). This is encapsulated by the following quote from an interview with a local individual, who said: 'They took away half of our culture but at the same time they taught us how to defend the other half against the Whites' (Grünberg 1994: 172; cited and translated by Brandhuber 1999). The process of *conscientisação* and *praxis* has taken a long time, but it appears to be bearing fruits now as native groups start to reassert their 'identities' and strengthen their 'way or form of life' through new and innovative educational initiatives.

After 2004, when the report on indigenous education was distributed to all native communities in Brazil, some groups in the Alto Rio Negro area of the Amazon region of Brazil started to take over the schools from the Salesians, and this has led to an important re-*contextualization* of the education provided to those indigenous groups (cf. Rezende 2004; Johannessen 2009; Sumiya 2005).

The use of native languages in schools within these communities has become something central. Most of the teaching and learning is done in the local language, but these schools continue to teach the Portuguese language, and sometimes other local languages, as a second language. New books and other pedagogical materials are currently being written and organized by both teachers and students in their respective local language, which helps individuals' command of the language and access to cultural materials–and it is arguable that this can only strengthen their 'identity'. Therefore, the direct consequence of switching from a Portuguese-focused to a native language–focused teaching and learning environment has revitalized not only the language but also the culture and community because when adults and children learn the language, they also learn the culture and connect themselves to the community; that is, they learn, as Wittgenstein would say, 'a form of life', and reaffirm their 'identity'. Another development connected to this change to native language as the medium of teaching and learning is that the Universidade Estadual do Mato Grosso (UNEMAT) has implemented teacher-training courses aimed solely at forming native indians as teachers, which further reinforces the re-*contextualization* of the education provision for native communities, and as such the teacher is no longer 'the white man' but someone from the community itself (cf. Januário 2002), who shares students' 'identity' and is better able to understand it.

Another change that occurred in these schools managed by native groups is that the school calendar is very flexible and takes into account their specific social and economic context; for instance: (i) the calendar is set around traditional festivities and the period of preparations leading to these; (ii) the calendar can be easily modified for economic reasons (e.g. need to go fishing because fish is plentiful). As such, the school and school calendar work with the community and not against it, as it was the case in the past under the previous provision since it followed the calendar set by the central government and more appropriate to the urban areas of the south and coastal areas, as well as to the traditional 'white men's festivities' (e.g. Easter Week; Christmas period).

Yet, another development is that the larger community has become an extension of the school and classroom. This is so because it welcomes teachers (some are members of the community, others come from surrounding ones) and local students, provides them with school meals, is considered a true teaching and learning environment and participates in the assessment of students. Thus, when food for school meals is short, teachers and students can go fishing (boys) or harvesting (girls), and this becomes a teaching and learning experience that prepares students to live in their local communities. That is, they learn to fish, but they also learn the types of fish available in their local rivers and streams; or they learn to harvest, but they also learn the fruits and vegetables of the local area. As for the students assessment, the teacher, student, parents and wider community are involved in assessing the student's progress, which takes away from the teacher the ownership of knowledge and democratizes it with the community, creating less asymmetrical relations that are the very foundation of oppression and of Freire's 'banking education'. It is arguable that all these changes alight in the teachers, students and wider community a sense of interdependence, which, once again, stimulates their own sense of belonging and of 'identity'.

Finally, the pedagogical methodology employed in these new initiatives is research based, something that is at the very heart of Freire's 'dialogical education'. Hence, teaching and learning activities are developed through research and investigations set by the teacher around topics that are important to the native community. These activities are not restricted to the school and classroom, encompassing also the immediate surroundings of the native village (e.g. rivers, woods). Most important is the fact that these activities always aim at establishing a direct practical connection with the daily routine of the community as well as encouraging a sustainable and environmentally friendly outlook in the students. For instance, if the students are learning about volume of liquids, then they might refer to the local fishing tanks kept by the community.

All the above-mentioned changes have had a positive effect on the vitality of these native languages, cultures and communities, not to mention on these groups' 'identities', and as such attention should be paid to these ventures in Brazil and what further developments might occur.

Conclusion

It has been argued that 'language revitalization' will be one of the most important social trends of the coming decades (cf. Harrison 2007, 2010). If this turns out to be indeed the case of things to come, then it would represent a reaction against the current hegemonic process of globalization and a *monoculture of minds* implied by it (e.g. Western brands and habits being adopted across the world; English becoming the 'medium of learning' in many non-native English-speaking countries), which seems to be 'standardizing' (meaning, 'Westernizing') peoples' 'identities' (Shiva 1993). As such, it is contended here that this issue will be a major preoccupation on our intellectual life as we seek new and innovative ways of revitalizing *endangered languages, cultures* and *communities*, and consequently, of strengthening peoples' 'identities'.

Accordingly, it could be argued that these new educational projects in the Alto Rio Negro area of the Amazon region of Brazil are the first 'green-shoots' of this developmental trend and as such they might be seen both as templates for other countries and peoples trying to reinvigorate their 'forms of life' and as a sign of things to come. Certainly, the complete avoidance of 'language, culture and community death' is something that is impossible – to defend this, would be to defend a utopia and history has already taught us that 'languages, cultures, and communities' have emerged and died since time immemorial. However, as I said previously, we are now faced with the 'mass extinction' of languages, cultures and communities and therein lies the importance of finding ways of providing peoples with ways for their sustainable existence, and this can only be done through the strengthening of their 'identities'. These new ventures in the Amazon might not put a complete stop to this phenomenon of mass extinction, however they provide native communities with hope that their languages, cultures and communities – their very 'identities' – will not die. This might just be enough to provide their 'forms of life' with 'a chance for survival'.

References

Albuquerque, J. G. (2007), Educação Escolar Indígena: do Panóptico a um Espaço Possível de Subjetivação na Resistência, PhD Thesis, http://www.iel.unicamp.br/revista/index.php/sinteses/article/viewFile/841/580 (last accessed 30 January 2012).
—(2009), Resistência Tuyuka nas Políticas de Ensino da Língua, IV SEAD – Seminário de Estudos em Análise do Discurso, http://www.discurso.ufrgs.br/anaisdosead/4SEAD/SIMPOSIOS/JuditeGoncalvesDeAlbuquerque.pdf (last accessed 15 March 2012).
Archer, D. (2007), 'Education or Banking?', *Adult Education and Development*. Vol. 69. Bonn: Institut für Internationale Zusammenarbeit des Deutschen Volkshochschul-Verbandes, pp. 9–12.
Azevedo, M. (2009), 'Indigenous Education in Brazil: History and Recent Developments', in Eva Marion Johannessen (ed.), *Schools in the Rainforest: Innovative Indigenous Education in the Amazon*. Oslo: Rainforest Foundation Norway.
Boff, L. (2011), *Virtues for Another Possible World*. Eugene, OR: Cascade Books.
Borges, AA da Cruz (2011), 'Efeitos de Sentido da Temporalidade: Determinação do Lugar Indígena'. *Anais do Seta* 5: 18–27, http://www.iel.unicamp.br/revista/index.php/seta/article/view/1932 (last accessed 30 January 2012).
Brandhuber, G. (1999), 'Why Tukanoans migrate? Some remarks on conflict on the Upper Rio Negro (Brazil)'. *Journal de la Societé des Américanistes*, Tome 85: 261–80.

Camargo, D. M. P. and Albuquerque, J. G. (maio/ago 2006), 'O Eu e o Outro no Ensino Médio Indígena: Alto Rio Negro (AM)'. *Educacão e Sociedade.*, Campinas 27(n. 95): 445–69.
Crystal, D. (2007), *Language Death*. Cambridge: Cambridge University Press.
Fanon, F. (1967), *Black Skins, White Masks*. New York: Grove Weidenfeld.
—(1963), *The Wretched of the Earth*. New York: Grove Weidenfeld.
FAO (2006), 'Impact of international agricultural trade and gender equity: Selected country case studies', Rome: FAO. http://www.fao.org/docrep/009/a0493e/a0493e04.htm (last accessed 07 March 2012).
—(2006a), 'Brazil: Country Pasture/Forage Resources Profile', http://www.fao.org/ag/AGP/AGPC/doc/Counprof/Brazil/Brazil.htm (last accessed 07 March 2012).
Foucault, M. (1979), *Discipline and Punishment: The Birth of Prison*. New York: Vintage Books.
—(1982), 'The Subject and Power'. *Critical Inquiry* 8(4): 777–95.
Freire, P. (1972), *Pedagogy of the Oppressed*. London: Penguin Books.
FUNAI (2012), 'Os Indios', http://www.funai.gov.br/indios/conteudo.htm (last accessed 15 March 2012).
Giaconne, A. (1949), *Os Tucanos e Outras Tribos do rio Uaupés Afluentes do rio Negro Amazonas – Notas etnográficas de um missionário Salesiano*. São Paulo: Imprensa Oficial do Estado.
Grünberg, Georg (1994), 'Indigene Rechte, Ôkologie und die entwicklungspolitische Praxis im tropischen Waldland. Beispiele aus Brasilien und Guatemala', in Doris Cech, Elke Mader, Stefanie Reinberg (eds), *Tierra – indigene Volker, Umwelt und Recht*, Frankfurt and Sudwind, Wien: Brandes und Apsel, pp. 159–74.
Harrison, David K. (2007), *When Languages die: The Extinction of the World's Languages and the Erosion of Human Knowledge*. Oxford; New York: Oxford University Press.
—(2010), 'The Last Speakers: The Quest to Uncover the World's Most Endangered Languages'. Washington, DC: National Geographic Society.
Hoxie, F. (1984), *A Final Promise: The Campaign to Assimilate the Indians, 1880–1920*. Lincoln: University of Nebraska Press.
Hurtado, C. N. (2007), 'The Continuing Relevance of Paulo Freire's Ideas', in *Adult Education and Development*. Vol. 69. Bonn: Institut für Internationale Zusammenarbeit des Deutschen Volkshochschul-Verbandes, pp. 51–78.
IBGE (2013), 'População residente, por cor ou raça, segundo o sexo, a situação do domicílio e os grupos de idade', ftp://ftp.ibge.gov.br/Censos/Censo_Demografico_2010/Caracteristicas_Gerais_Religiao_Deficiencia/tab1_2.pdf (last accessed 21 December 2013).
Janse, M. (2003), 'Introduction', in M. Janse and S. Tol (eds), *Language Death and Language Maintenance: Theoretical, Practical and Descriptive Approaches*. Amsterdam: John Benjamins.
Januário, E. (2002), 'Ensino superior para índios: um novo paradigma na educação'. *Cadernos de Educação Escolar Indígena*, UNEMAT 1(1): 15–24.

Kahn, M. (1997), 'Educação Indígena'. *Cadernos de Pesquisa* 7: 49–63.
Lasmar, C. (2009), 'Conhecer para transformar: os índios do rio Uaupés (Alto Rio Negro) e a educação escolar'. *Tellus*. ano 9, n. 16, pp. 11–33.
Malcolm, N. (1954), 'Wittgenstein's *Philosophical Investigations*'. *The Philosophical Review* 63: 530–59.
McGinn, M. (1997), *Routledge Philosophy Guidebook to Wittgenstein and the Philosophical Investigation*. London: Routledge.
Milloy, John S. (1999), *A National Crime: The Canadian Government and the Residential School System 1879–1986*. Winnipeg: University of Manitoba Press.
Morgan, W. J. and Guilherme, A. (2013), 'Martin Buber et Frantz Fanon. Le politique dans l'éducation: dialogue ou rébellion', in *Diogéne*, no. 241, Janvier-Mars, pp. 35–57.
Nielsen. K. S. (2008), *The Evolution of the Private Language Argument*. Aldershot: Ashgate.
Rezende, J. S. (2004), 'Repensando a Educação Indígena', *Inspetoria Salesiana Missionária da Amazônia*, http://www.isma.org.br/artigos/educacao_indigena.pdf (last accessed 15 March 2012).
Rhees, R. (1954), 'Can There Be a Private Language?'. *Proceedings of the Aristotelian Society* 28: 77–94.
Rodrigues, Aryon Dall'Igna (1986), *Línguas Brasileiras: para o conhecimento das línguas indígenas*. São Paulo: Loyola.
Shiva, V. (1993), *Monocultures of the Mind: Biodiversity, Biotechnology and Agriculture*. New Delhi: Zed Press.
'Stolen Children' Report (1997), Australian Human Rights Commission, http://www.hreoc.gov.au/social_justice/bth_report/index.html (last accessed 30 January 2012).
Sumiya, L. A. (2005), 'Projeto Educação Indígena no Alto Rio Negro AM', in Marco Antonio Carvalho Teixeira, Melissa G. de Godoy, Roberta Clemente (eds), *20 Experiências de Gestão Pública e Cidadania 2005*. São Paulo: Programa Gestão Pública e Cidadania.
—(2005a), Educação Indígena Fortalece Identidade e Promove of Desenvolvimento, EAESP, Fundação Getulio Vargas, www.eaesp.fgvsp.br/.../013projeto_educacao_indigena_do_alto_rio_negro.pdf (last accessed on 26 June 2010).
UNESCO (2012a), *Endangered Languages*, http://www.unesco.org/new/en/culture/themes/cultural-diversity/languages-and-multilingualism/endangered-languages/ (last accessed 14 January 2012).
—(2012b), *Atlas of the World's Languages in Danger*, http://www.unesco.org/culture/languages-atlas/index.php (last accessed 14 January 2012).
Villas Boas, O. and Villas Boas, C. (1990), *Xingu: os índios, seus mitos* – Porto alegre: Kuarup.
Wittgenstein, Ludwig (1953), *Philosophical Investigations*. Malden: Blackwell.
Wurm, S. A. (1991), 'Language Death and Disappearance: Causes and Circumstances'. *Diogenes* 39(1): 1–18.

Part Three

Critical Pedagogies

8

The Language of Leisure and Physicality: Constructing and Re-constructing Identity

Wendy Bignold

> ### Editor's Introduction
>
> Wendy Bignold explores alternative discourse and identity in the leisure activity of unicycling. She shows how this particular activity forms the nucleus of a youth discourse expressing styles, of dress, music, gesture, speech and ways of being. This discourse stands in opposition to hegemonic mainstream in that it is unplanned, spontaneous and existential, capturing life in the moment.

Introduction

A recurring theme in this book is the significance of language, both linguistic expression and non-verbal communication, to the construction and expression of identity. This chapter examines this in the social realm of leisure by exploring the use of language by adolescents engaged in physical activity. Identity is constructed by individuals and co-constructed further by their interactions with others. It is through social situations, such as work, school and family, that we build and express our identities. For adolescents who are moving out from the social security of the immediate family, their leisure time takes on increasing significance and influence in the construction, or renewal, of identity. The significance of leisure time for young people is that it is here that they select the activities and the peer groups they wish to interact with. These decisions are increasingly theirs to take and are not imposed on them as they are at school or in family relations arranged by their parents or senior family members. Many young people choose to engage in physical activity of one kind or another as part of their leisure time. Indeed the selection of which physical activity or sport to engage with can itself say much about someone's identity. This chapter examines the sport of unicycling and its impact on motivation, self-esteem and identity in young male riders, and the role of language in this.

This chapter draws on an international study of unicycling carried out over a 6-year period (Bignold 2009). The research indicates that unicycling is a sport which motivates and inspires young riders, that makes them feel good about themselves and what they can do and so has the potential to impact positively on them. However it is an activity which is often dismissed as being something for clowns, and which teachers appear not to be valuing in their pupils who do ride. As such, the potential of unicycling is going unnoticed.

According to Furlong and Cartmel (2007), traditional means of young people's socialization such as school, family and community are becoming weaker. They may be marginalized by family or peers or they may choose to marginalize themselves. To such individuals an alternative group can provide an appealing identity. This chapter will explore the development of group identity and its impact on self-identity and self-esteem by investigating the culture and language of unicycling and the sub-cultures of the different disciplines within it, particularly those which are popular with young riders.

Leisure: A place for reconstructing adolescent identity

In adolescents, self-identify and self-esteem become hugely important as peer pressure and acceptance becomes increasingly significant to individuals (Geldard and Geldard 2004). It is at this age that children, then youth, start to develop stronger, sometimes new or renewed, self-identities often based around activities outside of school; a key text for youth practitioners emphasizes this: 'It is in the realm of leisure that young people truly become themselves' (Hendry et al. 1993: 2). A sense of self is key to children and young people's personal achievement both in school and out of it. The 'self' is a complex and multidimensional concept and has traditionally been considered as embodied, as an inner essence (Pini 2004). A more recent, post-structuralist view is that the 'self' is socially constructed. Foucault (1988) and Pini (2004) describe selves as not emerging naturally, but being produced within wider historical and social contexts. There are different ways an individual can 'work upon' his or her body to become a 'self' and achieve a sense of personal fulfilment and identity. There are a number of elements within the sense of self that Foucoult refers to, the two most significant being self-identity and self-esteem. Gibson and Jefferson (2006) acknowledge that these two are often strongly entwined in adolescence.

There are two elements to self-identity; these can be simply described as self-concept (a developing awareness of oneself) and self-knowledge, (recognizing one's strengths and weaknesses) (Bignold 2006). Self-identity is constructed from an individual's sense of self, based on his or her personal, family and community history and his or her belonging to one or more social groups (Hill and Tisdall 1997). Young people's developing identities are significantly influenced by their leisure activities, consumption, style, music, friendships and language (Hill and Tisdall) – all elements of unicycling culture. It is necessary to have a positive and accurate identity in order to achieve a holistic sense of self and high self-esteem. This can be problematic for a young person whose sense of who he or she is, is threatened by 'negative social images, discontinuities of life experiences or conflicting loyalties' (Hill and Tisdall 1997). Adolescence can be, for many, a time of conflicting loyalties as peers take on increasing significance, often over and above the family. Traditional contexts of socialization for adolescents, such as family, school, church and community, are becoming less significant as the influence of peers, the media, and particularly today electronic and social media, become more significant. Given so many different messages, contradictions, choices and freedoms, young people can feel overwhelmed as they look to find their own place in their world.

Social identity, how someone sees his/her relationships with others or how he/she thinks others perceive him, is an important part of self-identity (Furlong and Cartmel 2007). Leisure and youth cultures are significantly important here as they are central to renewing social identities among young people. Being able to choose which activity to pursue is, in itself, significant to self-identity as it is one means by which young people are empowered. The influence of peers on social identity is important because of the dialectical interplay here, based on communication (Thompson 2003). The messages an individual receives from others about himself are greatly influenced by the messages he gives out to others about himself.

Given then that the realm of leisure is important for the development of self-identity, let us consider specifically the place of sport, or physical activity, within this as many young people choose to pursue sports in their leisure time. Sport has traditionally had a major impact on youth identity, particularly boys' identity, with established mainstream sports, such as rugby and football, dominating the compulsory PE curriculum in schools (Mills 2001). The valuing of sports which are hegemonized, promoting aggressiveness, strength, speed, competitiveness and the domination of one group or team over another can inadvertently create an atmosphere of aggression within the playground generally or among specific groups. If you are an individual, or social group, who does not value such things yourself then adolescence, with its time of changing identity, can be even more difficult. Unicycling has the potential to provide an alternative identity which is not based on violence, aggression or competitiveness, but creativity, aesthetics, individualism and cooperation.

Unicycling: A lifestyle sport

Unicycling is an activity which many people associate with the circus; however, to those who ride regularly it is a serious sport which is highly motivating, demanding and challenging, but fun and exciting, social and creative. It requires significant commitment to develop higher level skills. Imagine the perseverance needed to be able to do a 360 degree spin with your feet, not on the pedals, but on the cranks or frame. Imagine the drive needed to walk up Snowdon, the highest mountain in Wales, carrying a unicycle over your shoulder so that you can ride back down it, bouncing over rocks and flailing onto rough ground.

Lifestyle sports, also known as extreme sports or adventure sports, among other things, have been credited with largely developing out of the Californian surfing scene of the 1960s. The interest in surfing inspired the transformation of this sea sport into land-based activities, such as skateboarding and BMX biking (Chandler et al. 2002). As these new activities were practised more widely new variations were developed. A developmental link can be seen here between skateboarding and Street unicycling, both of which take place in an urban street environment, indeed Trials, Street and Flatland are all disciplines within biking as well as unicycling. Lifestyle sports consist of an increasing range of activities outside of traditional mainstream sports. They differ from traditional sporting and physical activities in that their emphasis is on location, equipment, endurance and sometimes the danger involved. In addition to these practical differences they also provide other approaches to thinking about sport. Despite being acknowledged as alternatives to mainstream sport they are being taken up by increasing numbers of people, and particularly, although not exclusively, young people (Wheaton 2004). Sport England recognizes the rapid increase in lifestyle or alternative sports over the last two decades and acknowledges the role that they have to play in engaging young people in physical activity;

> There has been a proliferation of new sporting forms over the (last) two decades that have challenged traditional ways of conceptualising and practising sport. These new forms, variously labelled 'action', 'new' 'whizz', 'extreme' and 'lifestyle' sports have commercial and competitive dimensions, but are essentially understood by participants as bodily experiences – about 'doing it'. (Tomlinson et al. 2005: 2)

Despite this there has been little research into them or the people who participate in them. The term 'lifestyle sport' also implies a long-term commitment to the activity; unicycling is rarely taken up as a fad. The perseverance and time usually required to be able to ride a unicycle competently and then to succeed at your chosen trick or discipline requires a significant investment in time.

The unicycle was invented in the late 1880s, a descendant of the penny farthing bicycle, its emphasis was on trick riding. Since then a whole range of unicycling disciplines has evolved with new ones still being developed. Currently, seven different disciplines are recognized in unicycling; which are summarized as:

- Neighbourhood: basic unicycling in the street
- Freestyle: doing skills, stunts or tricks
- Trials: hopping and riding over obstacles
- Street: using a variety of objects from urban settings, such as stairs or handrails, to do tricks
- Mountain: riding over rough terrain, like mountain biking
- Touring or commuting: mainly meant as distance riding with speeds of 10 to 15 miles per hour reached with ease, depending on the wheel size.
- Flatland: a combination of Street and Freestyle

In addition to the riding styles, listed disciplines also include variations of other sports, the most popular being unicycle hockey and unicycle basketball.

Over the last 10 years unicycling has increased in popularity (Monney 2006) with riders moving away from the traditional performance base of circus and parades and creating new forms of unicycling based on the riding styles, which have resulted in identifiable disciplines. Unicyclists tend to ride more than one style, pursuing several disciplines at a time. Once competent at riding unicyclists often try out new activities in different disciplines. The disciplines most popular with adolescent riders are Trials, Street and Flatland.

Trials unicycling is based around bicycle trials and motorcycle trials, in that the rider hops or rides over obstacles without putting down a foot or hand. A trials course can be over a natural environment, such as hopping along or over fallen tree trunks in a forest, or in an urban environment, jumping over railings or onto a pile of wooden palettes either stacked for storage or positioned to create a trials course.

Street unicycling is defined as a discipline which uses trial obstacles to create freestyle moves; however it does have moves of its own, for example rail grinding, sliding down or along a railing with one pedal resting flat on top of the rail and grinding along it, or stair hopping. Basic street moves include crankflips, unispins and twists which are then combined to make more complex moves, such as a 180 degree twist with a crankflip at the same time. Both Trials and Street are particularly popular with young males in the UK, France and Denmark.

Flatland is the newest discipline to emerge within unicycling, combining Street and Freestyle. Indeed it has been credited to those Street enthusiasts who struggled to hop onto or over obstacles but enjoyed doing tricks on the flat (Bignold 2009). They persevered at their own strengths and focused on trick riding on flat ground but with a distinctly urban flair to it rather than the aesthetic flair of Freestyle.

As with other sports unicycling has its own 'celebrities' who are role models to young riders and who are promoted mainly through DVDs mainly but in a far less aggressive marketing style than with many mainstream sports. The DVDs are popular as they show new tricks and the extent to which boundaries can be pushed. They are a significant element in the development of the different disciplines and the related styles, dress and music that become associated with each and as such are significant in building a subculture.

Identity: Developing a sense of self

A stable, high self-esteem can have a positive impact on personal achievement, academic or otherwise (Lawrence 2006), which in turn impacts on motivation and enjoyment or satisfaction. There is general agreement that self-esteem is based on self-identity and how this fits with someone's ideal self (Lawrence). Self-esteem is sometimes fragile in nature, particularly during adolescence as the earlier reference to conflicting loyalties often felt during this period emphasizes.

Self-esteem can be global, an all-round feeling of self-worth and confidence, or specific, with regard to a specific activity or behaviour. Key elements of self-esteem are academic ability, physical appearance, perceived language mastery and popularity among peers and the importance of each of these is based on what the individual values and defines as worthwhile. Much research, including that by Marsh et al. (2006), concludes that a person's 'context, environment and life-events' are highly influential. The values held by society and/or significant others, such as parents or peers, form part of the context in which the individual operates.

The importance of leisure as a place or space for young people to build their identities has been discussed. The physical activity, or physicality, which is often pursued in such space has its own contribution to make to identity; such activity is usually expressed through sport. Collins and Kay (2003) confirm the consensus that sport has the potential to raise self-esteem and have a positive impact on mood and perception of competence or mastery. It can also improve socialization with peer groups and adults. In most cases it can improve educational attendance and performance. All these aspects are linked to a sense of one's self, one's strengths and weaknesses. Sport provides opportunities for young people to experience challenge, fun and enjoyment while enhancing their self-esteem and reducing stress. It develops citizenship, social success, positive peer relationships and leadership skills (Elley and Kirk 2002; Wright and Cote 2003), all of which can have appositive impact on self-esteem, and as such on identity.

Some of the above benefits may apply to sports which involve team work rather than individual performance. Unicycling is predominantly an individual activity, although there are opportunities for team sports, such as Unicycle Hockey, or competing as a team in a 400 metre sprint relay race, representing country in an international competition, for example, or just participating with friends. The benefits identified in relation to social development may still be significant for unicycling as the social opportunities it provides are important to many riders. Interestingly the United Kingdom has seen a sudden rise in Street Sport initiatives seeking to exploit the potential impact of sport on urban youth who are looking for an identity and who are seeking to make sense of the spaces they inhabit (Bignold 2009). This is of particular significance to certain disciplines of unicycling which encourages youth to redefine the purpose of urban spaces within a leisure context.

A certain style of riding is shared by all unicyclists once the early wobbles are mastered; and a language characterized by technical terms and a positive outlook on life unites those who ride and those who support. As a new rider progresses in his skill so his ability to walk the walk, ride the ride and talk the talk increases; he becomes more familiar with the culture and subcultures and their specific language, verbal or otherwise. Unicycling, like many other physical pursuits, provides activities, rules and a terminology of its own which join together to form a culture or subculture. This culture – a way of riding, of talking – provides an identity for both individuals and groups.

Culture and subculture: The link with language

Culture is a combination of background, traditions, values and lifestyles which individuals share with others in a particular group. All of these can vary between different groups in society, according to elements of ethnicity, economic status, regional location and so on. Culture is learnt as part of the process of socialization. This chapter has already established that young people's socialization occurs in increasingly different settings with different agencies, such as leisure and the influence of peers or social media. A subculture is a group within a society or culture, related to it and yet distinctive from it.

Bourdieu's concept of culture as capital has been discussed already in this book in several places. According to Bourdieu, as well as being cultural, capital can also be social, economic or physical. Within his conceptual framework people occupy a *habitus*, a sphere in which they operate. Each person's habitus is unique to them and is built by individual histories, personal current contexts and future contexts (Raey 2006). Individual histories include early childhood experiences and subsequent socialization within the family. For an adolescent this individual history will be influenced by his or her current context, that is, changing relationship with the family. A poststructuralist perspective on identity describes how a person understands his or her relationship to the world, how that relationship is constructed or reconstructed over time. When someone invests time to learn a new skill, such as unicycling, they do so with the understanding that they will develop a wider range of resources, which will enhance their cultural capital, their identity, and may enable them to join new social groups through the acquisition of new language (Norton 2000). 'Language of membership', competence in the language of membership is important for new members and those already part of a group who wish to remain in it (Riley 2008). Competence in the language of membership is often more important than pronunciation or syntax.

Different social groups value different cultural capital. The assumption is that those groups who hold 'power' value their own culture and so to get on in that group anyone entering it must hold, or be able to gain, the same cultural capital. As such it is often white, middle-class values which other groups have to adhere to or be able to fit in with (Stevens 2006). However, Robbins (2000) warns against the frequent misinterpretation of Bourdieu's ideas which imply that cultural capital is a direct expression of class position. With respect to this study it may be argued that in current British society traditional sports are seen as having higher status than newer lifestyle sports and so the cultural capital of those who play traditional sports is worth more than those who take part in lifestyle sports. This is evidence, for example, in the significance given to traditional sports by mainstream society.

Thornton (1996) has adapted Bourdieu's thinking on cultural capital to consider subcultural capital. She identifies it as knowledge, goods or behaviour which give status or social advantage to an individual with regard to a subculture they belong to or aspire to be a member of. She gives the example of a fashionable haircut or CD collection to 'clubbing' subculture. In unicycling, it may be a particular saddle, endorsed by a current role model, or a t-shirt from a certain meet. When cultural capital is considered with specific regard to subcultures, as described above, it could be seen to be significant to unicycling. Thornton also establishes a hierarchy of dance moves within club culture as having different levels of subcultural capital. A direct comparison can be made to unicycling here; for example, a 360-degree turn in Freestyle holds greater status than a 180 degree turn, or a grind followed by a back-flip in Street is seen as more impressive than a grind with a simple drop-off at the end, as each is related to a different skill level. With regard to social capital Bourdieu regarded trust, collaboration and cooperation as key values (Grenfell 2006). These are all qualities which are important in the sport of unicycling.

Sport does not exist in a world of its own, it is part of society (Beard 1998), occupying different spaces and statuses depending on the sport itself and those who are playing it and watching it. Sport is part of our culture, but it can also be a culture or subculture in its own right; individual sports can be described as cultures or subcultures too.

Subculture and lifestyle theories have been analysed in relation to sport studies with a number of different approaches emerging. Some of these have been identified by Ford and Brown (2006) as interpretative approaches which seek to understand sport behaviours in terms of the meanings that participants place on their actions. Such interpretative approaches are appropriate for the sport of unicycling where concerns with authenticity and individual expression are central. Hermeneutic textual and discourse analysis approaches consider the way in which sporting social worlds are continually constructed and reinvented. In contrast human geographical approaches focus on traditions rather than re-inventions. They explore the significance of sports as representations of places and rituals. Ethno-methodology approaches consider sport subcultures as a process of socialization with an emphasis on an individuals sporting 'career' or time spent progressing in the sport, with the focus on the person rather than the place. Within the interpretative approaches Ford and Brown (2006) regard a sociological framework developed by Elias as significant. This framework views sport as a means of 'increasing exercise of self-control over feeling and behaviour, in a cultural shift from external to internal constraints' (Ford and Brown: 27). It explores sports cultures as groups of people 'bonded in dynamic constellations' with fairly high levels of individual autonomy but at the same time reliant on networks of interdependence. This framework would certainly fit the social structure of unicycling, where people participate as individuals but rely on others for social sporting opportunities.

An interesting element of urban unicycling is the alternative use of space, using the urban street environment not what it was intended for, but as a prop for extreme physical activity. This urban space, or hard landscape, is part of the urban culture of skateboarding and related activities. Part of the attraction of such spaces, Wells (2002) suggests, is that they are not of interest to adults and so youth can easily demarcate them as spaces of their own, as places to establish their own subculture. The importance of space as an influence on identity has its origins in post-structural and postmodern perspectives on identity. This draws on Foucault's thinking, that it is space, rather than time, that is of most significance. This acknowledges an experiential and cultural significance of space and place in the construction of identity. Benwell and Stokoe suggest that 'not only do people make spaces, but also spaces make people' (2006: 211). As such spaces offer opportunities for identity construction and for discourse which contributes to this. It is no accident then that young unicyclists, as young skateboarders or BMX riders, use urban spaces, streets, shopping centres and so on, in ways which they were not intended for. They are interacting with them in new ways, reinterpreting them in ways which enable them to create new, alternative identities for themselves, different to mainstream society.

Sport, music, politics and leisure are all undergoing rapid change and development in today's 'postmodern world' and consequently it is argued by some that this requires a new approach to theorizing about young people and the activities they take part in (Weinzierl and Muggleton 2003). This approach is known as 'post-subcultural studies'. It identifies the

> shifting social terrain of the new millennium, where global mainstreams and local substreams rearticulate and restructure in complex and uneven ways to produce new, hybrid cultural constellations. (Weinzierl and Muggleton 2003: 3)

Weinzierl and Muggleton's hybrid cultural constellations are the mixing of different subcultures and the close cohabitation of different social groups – so much so that boundaries between them become blurred at the edges. The approach argues that with the coming of globalization the parameters that defined cultural practices in the past have been radically altered. Cultural, or subcultural, theory must therefore be able to describe the 'elasticity and fluidity' of twenty-first-century subcultures (Stahl 2003), whether they are youth subcultures or sports subcultures. The localized context is seen as less important today than the interrelated and interdependent contexts which exist within global processes. This notion of fluidity is particularly relevant when considering young people and their cultural or subcultural memberships.

In the past the media were seen as critical to the success and continuation of the dominant culture by groups such as the Centre for Contemporary Cultural Studies (Stahl 2003). They were regarded as an integral tool which labelled and reinforced the negative status of the 'other' groups. In contrast, post-subcultural theorists recognize that the media are

> integral to the formation of subcultures, playing a significant role in both their origin as well as prolonging their lifecycle. (Stahl 2003: 31)

This is in part due to the development of different forms of the media including virtual media such as the internet. They enable communication of ideas and images critical to the survival of subcultures and no longer restrict cultural activity to physically bounded sites. This opens up the spheres of language interaction. Indeed Maguire (1999) recognizes the impact that globalization is having on the exchange and 'interweaving' of cultures and subcultures 'facilitated by and within sport' (p. 7). A second change in theory is the shift away from a linear description of the development of group identity or individual identity within a group. Instead there is a greater emphasis on non-linear development acknowledging more multidimensional influences and building on Bourdieu's recognition that activities occur within and between groups.

Interestingly Weinzierl and Muggleton, when promoting post-subcultural theories, do not make any reference to sport and its place within subcultures. Instead they focus on music, politics and dress as the central identities within youth subcultures today. There are a variety of factors, or identities, which have a significant impact on subculture as it applies to youth, and particularly to young people unicycling. These include language, as well the influence of the media, visual imagery and dress. These last two can be classed as non-verbal language, a subdivision of kinesics, with kinesics being the study of movements in general. There are a number of components in non-verbal language (Thompson 2003) – these are facial expression, eye contact, posture, orientation, proximity, fine movement, gross movement and clothing and artefacts or objects. Thompson argues that non-verbal communication is often over-simplified and treated in an uncritical way. Non-verbal communication is more powerful than verbal communication in that when a statement is made verbally which is contradicted by the accompanying body language it is generally the body language that is given credence. Indeed in unicycling there is much non-verbal communication as peers watch and encourage each other using facial expressions, eye contact, orientation, proximity and fine movements. Examples of this can be seen in both narratives.

The media are a significant element in communication between peers, locally and over vast global distances now made possible by the internet. 'The media' includes the internet and has already been acknowledged above as having a significant role in the survival of subcultures today. In today's global world people can consume media from around the world and this has a significant impact on both individual and group identity (Rizvi 2006). Although Rizvi discusses this phenomenon of global mobility with regard to education, it can equally be applied to unicycling. Local cultural practices are being shaped by globalization which has a hugely significant impact on the development of motivation, identities and culture as illustrated in the second narrative.

Unicycling is recognized as a subculture by many who participate in the sport and who give thought to such things. Like other sports it is a social practice; it provides a common activity in which internal values are realized in the pursuit of excellence. (Excellence may be at many different levels and may simply be basic mastery to some.)

Unicycling is a physical activity which brings young people into contact with others. Because of the intensity of it there are frequent interludes of rest and recovery which provide natural opportunities for social interaction. The common interest or ability (or initial lack of ability) unites those who do it. It provides a group identity but not necessarily a formal group identity in the way a team game might. Unicycling is a social practice; it is not a social institution. Many people unicycle on their own, but a lot will come together on a monthly or yearly basis to meet with other unicyclists. There are unicycling clubs in existence for those who want a greater, or more frequent, degree of social interaction. Observations of mine suggest that these tend not to be highly structured and so they do not form an institution (Bignold 2005). Instead they create space for individuals driven by intrinsic values and do not seek extrinsic values for club recognition.

Unicycling provides social interaction for those who want it and an identity, either group or individual. One example of this is Trials unicycling; observations at British Unicycle Conventions show that this is the most popular form of unicycling among young people in the UK at present. It has an element of urban identity about it and those young people who take part in often dress in a particular style, with a particular stance, Hobo, which is the same as skateboarders and which gives them a clear identity. This does indicate how consumption forms a part of the subculture.

While many young unicycists do adopt a Hobo style of dress, more of them choose clothing (t-shirts or hoodies specifically), which link them to unicycling by logos or brands. T-shirts or hoodies showing allegiance to a particular unicycle discipline, role model or club are an important visual element of the subculture. T-shirts indicating attendance at a certain national or international meet are used to demonstrate Bourdieu's cultural capital by those who wear them.

This chapter has explored various theoretical approaches to identity, self-esteem, culture and language. Two narratives will now be shared to illustrate the relationship between these different elements.

Unicycling narratives: Constructing and reconstructing identity

The research on which this chapter draws was concerned with the experiences of young people who unicycle. The themes of identity and language, of motivation and self-esteem were at the centre of the study. It was the young people's lived experience of unicycling which would shed light on these themes, their stories, rather than a technical deconstruction of the language they used. A narrative approach was used to tell the stories of the young riders' experiences, based on the definition of 'narrative' as used by Shacklock and Thorp (2005):

> Narrative inquiry is concerned with the production, interpretation and representation of storied accounts of lived experience. (Shacklock and Thorp 2005: 156)

Narratives as a research tool recognize the strength of language to articulate identities. This method of data presentation allows the researcher to locate life experience, identity and cultural formation within a narrative frame, co-constructed by the young riders themselves. The first chapter discussed the idea that language tells us more about how we perceive the world than the world itself. The narratives of the unicyclists capture the world as they perceive it.

It is through language, narrative and dialogue that experiences and stories are constructed, perhaps in a formal interview or in a passing conversation. The primary source of data for the life stories was interviews, a two-way process which enables stories to be assembled by the interviewees in response to the interviewer's questions. Heikkinen et al. (2007: 13) regard the dialogue as key to the construction of narratives; 'social reality is constructed as a dialectic process in interpersonal discussion'. They refer to this as 'the principle of dialectics'. Credible narrative research is based on how well the informants' or interviewees' voices are heard, which is why it is important to acknowledge the dialogue as a two-way process in which the researcher and interviewer hold equal status.

The narrative accounts sought to capture the identity of and influences on the individual unicyclists, exploring their personalities through their experiences of the sport and suggesting social meaning in their actions linked to identity. The narratives constructed in this study can be categorized as 'creative non-fiction'. They are directly based on the individuals interviewed, their stories and experiences and observations of them at actual events. However, they are told using creative literary techniques to help the reader feel something of the lived experiences.

Taking an ethnographic approach in the research allowed for participatory interviews and observations. The semi-structured interviews enabled the interviewees to tell their stories at their individual paces, unrestricted by time schedules and closed questions. I have analysed the dialogue created thematically and the observations, based on themes I identified linked to my underpinning research questions. Alongside this individual data other information was collated from a range of sources and the narratives were co-constructed with the young riders. Below are two extracts from the narratives, followed by a discussion of each to explore the importance of language and the development of identity, motivation and self-esteem.

The first extract is part of Pete's story. He was a young man who had started unicycling as a teenager looking for an identity at school in England and motivated by a desire to belong to a group. His narrative is set in the context of an international unicycle marathon race.

> Those first three miles were pretty good today, he got into a good pace, a comfy stride; he just had to keep this up for another 23 and it'd be in the bag. It was going to be OK. He was riding on his own, most of his group having raced off in the first mile, so it was pretty quiet, the roads were pretty rural. A car passed him every now and then, the windows wound down to let a breeze in on this hot morning, passengers cheering out of the windows, the driver piping the horn. Great, a bit of encouragement always helped. That had been the great thing about learning with the Guys: the encouragement for each other, the support, the camaraderie. Right from the beginning at the school circus club they had egged each other on. Who had he first gone along with? Was it Ben? No, it was Lou, definitely Lou. Lou had been really into juggling, was pretty good, could do five balls, and Pete had gone along with him to learn to juggle but from the very first session the unicycle had just seemed so much more appealing, it seemed to be calling him, it had his name on it. Lou had practised with six balls and Pete had practised with the unicycle for a few weeks. He could remember the frustration though, he just couldn't get it, couldn't stay on; God, it had annoyed him. He had become determined to do it, not to be beaten. Then a friend's relative was selling one, a really old Pashley, a bit battered about but Pete had bought it and practised at home every day. That was the breakthrough, the perseverance. He could recall the feeling of balance as he rode a few feet; then he'd fall off on the grass but that great sense of satisfaction was what made him have another go and another go. Within a week he was riding down the drive and within a month he was riding competently. At last he was like that kid the year below him, who could ride. Pete had watched him messing about on his uni in the playground – God, he was cool. No-one else at school could do that, come to think of it Pete didn't know anyone outside school who could do that, jumping up and down the steps, bunny-hopping along the path. Looking back it was a bit sad wanting to be like someone else, now he liked to forge his own way, no longer so bothered by what others thought.
>
> The Guys had really got together at that time, at school. They started doing stuff on the unis from the circus club; riding round the gym, trying to turn left – it

was so much harder than turning right, something to do with the way your body works; they were all right-handed. He remembered how much they'd laughed in those early days, trying to ride round in a left-handed circle and forever ending up on the floor, they laughed and laughed at each other, looking so funny as they fell off those little wheels, not yet good enough to fall with grace, arms and legs flailing everywhere!! They'd started playing a bit of hockey at school, just amongst themselves, knocking the ball about, not much of a game when none of you could turn left!!! How they'd laughed! Pete remembered the ramp they had made up the sports-hall steps with that old plank of wood from the workshop. They'd practised riding up and down it for ages before they'd agreed to take it away and progress to hopping up and down. What fun! They were learning tricks together, pushing their own little boundaries together, having a laugh together and, without realising it, really bonding together. Thinking back now as he sat in that easy rhythm, riding through Farum on that hot sunny day, he remembered those times as good times. They were a group, a gang, mates. Pete realised now how much those friendships had meant to him at the time. He had been feeling awash in a year of people, boys, drifting amongst others, not really sure who he was or where he belonged. The Guys had changed all that, given him a defined group, good friends.

They shared a common interest, a group identity; gave him an identity, no longer drifting, now forged with others. They stuck together, had to stick together: they were different from the rest and that wasn't always a good thing. Being different at school wasn't always a good thing; you felt like a party in the wilderness, you had to keep together or you'd die. He realised early on that he couldn't get along with everyone so he forged strong relationships with those he did, the Guys. There were six of them, Pete, Ben, Zach, Nick, Jonnie and Tom. Jonnie could already ride, had been riding since he was 8 or 9. They always used to tease him – it was all those folk festivals his hippie parents had taken him to as a child. Some guys in the year below had gotten into it to, almost a uni club at school. The maths teacher who ran the circus club was really pleased, he'd been so encouraging from the start. Come to think of it though, it was only last year Pete had actually seen him on a unicycle; strange, that. He'd always seemed bewildered by the stuff the Guys did, the tricks and that, guess he wasn't really into unicycling, any more than doing a bit of juggling on one, and had been surprised at the Guys then. He had helped the kids in the circus club who wanted to juggle or poi or stuff and so he had rarely come out into the playground to watch them practise.

Pete's extract illustrates clearly the importance of non-verbal language and the role it has in building relationships and shared identities, discussed earlier in this chapter. As Peter recalls his early unicycling days with his friends in the circus club at school you can hear the warmth in his memories of their interactions and particularly their encouragement of each other. This takes place through facial expressions, eye contact between the boys, their close proximity to each other as they ride around and their gross and fine movements, a hand on Pete's shoulder to encourage him, a high-five slap to congratulate. Their unspoken support, their laughter; 'Well done!', 'Go for it!', 'Keep trying!'. The language is non-verbal, the communication simple, but the impact significant. This encouragement builds group identity and the physical skills of unicycling. As such Pete and his friends each develop their cultural capital as Bourdieu described it, or in this case their subcultural capital. As their unicycling skills grew so did the status each of them had within their group, their gang; it gave them credibility. The language of unicycling enabled each of them to express their identity as well as build a group identity in their chosen leisure pursuit.

The second extract is from Sangay's narrative. Sangay was a Nepalese youth, who had been riding for about a year and who was drawn to the virtual, global community of unicyclists, looking for an identity beyond his immediate environment of Kathmandu. Sangay's narrative is set in the context of unicycling with his friend at their boarding school. He takes the nick name Flames, and his friend, Animal.

> It was a typical unicycling scene; a couple of friends practising together, urging each other to go faster, or higher, or further, depending on what the goal was, usually boys, young lads mostly, just like Flames and Animal, in their teens, riding Street or Trials. The baggy trousers, hanging low, were a trademark style for male, adolescent unicyclists, borrowed from the skateboarding and BMX cultures they sometimes rode with. Usually a hoodie was worn on top, typical youth subculture today, anti-establishment almost given the menacing, negative stereotypes of hooded youth in the media. Without a hoodie on, shirts had to be cool, like Flames' and Animal's. You were making a statement after all, even if you didn't realise it. Unicycling was cool and you had to look cool, look the part – it was the same wherever you were. Something about riding on one wheel, the feeling of being different, unique, you had to look the part; it just went with the riding. The websites, official and unofficial, kids posting photos and videos of their tricks online, all reinforced it as part of the subculture. The images in the few magazines that took any interest in it fuelled it too. Unicycling was cool and if you rode you were cool (or whatever the latest youth expression was – 'mint'?). It was the same wherever you were, all part of the universal unicycling male, youth subculture. Of course that was how lots of adolescents dressed

today anyway, the larger youth culture, mainstreamed now to some extent. Still, Animal and Flames knew they looked cool and were happy to be so. They knew the look they wanted and had scoured all the secondhand stalls to achieve it – their meagre clothing allowance being spent creatively. They'd been on Facebook and YouTube, websites of Kris Holms and others. They weren't really interested in the speed or long distance practical clothes, which didn't look cool, and anyway they wouldn't have found those second-hand locally. Instead they had studied their contemporaries on the internet, other young lads, pictured with their mates, doing their thing on a uni and looking cool at the same time!

There was a new post on YouTube, a French lad, Francois; he was riding off the roof of a building, a good three metres high Animal reckoned. It had a flat roof; Francois rode along it and stopped close to the edge. His friends were on the ground shouting up to him, encouraging him, goading him, whistling, clapping. He took very small hops getting closer and closer to the edge, then paused. His friends fell silent and Francois hopped off the edge. He kept his body upright but bent his torso forward slightly, his feet on the pedals still, his arms out to balance. He landed upright and on his uni still and rode off screen. His mates applauded. 'Mon dieu!' 'Fantastique!' Francois rode back on screen; the film was a bit shaky as the cameraman, presumably one of his mates, got him back in the viewfinder. He beamed with satisfaction and gave one of the spectators a high five slap. He was cool, he looked cool, baggy jeans and a faded t-shirt, 'Koxx'. Animal and Flames had come across Koxx on the internet too; a French company that made unicycles and had some amazing clips of tricks on their website. Yogi, he was in a lot of the Koxx clips. He usually rode bare-chested, his long hair tied back in a pony tail. He looked really cool but the friends knew they wouldn't get away with that look here! Francois was certainly impressive with his amazing drop – what a feat, they wished they could do that. But after that clip were several seconds of Francois on other attempts to hop off the roof. Each time he had not made it; he'd fall on landing – sometimes pretty hard, 'Ouch!' – or he'd land on his feet, his unicycle crashing to the ground nearby. Animal and Flames watched the successful drop over and over again. 'Hey, perhaps we could post on the internet!' Animal suggested.

Sangay's narrative illustrates the role of the media in facilitating communication over long distances. In particular it illustrates the significance of the internet for young people today and its part in the development of sub-cultures. For Sangay in Kathmandu, his local cultural practices are shaped by global influences, the French rider in the posted video clip for example. As with Pete's extract the 'language' illustrated in this second narrative is non-verbal communication; a key component here is the young riders' dress. They have scoured the second-hand clothes stalls of Kathmandu to find the appropriate western cast-offs which capture the urban image they want to express their identity with. In Sangay's story the urban identity is important. As well as dress and style this is expressed in the use of the environment by Francois and which Flames so desperately seeks to emulate. Unicyclists use urban spaces to create a different leisure environment for themselves. They ride along and jump off steps, walls, railings and such. Wells (2002), discussed earlier, regards the use of urban environments for such leisure activities as critical to young peoples' reinterpretation of street spaces and demarcation of them as their leisure environments.

Conclusion

Language, both linguistic expression and non-verbal communication is used by individuals and groups to construct and express identities which can create a sense of self and of belonging. Language in unicycling is spoken more than written; it is immediate and spontaneous rather than planned. This relates to Derrida's view of language discussed in the first chapter, that authentic language is not constrained by a written form. It is natural, unplanned and can create a sense of being and belonging in the impulsive way it is used within friendship group. This link between being and language is articulated by Heidegger and illustrated in both narratives, not so much in the spoken word even but in the non-verbal communication among the two friendship groups in the stories. Language in its daily use is much more than words and phrases it is a social practice within a culture, or subculture as presented here.

Unicycling is very much about the riding, the physical skill and activity. While there is specialist language, mainly technical to describe aspects of this or the equipment used, non-verbal communication plays a much more significant role in developing and maintaining its subcultures. For individual riders it enables them to construct or reconstruct an identity within the realm of leisure.

References

Beard, A. (1998), *The Language of Sport*. London: Routledge.
Benwell, B. and Stokoe, E. (2006), *Discourse and Identity*. Edinburgh: Edinburgh University Press.

Bignold, W. (2009), *Unicycling & Identity: Narratives of Motivation and Achievement in Young Riders*, PhD thesis. Liverpool: Liverpool Hope University.

—(2006), 'The Child, Family & Society', in J. Sharp, L. Hankin and S. Ward (eds), *Education Studies: An Issues-based Approach*. Exeter: Learning Matters.

Chandler, T., Cronin, M. and Vamplew, W. (2002), *Sport and Physical Education: The Key Concepts*. London: Routledge.

Collins, M. and Kay, T. (2003), *Sport & Social Exclusion*. London: Routledge.

Elley, D. and Kirk, D. (2002), 'Developing Citizenship Through Sport: The impact of a sport based volunteer programme on young sport leaders'. *Sport, Education and Society* 7: 151–66.

Ford, N. and Brown, D. (2006), *Surfing and Social Theory: Experience, Embodiment and the Narrative of the Dream Glide*. Abingdon: Routledge.

Foucault, M. (1988), *The History of Sexuality, Vol. 3, The Core of the Self*. London: Allen Lane.

Furlong, A. and Cartmel, F. (2007), *Young People and Social Change: New Perspectives*, 2nd edn. Maidenhead: Open University Press/McGraw Hill.

Geldard, K. and Geldard, D. (2004), *Counselling Adolescents*, 2nd edn. London: Sage.

Gibson, D. and Jefferson, R. (2006), 'The Effect of Perceived Parental Involvement and the Use of Growth-fostering Relationships on Self-concept in Adolescents Participating in Gear Up'. *Adolescence* 41(161): 111–26.

Grenfell, M. (2006), 'Bourdieu: Educational Explorations in Field Theory', BERA Conference, University of Warwick.

Heikkinen, H., Huttunen, R. and Syrjala, L. (2007), 'Action Research as Narrative: Five Principles for Validation'. *Educational Action Research* 15(1): 5–19.

Hendry, L. B., Shucksmith, J., Love, J. and Glendinning, A. (1993), *Young People's Leisure and Lifestyles*. London: Routledge.

Hill, M. and Tisdall, K. (1997), *Children & Society*. Harlow: Prentice Hall.

Lawrence, D. (2006), *Enhancing Self-Esteem in the Classroom*, 3rd edn. London: Paul Chapman, p. xvii.

Maguire, J. (1999), *Global Sport, Identities, Societies and Civilisations*. Cambridge: Polity Press.

Marsh, H. W., Trautwein, U., Ludtke, O., Koller, O. and Baumert, J. (2006), 'Integration of Multidimensional Self-Concept and Core Personality Constructs: Construct Validation and Relations to Well-Being and Achievement'. *Journal of Personality* 74(2): 403–56.

Mills, M. (2001), *Challenging Violence in Schools: An Issue of Masculinities*. Buckingham: Open University Press.

Monney, J. (2006), 'The Future', *Uni, The Unicycle Magazine*, issue 1, 30–1.

Norton, B. (2000), *Identity and Language Learning; Gender, Ethnicity and Educational Change*. Harlow: Longman.

Pini, M. (2004), 'Technologies of the Self', in J. Roche, S. Tucker, R. Thomson and R. Flynn (eds), *Youth in Society*, 2nd edn. London: Sage, pp. 160–7.

Raey, D. (2006), 'From the Theory of Practice to the Practice of Theory: Operationalising Bourdieu's Concept of Habitus in Research on Higher Education Choice', BERA Conference, University of Warwick.

Riley, P. (2008), *Language, Culture and Identity*. London: Continuum.

Rizvi, F. (2006), 'Internationalization and the Assessment of Research Quality in Education', BERA Conference, University of Warwick.

Robbins, D. (2000), *Bourdieu and Culture*. London: Sage.

Shacklock, G. and Thorp, L. (2005), 'Life Histories and Narrative Approaches', in B. Somekh and C. Lewin (eds), *Research Methods in the Social Sciences*. London: Sage, pp. 156–63.

Stahl, G. (2003), 'Tastefully Renovating Subcultural Theory: Making Space for A New Model', in D. Muggleton and R. Weinzierl (eds), *The Post-Subcultures Reader*. Oxford: Berg, pp. 27–40.

Stevens, P. (2006), 'Institutional Characteristics and the Development of Teachers' Ethnic Stereotypes', BERA Conference, University of Warwick.

Thompson, N. (2003), *Communication and Language*. London: Palgrave Macmillan.

Thornton, S. (1996), *Club Cultures: Music, Media and Subcultural Capital*. Middletown, Conn: Wesleyan University Press.

Tomlinson, A., Ravenscroft, N., Wheaton, B. and Gilchrist, P. (2005), 'Lifestyle sports and national sport policy: An agenda for research', *Report to Sport England*. London: Sport England.

Weinzierl, R. and Muggleton, D. (2003), *The Post-Subcultures Reader*. London, Bloomsbury Academic.

Wells, K. (2002), 'Reconfiguring the Radical Other: Urban children's consumption practices and the nature/culture divide'. *Journal of Consumer Culture* 2(3): 291–315.

Wheaton, B. (ed.) (2004), *Understanding Lifestyle Sports; Consumption, Identity and Difference*. Abingdon: Routledge.

Wright, A. and Cote, J. (2003), 'A retrospective analysis of leadership development through sport', *The Sport Psychologist* 17(3): 268–91.

9

Drama and the Identity of the Language Learner

Bernie Hughes

> ## Editor's Introduction
>
> Bernie Hughes writes about the performance of foreign language identity through a drama pedagogy in foreign language learning. She advocates drama as the opening up of a 'third place' for the foreign language learner. This is a personal learning space where the learner is able to make his/her own personal representation of the learning process and develop her/his learner identity. There are similarities between Bernie's evocation of 'third place' and Wendy Bignold's account of spontaneous discourse of the last chapter. Both chapters evoke the cultural discourse of playfulness and experimentation where identities are constructed existentially in the space of the learner-actor, through dialogue in this chapter and through physical engagement in Chapter 8. Both unicycling and drama connect identity to a discourse of performance.

Introduction: Language learning, dramatic play and identity

'It's like playing a game. You've got to know all the moves. . . . Like playing a really difficult game'

The notion that foreign language learning, as articulated here by a 16-year-old 'A' level trainee of French, equates to a game, suggests an interesting view of the foreign language learner experience and the identity of the same language learner in the process of L2 acquisition. The implied notion of performer/player in this process further hints that in engaging in foreign language culture, the learner needs particular skills in order to present himself/herself well, and faces a challenge in the process.

In Kramsch's (2009) positioning of Third Culture within Language Education, the learner is indeed identified as 'performing' in the mother tongue/first language (L1) and the associated first culture (C1) and then engaging in performance of the second language (L2) and related second culture (C2).

As the learner brings one language and culture up against the other, there are conflicts which may arise between the individual learner and self, the language, culture and in the process of social interaction with the wider group of interlocutors. Establishing a 'Third Culture' as Kramsch sees it, sets up a space in which meaning and identity can be negotiated, to dispel tension, between the individual in relation to the wider group, the sense of self, sense of other and the conflict between native/non-native speaker.

'A third culture pedagogy leaves space for mischievous language play, carnivalesque parody, simulation and role-play and the invention of fictitious, hybrid identities that put into question NS claims on authenticity' Kramsch (2009: 234).

The focus of this chapter is on how learners relate to their learning process and perceive their language development, and can be supported to become more at ease with their identity as foreign language learners, moving more confidently towards autonomy. The subjects of the discussion are teacher trainees, who as primary practitioners have multiple roles in the primary classroom and who, in language learning terms, must engage with and in many cases renew their identities within foreign language cultures, reviving their school experience, as well as developing and understanding current modern foreign language pedagogy for the primary setting.

To explore this question further, the intention is to draw on theories of language learning instruction as outlined by Ellis (2005) and examples from undergraduate trainee work and testimony, including trainees' own statements about how they feel when speaking a foreign language and respond to interactive workshops based on dramatic techniques. This is set against the aforementioned theoretical notion of 'Thirdness' as seen by Kramsch, including the manner in which the learner perceives the language learning process and makes sense of it as an individual.

With trainee teachers in mind, there is no doubt that tensions exist in negotiating identity, culture and language in the foreign language learning setting and 'thirdness' has the potential to have a liberating effect. Here the use of drama can further help the language learner.

The pedagogy of drama and its imaginative power is widely acknowledged as appropriate for language learning (Winston 2012) and as a means of developing language. Drama promotes interaction, spontaneity, but also provides an invitation to establish an individual 'game-plan', and engage in reflection and collaborative work with peers/other learners. This is an important aspect, as trainees need to build confidence. In parallel, is the idea that within the foreign language communication situation the learner develops as an actor or performer with the FL learning situation to become a more confident self.

There are a number of tenets in the use of drama which are highly relevant to the foreign language learning situation and which can support the process of engaging in foreign language work. Basom's (2005) list on the benefits of Drama Education includes the notion of the development in the learner of self-confidence which comes through risk-taking and leads learners to trust in their own capacities. There is, furthermore, the development of the imagination since drama encourages working on creative choices and looking at the familiar in a new light. Drama further develops empathy and co-operation and collaboration and non-verbal communication skills

Negotiating 'Thirdness' through drama and game

Language as 'game' suggests such learner identity has both a playful, and yet unreal quality for the British non-native speaker of a foreign language, one in which this learner throughout is in role, in keeping with Cook's (2000) stance, which emphasizes the importance of play in the L2 language learning domain, along with the intellectual and creative aspects of engaging with language and culture. What is more, the learner's feelings about interaction in the target foreign language are important in order to understand how best to support language development.

Like many games, it is likely such learning presents a competitive element, requiring an accumulation of skills and pressure to achieve results. The learner may well compare performance with others and be led to focus on negative features of his/her errors in developing the L2. Thus the notion of affect comes to the fore and is a key aspect in this kind of language learning (Arnold 1999; Dörnyei 1999).

Wernicke (2009) reports on how trainees translate between language and cultural contexts and while they act as learners of the language in question, their meaning-making is drawn from their own life experiences. Wernicke thus highlights the different identities trainees come across within the classroom and how they meet boundaries or crossings within this learning context, citing Kramsch's (1993) reference to the classroom as a place of cross-cultural fieldwork.

Teacher plays a leading role

Within a classroom day the teacher also constantly engages in different roles. Within multiple identities the teacher's use of language is constantly changing according to the subject taught. The teacher leads the children and invites them into role as 'mathematicians' 'scientists' or 'artists' etc. in order to define the parameters of the work and to focus learning tasks in a meaningful way.

This is however more difficult to achieve in the foreign language. The invitation into role requires subject knowledge to be in place. When this is the case it can free the teacher and children to be experimental and engage in work as co-learners.

In the course of her exploration of trainee foreign language learning experience, Allais (2012) refers to the transcultural and translingual navigation in which foreign language learners engage. Referring to the work of Bhaba, Derrida and Said, Allais highlights the conflicts and tensions multilinguals undergo in negotiating the Third Space; Said, for example, expresses the idea of the multilingual as a 'prisoner', while Kramsch's re-framing of third place in relation to education suggests that the Third Place opens up spaces of possibility within everyday language practices, for the teacher/leader/learner. As non-native speakers, trainees are crossing not only linguistic and cultural borders, but also pedagogical borders, as emerging leaders in Primary Modern Foreign Language (PMFL).

The third culture of the foreign language learner

Kramsch suggests that it is the experience of Thirdness that allows the learner to make connections with emerging patterns, to reflect and derive meaning, whereas in 'Firstness' the learner is in receptive mode to surrounding information and in 'Secondness' the learner is in response mode where there is interacting and role playing with interlocutors. A sense of 'Third Culture' evolves and it is in this Third Space the learner, with an openness to creative exploration has an opportunity to discover and uncover identity. It can be a creative and inventive space for the non-native speaker who is attempting to grasp, work with and understand a foreign language. In this Third Space conflicts and tensions continue, but there is opportunity to construct, manipulate, critique, invent and understand. Such pedagogy invites multimodal and inventive practices.

Trainee confidence in L2 – class profile

Many trainees refer to lack of confidence in relation to their knowledge of foreign languages and need to find ways of overcoming such tensions. Profiling one non-specialist language group's characteristics as an example, most trainees have English as their mother tongue, some have learnt a foreign language at primary school (just under a quarter of the group), this language being mainly French.

The majority of trainees have already studied a foreign language in secondary school, including mostly French, some Spanish, some German with Irish and Latin or Greek also represented. Three quarters have observed a primary foreign language lesson. Most trainees do not use any language other than English regularly, and all trainees when asked to note their level of confidence in teaching a foreign language lesson state that they are not confident in this aspect, and they are not confident in their subject knowledge.

This issue of confidence is of critical interest in working with trainees in preparation for work in the primary classroom. The affective elements influencing language acquisition, as theorized by Krashen's (1982) Affective Filter Hypothesis can also be seen as key underpinning factors to such new situations of language learning. The challenge for the teacher is to reduce anxiety and tension (in Krashen's theory, lowering the filter) and facilitating the creation of the right atmosphere for optimum language learning.

For the trainee there are therefore perceived limitations in subject knowledge and culture awareness which are barriers to linguistic progress. Harris (2000) highlights the grammatical, sociolinguistic, discourse and strategic competences needed to know a language:

A learner cannot be said, for example, to 'know' a language if they are unable to engage in a conversation without whispered prompts from the teacher, or to repair for themselves breakdowns in communication, or to read authentic (rather than 'doctored') materials from the target language country, without constantly needing to resort to a dictionary (2000: 220).

In terms of exploration of identity, this is also reminiscent of Brian Friel's (1980) play 'Translations' which explores this idea of impossibility of communication, faced with a language that is not one's own. The fact that experience suggests that trainee language learners frequently refer to the notion of 'struggle' when negotiating language learning is significant. There can be a discomfort in learning a foreign language, as a more mature student learner, which is a challenge to overcome.

This presents young trainee teachers with a dilemma, in that their previous knowledge of the language needs refreshing, and time does not allow an extensive number of sessions in order to focus on advancing language learning. Trainees also have concerns about speaking the language even one with which they are familiar, and yet ultimately developing subject knowledge confidence and working towards teaching a lesson are important objectives, so that confident learners may instil confidence in their pupils, as teachers. Their language knowledge is dormant and linguistically speaking they are static. This 'static self' needs help to re-acquaint with past knowledge, re-define the experience and allows them to move forward in confidence.

Developing L2 identity through drama: The challenge

The infusing of language with drama to support the negotiation of L2 is appropriate therefore but not without its challenges. Trainee trepidation of low-level language subject knowledge is an issue of which to be highly conscious in approaching such work. Notions of 'Performance' and 'Self' are foregrounded at every turn. Such psychological factors have also long been identified as part of the general language acquisition process. Bialystok and Hakuta (1994) remind us of the complexity of language learning. Therefore, while for many advocates the combination of drama and language can enhance communicative competence and overall language learning (Winston 2013) it can also be seen as exposing the participant to new challenges. In addition clearly individual differences in language learners play an important part, as emphasized by Gillette (1994), but seen from a positive perspective successful language learners can be seen to fix language learning as a personal goal and therefore are often willing to make an effort.

Learner subjects in this discussion: The trainee teacher

The examples of learning situations presented in the following discussion, relate in particular to undergraduate learners who are also trainee teachers, and who therefore need not only to assume multiple identities as primary practitioners, but also in turn to support young learners to find their own language learning identities in the primary setting. They therefore perform a dual role of learner and teacher. In this complex, multi-layered process, finding a voice in the foreign language in question, is a challenge. Referring to the background picture of foreign language learning national policy is a useful starting point for this exploration of trainee identity in language learning, as nationally the uncertain status of language learning is relevant to trainees' perception of languages and consequently their own position.

The developing picture of language learning in the United Kingdom

The advent of the statutory teaching of foreign languages in Key Stage 2 of the primary curriculum from 2014 will require many primary school teachers to re-acquaint themselves with foreign languages first learnt at school and develop ways of teaching and learning an Modern Foreign Language (MFL) with their primary class. While investing in visiting experts to provide language lessons for primary learners is a model used by many primary schools, research and policy documents in the United Kingdom indicate a preference for the use of the class teacher to provide such lessons.

According to the Department for Education (DFE), the number of children taking an MFL at General Certificate of Secondary Education (GCSE) will be almost a third higher in 2013 than it was in 2011 and is forecast to continue to grow, so there is a real need for talented language teachers. The new policy of statutory provision at KS2 will likely have an impact on the ways in which young people are taught a foreign language subsequently at KS3 and KS4 and come to uncover an L2 identity in the process. As long ago as the 1990s, Hawkins (1991) provided the example of there being in some secondary settings five kinds of language teaching, including teaching English as mother tongue, teaching a foreign language (e.g. French), teaching English as a foreign language (EFL) (for ethnic minorities), teaching of ethnic minority mother tongues (e.g. Arabic, Chinese etc.), teaching of Latin. As new policy evolves so will language teacher identity. There has therefore never been a more appropriate time for trainee teachers to engage in MFL and to assimilate a new role as language teachers and to develop a stronger L2 identity, within the primary school setting.

The primary practitioner: Complex identity

The primary practitioner contends with many subject-oriented identities, across a range of curriculum and foundation subjects, switching from one to another, and has to negotiate competing discourses (Woods and Jeffery 2002). The primary teacher also faces many pressures, such as Office for Standards in Education (OFSTED). A new wave of accountability is emerging in relation to the 2014 Curriculum and the primary teacher's role is evolving with a constant need for the teacher to establish and reappraise his/her professional identity and sense of self. The trainee comes with a residual core of language, which varies considerably from one learner to another and some wider awareness of other languages. Injecting confidence is the key. In keeping with many first-hand narrative accounts of negotiating of the self in the contemporary multicultural world is therefore the notion of challenge and struggle.

In a poem entitled 'Puzzle' about her own language learning experience, Myrna Nieves describes writing in a foreign language (in this case English) as 'a wave where spaces open into a void and you just need to jump off a cliff' (2000: 11). Gaps in understanding, which can be both linguistic and cultural act as barriers to L2 acquisition, and the learner has to make a dramatic leap into the unknown. Lack of subject knowledge in respect of trainee teachers is a key issue. Affective learning becomes an important underpinning principle in addition to needing support and encouragement

Drama in foreign language learning

The use of dramatic techniques to relieve such pressure and to facilitate the learner in growing into his/her role as language learner is part of a growing body of work in Second Language Acquisition (SLA). From the early work of Maley and Duff (1982) drama has long been linked to language learning as a demonstration of effective pedagogy.

Brash and Wernicke (2009) examine the notion of identity formation in L2 and the relationship between role-play and identity, and see drama-based role-play functioning as a bridge between the first language/first culture and target language/target culture. They also see silences as permitting a space for learners to reinvent themselves in the target language. Social and affective strategies are brought to the fore. As a long-time advocate of the use of drama in learning from secondary MFL experience and within the EFL setting, the way in which drama can lift confidence and free learners creatively was brought home to me during one of the first storytelling sessions I conducted with second-year undergraduate MFL specialists. The trainees had worked on the story of Goldilocks and the Three Bears and were in the process of animating and trying out the pedagogical approaches in two groups, one in French, one in Spanish. Now familiar with the story and having practised the language, I asked one group to perform the story as if they were in a circus and one group to perform as if they were telling a horror story. Physical presence, voice and gesture changed completely to impact on the revised performances.

Constructing a language portrait: First steps in overcoming lack of confidence

In this model, the Mother Tongue is central to the trainee primary practitioner. Identifying instances of language awareness points trainees towards languages around them and encourages them to think of their quite extensive peripheral knowledge of foreign languages. This is evidenced by trainees comments following this workshop experience. The sense of separate bodies of knowledge is eroded to give trainees insight into their passive knowledge.

One way of overcoming this negative initial self-appraisal of knowledge of languages is to ask trainees to construct a language portrait of their experiences of engaging with other languages at the beginning of their first session. Language portraits feature within the Qualifications and Curriculum Authority (QCA) Unit 1 scheme of work, across the range of foreign languages, as a mother-tongue activity with primary language learners. It constitutes a visual, annotated audit

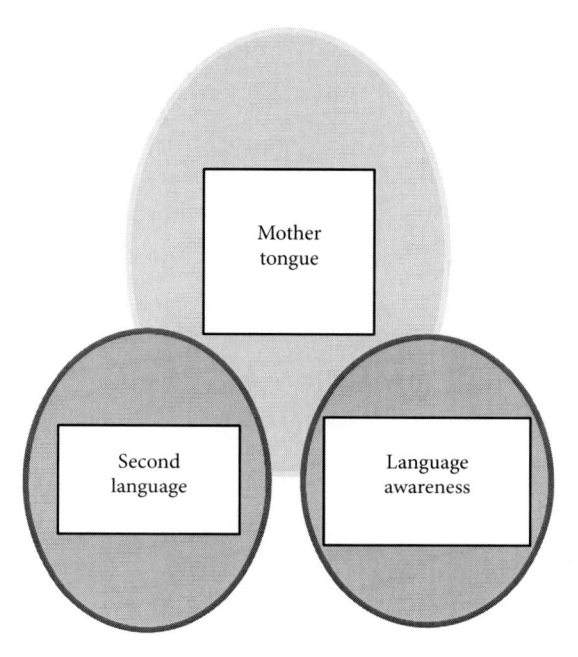

Figure 9.1 Distinct elements of the trainee language learner profile.

of trainees' previous language learning and invites trainees' recall of everyday language encounters.

A feature of this work is to introduce trainees to storytelling across languages, including references to French, Spanish and German story titles to allow trainees to compare with their mother tongue and to explore cross-cultural differences in translation. However, I would add that the gap in trainees' subject knowledge is one which can aggravate silence and lack of confidence. Through circumstance, many learners in the United Kingdom engage intermittently with their foreign language so that they build up patterns of unfamiliarity and growing uncertainty in relation to their subject knowledge and ability to interact and engage with a second language. Yet by virtue of effortless first language acquisition and many unnoticed intercultural encounters, trainees are complex learners of language.

Trainees draw an outline figure and detail their experiences of other languages, including the language in which they think, their 'head' language, their 'heart' language and other languages with which they have contact. They are therefore invited to record all languages no matter how fleeting, which they have encountered. Prompted to think in this way beyond the foreign language which may be a distant memory, trainees refer to numerous complex encounters with language on a daily basis.

Written comments relate particularly to the developing of subject knowledge:
'I dream of learning many languages and broadening my knowledge.'

Comments also demonstrate affection for mother tongue and passion for foreign language learning:
'communicate with friends and family- grown up with the language'
'Language in my Heart – Spanish – Loved the language ever since I was younger- beautiful with lots of emotion. Love Spain itself – family holidays.'

In the course of this process trainees also record interesting instances of everyday language encounters, such as listening to Chinese while working in a restaurant, languages heard in sporting settings such as Spanish football chants, instructions in Hindi on a cricket pitch, and conversations overheard from neighbours, such as Polish, Ukrainian. This exercise reveals that their language learning spectrum is seen to be much wider and their peripheral language familiarity is built up in a positive manner.

Accepting that the classroom can only provide trainees with a basis of language learning, learners need nonetheless to try to maximize their opportunities for language use and encounters beyond the classroom (Macaro 2001), progressing beyond their core foreign language identity to recognize the many everyday instances when they engage with language.

To counter the perceived lack of confidence, workshop opportunities are provided to support subject knowledge and pedagogy with a focus on the creative aspects of primary modern languages experienced in drama. Trainees complete a short audit of their language background and experience prior to the class and then post class. Shared class written notes are also analysed.

Workshop encounters with language learning

The workshop situation allows trainees to collaborate and compare practitioner identities, seeing similarities in lack of subject knowledge, which far from de-motivating is galvanized by drama, due to the physical and non-verbal interaction. Work can take on a new dimension and can present trainees with a space in which to reinvent themselves in the target language.

Perceived limitations in language subject knowledge

As a nation challenged by foreign language learning, repelled and attracted to languages in equal measure, one is aware that the position of English as a world language means that learners question the importance of learning a foreign language and are easily demoralized. For those who take up the challenge there is a need to develop coping strategies and drama may well offer a means of comfortably becoming another and developing confidence.

From experience of running language sessions with trainees, post class evaluations frequently cite confidence as what the learner seeks most. Trainees tend to come to workshops conscious of gaps in knowledge and anxious about perceived limitations. Learner identity is often summed up by 'I only know a few words . . .'. As primary practitioners trainees are conscious that they are on a course to fill these gaps, reducing a perceived deficit.

Even postgraduate language learners abroad are conscious of gaps in language subject knowledge and need to re-discover their previous level of language learning. Their prominent strategy is to regain lost ground and become that which they were previously. Thus the learner is attached to their previous self in foreign language terms, a self which maintained a higher standard of linguistic accuracy. It is also the case that even experienced learners have anxieties about the first moment they walk into the classroom.

There is also a gap between what the learner sees and the words he/she wants to use. Berger (1972) expressed this in relation to our negotiating what we see and what we know . . . 'we are always looking at the relation between things and ourselves. Our vision is continually active, continually holding things in a circle around itself, constituting what is present to us as we are' (1972: 9). Trainees' immersion in a dramatic situation may allow themselves to relax, see differently and to respond and speak differently.

Paige et al. (1997) highlight the importance of trainees becoming effective language and culture learners who are learning how to learn. Trainees do not always see themselves as part of a professional process of language development, rather than acquiring fixed knowledge which will not change.

From ordinary to extraordinary stories

Trainees are provided with a short conversation along these lines:

Ça va?
Oui, mais j'ai froid. Et toi?
Ça va. Attention!

Are you OK?
Yes. But I'm cold. And you?
I'm OK. Look out!

After modelling the conversation they are asked to re-run the conversation using different characters. They are then alternatively:

Two astronauts
Two police officers on a stakeout
Two teachers having coffee
Two spies
Two marathon runners
Two prisoners

And to contribute their own ideas, learners focus on character and action and are therefore drawn away from starting with words. Vocabulary is not the prime focus and the scripted text is one they can make their own. The physicalizing of the text helps to free trainees from concentrating on the script alone, and results in bold performances in which humour can come to the fore.

The trainees were also asked to graffiti on four separate wall spaces, one allocated to French, one to Spanish, one to German and one to other languages. They were able to circulate freely between the four spaces and note words and comments at will. They were encouraged to keep moving and not to worry about spelling. Then they were asked to position themselves in front of the wall they felt most comfortable with and asked to create something from the fragments of language. They therefore circulate, interact and write on the graffiti walls. The proviso was that they were not allowed to merely present, they were encouraged to enact. The groups took very different approaches: from one group who created a cartoon strip in French using an animal scenario, of buying a pet, to a second group presenting a scene in German choosing a surreal cafe scene. Yet another group worked across languages in an airport scene combining different languages in a series of sketches. Overall they commented on creative ideas developed, alternative ways to teach MFL and new strategies that can be used in the classroom.

Into the unknown: How principles of learning are underpinned

Ellis identifies ten principles which underpin instructed language learning.

1. Instruction needs to ensure that learners develop both a rich repertoire of formulaic expressions and a rule-based competence
2. Instruction needs to ensure that learners focus predominantly on meaning
3. Instruction needs to also ensure that learners also focus on form
4. Instruction needs to be predominantly directed at developing implicit knowledge of the L2 while not neglecting explicit knowledge
5. Instruction needs to take account the learner's 'built-in syllabus'
6. Successful instructed language learning requires extensive L2 input
7. Successful instructed language learning also requires opportunities for output
8. The opportunity to interact with the L2 is central to developing L2 proficiency
9. Instruction needs to take account of individual differences in learners
10. In assessing learners' L2 proficiency it is important to examine free as well as controlled production.

In commenting on these it is clearly that these principles offer a strong framework for instructed language learning, but also create a certain rigidity in terms of approach. The following commentary aligns with the corresponding principle.

1. Trainees are able to recall set phrases from early language learning, however perceive this as limited. Power of recall of grammar is also an issue. Trainees find security in grammar and perceive their limited recall as weakness. However there is also an interest in moving away from overly structured learning. One trainee remarked that a freer structure had 'given me fun ideas as a more informal way to teach MFL rather than rote learning'.
2. Trainees bring familiarity normally with one foreign language. Focus on meaning becomes problematical when trainees are required to engage with an unknown language.
3. Scribing and noting ideas in written form without explicit focus on mistakes is helpful to instil confidence
4. Exploring culture-specific knowledge here is helpful
5. Trainees underestimate their pre-existing knowledge. The encouragement to reflect on their individual linguistic richness is an affirming aspect of the development of identity as an FL teacher and learner.

6. This can certainly generate ideas. But modest input can be very positive. Trainees need help and encouragement to believe that less can be more and that dramatic communication permits mistakes and promotes non-verbal means of interacting.
7. There is impact of sharing previously learnt, hitherto passive knowledge.
8. Re-acquaint themselves through others' presentations. Trainees learn a new way of behaving, with a focus on non-verbal interaction.
9. Ellis primarily has in mind catering for different learning styles although this is challenging. However it is a requirement that teachers differentiate effectively. In using drama, sensitivity to trainees uncertainties, as outlined at the start of this chapter, is important.
10. Drama certainly promotes the use of free production. This is seen by Ellis as useful in that it relates most closely to the real-life authentic setting. Trainees comment on the confidence-enhancing aspects of dramatic interaction.

Re-defining roles: From hesitant to confident L2 speaker

The trainee groups conduct a free – write on each of the walls. The use of graffiti walls gives licence to be experimental and trainees are less judgemental about their own work and of others. Anxiety diminishes and trainees draw on what they know in a non-threatening atmosphere. They move away from what Ellis (2005) terms the controlled practice exercises which reduce spontaneity, and can be limited in length and complexity. Although trainees are not looking for regularities in language in the graffiti exercise, they are led to discuss common points of culture and specific understanding, the group's sense of Frenchness or of situations they can exploit. The fragmentation also frees trainees to focus less on written text and more on use of non-verbal communication. Trainees are less hampered by accuracy of spelling and write about aspects of culture with which they are familiar.

Trainees refer particularly to their power of recall:

A   I remember a lot of French when revisited
B   Helped understand how to enunciate
C   Shown me I know more than I thought
D   Revisiting my own knowledge of languages I know
E   Jogged my memory and made me realize

F   That I do have some knowledge of French that I can build on
G   I have done more German today than in years. Remembered more than I thought I did
H   Realizing that with a little help you could teach a language you're not 100 per cent confident in
I   Remembering the French I already know
J   Reassured my knowledge I have attained since secondary school
K   good to see how we can decode other languages based on what we know
L   feel more confident in teaching
M   That you can make an interesting lesson without good knowledge of the language

Foreign language identity: A cross-language comparison

A group of first-year primary education trainees beginning an MFL specialist course were asked to note down in written form how they feel in relation to speaking French, Spanish and German, respectively. They were asked to free-write responses to three prompts:

When I speak French I feel . . .
When I speak Spanish I feel . . .
When I speak German I feel . . .

This group of trainees follow an introductory language awareness course and then a programme studying language acquisition alongside sessions on the French-speaking Spanish-speaking and German-speaking worlds. Trainees are therefore encouraged to think and work across languages, although they will be aware of their personal hierarchy of language familiarity, from first learnt foreign language, through to second foreign language etc. This data is analysed using a comparative method to draw out cross-cutting themes (Silverman 2005). The approach is reading and re-reading data, looking for similarities and differences between statements. The degree of generalization which can be made from such a sample is limited. However, it is possible to use such a small sample of data collected to theorize about the possible wider applicability of the findings by using 'theoretical inference' (Hammersley 2012).

The following are statements in relation to trainee feelings as they speak each language. (The number of years language learning experience of each trainee is in brackets)

When I speak French I feel

1. (7) French. I'm gaining confidence but still struggle with tenses
2. (9) Quite confident in my speaking and reading French but unsure of some pronunciation
3. (4) Like I can remember parts and that makes it feel good when I can speak it. However I struggle on a lot of different parts. I am not very confident except in some particular parts such as numbers, colours etc.
4. (8/9) confident in my language ability. I feel that I can talk well and freely and communicate with ease
5. (19) at home. French is a part of me and I feel proud to have that connection
6. (7) when I speak French I feel fairly confident and proud that I am able to communicate with others whom maybe don't speak my native language
7. (8) confident. I feel that French is an important part of my life and when I speak French I feel proud that I can think in French too
8. (2) gentle, elegant, educated as the language sounds delicate to me

It is notable that in spite of several years accumulated experience in the French language, feelings in relation to French are strongly bound up with the notion of confidence, which re-occurs in several statements. This confidence is in turn connected with accuracy of pronunciation, knowledge of vocabulary and

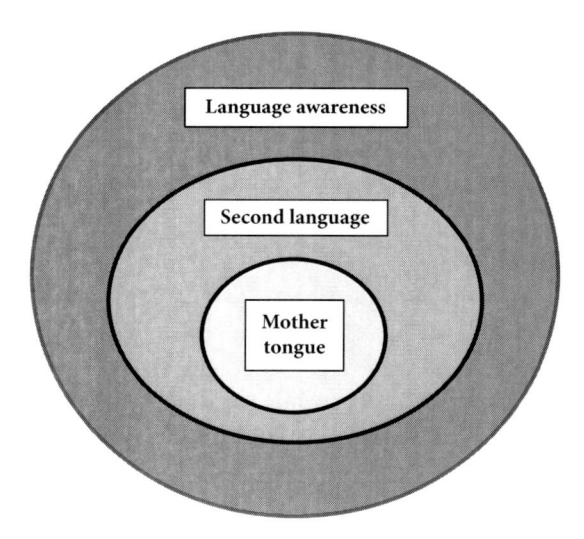

Figure 9.2 The blending of mother tongue, second language and wider language awareness.

communicative ability (Trainees 1, 2, 3, 4, 6, 7). A feeling of pride is emphasized (Trainees 3, 6, 7).

Speaking the French language is very much bound up with achievement and sense of success. The trainees' statements express high expectations of themselves in relation to the language. In addition, two of the views expressed by trainees with extensive experience (Trainee 5) and more limited experience (Trainee 8) suggest heightened positive awareness of language, which is to be expected from trainees who are motivated by MFL, but which raises questions about the less confident learner. Confidence underpins every aspect of the language learning experience. Language awareness, second language and sense of mother tongue language blend more fluently together (Figure 9.2).

The experience of speaking Spanish

When I speak Spanish I feel...

1. (0) Able to relate certain words to Italian but still struggle to get 'into Character'.
2. (0) Nervous because I have never spoken or learnt any Spanish before
3. (0) That I can speak some bits fluently but as never studying it in school, I only know things such as food and drink and basics so I feel I struggle with other bits
4. (7/8) Less confident than when speaking French but I am still able to communicate quite easily. I love the language and I love how I feel when I speak Spanish
5. (0) motivated to learn more of this beautiful language
6. (0) Happy. I've always loved the language and so when I speak it I enjoy doing so. I am always happy to learn more Spanish
7. (0) like it is something I struggle with – I feel like myself trying to speak another language as I only know basic vocab whereas with French I feel more comfortable
8. (0) exotic, mysterious as the language seems unique

In Spanish Trainees are more polarized in their responses to the language. Trainee 1 refers to language connections made across the Romance languages of Italian and Spanish, with a strong sense of being 'other' when engaging in Spanish, much as an actor or performer. Trainees 2, 3 and 7 express negative feelings in relation to Spanish, as opposed to Trainees 5, 6 and 8 who refer to happiness, motivation and intrigue. The notion of 'struggle' re-occurs in these statements and suggests that without words, trainees are inhibited.

The experience of speaking German

When I speak German I feel

1. (0) Confused! Can't grasp a lot of vocab and the tenses confuse me
2. (4) OK because I studied German but I'm a bit rusty at it
3. (5) That I understand the majority of it which makes me more confident in it and I feel I can speak it quite well
4. (0) excited to learn a new language but also anxious as I've never come across I before
5. (0) nostalgic, remembering my past knowledge, and eager to pick up the language again
6. (0) excited. I feel its pronunciation is very different from the other languages I speak so when I do speak it correctly it is exciting
7. (2) confident than with Spanish but still feel a 'distance' to the language I remember some vocab from school which gives me confidence, but I have no knowledge of tenses etc
8. (7) empowered as I am very confident speaking the language

In German certain new ideas emerge in the comments by the trainees in relation to nostalgia (Trainee 5), Excitement, linked to the new experience (Trainees 4 and 6) and empowerment (Trainee 8). However a sense of distance (Trainee 7) and confusion (Trainee 1) also prevails at the unfamiliar. Knowledge of vocabulary terms is seen as important and leads to confidence (Trainee 7).

The primary practitioner in the classroom setting: Learner and teacher role

Thus the learner's role as an individual teacher, as member of a group of training teachers, as learner teacher needing to understand MFL pedagogy and develop strategies to employ in the classroom and be able to reflect in order to improve practice, all come in to play. Trainee teachers are led to re-define their role in relation to the language learning situation and their teacher role within this learning experience.

In the foreign language learning situation the use of another voice can lead the teacher to a more confident place in which with pupils, celebration of the foreign language culture and language brings confidence in learning. The teacher is recalling, rethinking and enacting language from memory. This can lead to a more confident self-perception.

The use of dramatic techniques can help to free the learner to perform and interact more spontaneously and consequently move away from the perceived view of limited monolingual identity. Drama also allows for collaborative work, which allows developing practitioners to pool cultural notions and to refresh ideas and experiences. Trainee teachers both develop their L2 identity and their teacher identity. This in turn will permit more confident teaching of language and culture to primary age pupils. Drama in this way can be seen as a path to a more creative L2 self and can offer steps towards foreign language autonomy.

Language beyond words

In the poetic image of jumping off a cliff as the physical manifestation of engaging with a language may seem unduly dramatic, but is in fact a notion which equates to the risk-taking and exposing elements of an individual engaging with a foreign language.

Drama has an important role to play in order to permit moving beyond words, moving into explorations of the non-verbal and giving a sense of confidence. It also importantly brings laughter and humour into the room, so that trainees feel they can play with language and experiment. This creates an atmosphere akin to that in many early language learning classes in the primary setting, where children's curiosity is not bound up with restricted sense of self or of confidence.

Clearly, there are also a number of thresholds to cross in language learning, from beginner to early language learner, from early language learner to confident speaker, from confident speaker to fluent communicator. The emotional ties which language learning unearths and reveals need to be sensitively explored to facilitate confident engagement with a foreign language and its culture. But it is in the game-like and creative encounters with the foreign language in which deep learning has the opportunity to emerge that the confident language learner can emerge.

References

Allais, L. (2012), 'Third Place in the French classroom: A separate space for a new beginning?', http://blc.berkeley.edu/index.php/blc/postthird_place_in_the_french_classroom_a_separate_space_for_a_new_beginning.

Arnold, J. (1999), Affect in L2 Learning and Teaching. In elia (estudios de linguistic inglesa aplicada) 9, 2009, 145–51.

Basom, J. (2005), *The Benefits of Drama Education.* www.DramaEd.net.

Berger, J. (1972), *Ways of Seeing.* London: Penguin.

Bialystok, E. and Hakuta, K. (1994), *In Other Words: The Psychology and Science of Foreign Language Acquisition.* New York: Basic Books.

Brash, Barbel and Warnecke, Sylvia (2009), 'Shedding the ego: Drama-based role-play and identity in distance language tuition'. *Language Learning Journal* 37(1): 99–109.

Brown, G. and Yule, G. (1983), *Discourse Analysis.* Cambridge. Cambridge University Press.

Carter, R. (2004), *Language and Creativity: The Art of Common Talk.* London: Routledge.

Cook, G. (2000), *Language Play, Language Learning.* Oxford: Oxford University Press.

Cook, V. and Wei-Lei (eds) (2009), 'Contemporary Applied Linguistics', Vol. 1. *Langguage Teaching and Learning.* London: Continuum.

Department for Education: http://www.education.gov.uk/get-into-teaching/subjects-age-groups/teach-mfl [accessed 4 November 2013].

Dörnyei, Z. and Malderez, A. (1999), 'Group Dynamics in Foreign Language Learning and Teaching', in J. Arnold (ed.), *Affective Language Learning.* Cambridge: Cambridge University Press, pp. 155–69.

Ellis, R. (2005), 'Principles of instructed language learning'. *System* 33: 209–24.

Friel, B. (1980), *Translations.* London: Faber & Faber.

Gillette, B. (1994), 'The role of learner goals in L2 success', in J. Lantolf and G. Appel (eds), *Vygotskian approaches to second language research.* Norwood NJ: Ablex Publishing.

Hammersley, M. (2012), 'Troubling Theory in Case Study Research'. *Higher Education Research and Development* 31(3): 393–405.

Harris, V. (2000), 'Towards independence in language use and language learning', in K. Field (ed.), *Issues in Modern Foreign Language Teaching.* London: Routledge Falmer.

Harris, Z. S. (1952), 'Discourse Analysis'. *Language* 28: 1–30.

Hawkins, E. (1991), *Awarenes of Language: An Introduction.* Cambridge: Cambridge University Press.

Kramsch, C. (1993), *Context and Culture in Language Teaching.* Oxford: Oxford University Press.

Krashen, Stephen D. (1982), *Principles and Practice in Foreign Language Acquisition.* Oxford: Pergamon, http://www.sdkrashen.com/Principles_and_Practice/Principles_and_Practice.pdf. [accessed 3 November 2013].

Lantolf, James P. and Appel, G. (eds), (1994), *Vygotskian Approaches to Foreign Language Research.* London: Ablex Publishing, pp. 195–213.

Macaro, E. (2001), *Learning Strategies in Foreign and Foreign Language Classrooms*. London: Continuum.

Maley, Alan and Duff, Alan (1982), *Drama Techniques in Language Learning*. Cambridge: Cambridge University Press.

Paige, R. Michael et al. (1997), *Culture Learning in Language Education: A Review of the Literature*, http://gps.umn.edu/culture/resources/litreview.PDF [accessed 3 November 2013].

QCA Scheme of work Unit 1 All About Me, http://webarchive.nationalarchives.gov.uk/20100612050234/http://www.standards.dcsf.gov.uk/schemes3/documents/unit_1_french_moi.pdf [accessed 3 November 2013].

Silverman (2005), *Doing Qualitatatve Research*. London: Sage.

Wernicke, M. (2009), *The FSL Classroom as Third Space*. http://mwernicke.ca/Olbi08.pdf [accessed 11 December 2013].

Winston, J. (ed.) (2012), *Second Language Learning through Drama –Practical Techniques and Applications*. London: Routledge.

—(2013), *Drama Education and Foreign Language Learning Editors: Winston, J.* London: Routledge.

Woods, Peter and Jeffery, Robert (2002), 'The reconstruction of primary teachers' identities'. *British Journal of Sociology of Education* 23(1): 89–106.

10

Towards a Cultural Paradigm of Alterity in Modern Foreign Language (MFL) Learning

David Evans

Editor's Introduction

David Evans explores identity and foreign language learning and, following on from the last chapter, looks at cultural identity within foreign language as alterity or 'Otherness'. He argues that the student of foreign languages should not be framed only by a socio-economic discourse but should since viewed as a learner of culture. Learning language is then learning culture since culture not only surrounds language but also resides within it. Learning a foreign language is being a participator in a linguistic-cultural community which, for the learner, represents Otherness as well as similarity and is not just an extension of learner subjectivity. Foreign language is not therefore the mother tongue in translation but, recalling Philippe Chassy's Chapter 3, is conceptually and culturally different. Languages cannot be accurately translatable into each other and identities change as one moves from one language to another.

Introduction

Socio-economic motivation is, in secondary schools, a prevalent rationale for foreign language (MFL) learning. The notion of selling goods abroad to consumers in their own language is a compelling motivational tool employed by governments, industry and schools. The learner is framed as a socio-economic unit eager to transact through the discourses of tourism or business. This chapter's axiom, however, is that the student is not merely a tool of economics but rather a learner of culture whose own cultural identity and language evolve within the learning process. Notions of culture on the inside of language as well as around language as part of a cultural ecology, proposed by such writers as Kramsch (1993) and Van Lier (2000), are not widely acknowledged. Therefore socio-economics seems to become the cultural default for language learning. Unfortunately this economic motivation is instrumental and external to the language itself. This leads to a utilitarian view of language where the content of language is superficial as is the identity of the learner. An alternative perspective is proposed where MFL is predominantly a moral and cultural activity, an exploration of identities and an exploration of 'Otherness', not only of the community of speakers but of language itself.

Many educational commentators and policy-makers argue that Modern Foreign Languages should be compulsory throughout the secondary school curriculum as a means of increasing competitiveness in world markets in terms of marketing and exporting UK products. Modern Foreign Languages (henceforth MFL) are then often viewed within an economic term of reference as follows '. . . the time is right for the government to declare a clear commitment to setting a national policy agenda for languages, along with an enhanced international dimension in education, as a contribution to economic success and international understanding' Nuffield Languages Inquiry (2000: 64) This inquiry also points to 'an inadequate supply of language skills available to industry across a range of languages' (2000: 64).

Since MFL is frequently regarded as skills based rather than culturally based in content (Kramsch 1993), it is viewed and judged according to practical outcomes that are instrumental involving economic and functional transactions. Kramsch furthermore argues that teaching and learning MFL within a skills-based behavioural context tends to view language as ideologically and culturally neutral. However, as she points out, skills-based language is surface language and as such floats at the surface of the dominant culture. Far from being neutral, it puts into operation society's dominant ideologies. More generally, Ball (2008) argues that 'education is a servant to the economy. Education is now thoroughly subordinated to the supposed inevitabilities of globalization and international economic competition' (*Education Guardian*, 29 January 2008).

Fairclough (1989) asserts that in the United Kingdom, as in other European and Western countries, society's dominant ideology is free market capitalism and this is inevitably reflected in educational discourse. He argues that this is because socio-economics occupy an influential position in societal Orders of Discourse which in turn shape discourse types such as education, health, transport, public services and utilities. In fact these areas are social and public infrastructural ones that have been transformed into internal and external commercial markets. A recent example in 2013 of a state-owned utility being sold off to share holders is the privatization of the Post Office as a profit-making enterprise. Many other European countries, however, retain state-owned utilities as part of their infrastructure to be run as services to the nation such as railways, energy companies and postal services. However in the United Kingdom, recent history has demonstrated that capitalist ideologies now pervade the innermost functioning of state infrastructure. In 2012, the *Guardian Newspaper* quoted a top civil servant in the Department for Education, Sir David Bell as having 'no principled objection to profit-making companies taking over state schools' (*Guardian Newspaper*, 1 February 2012). Furthermore in the article he states, 'In those areas of systematic failure, where all other options have failed, can you object to somebody coming in and trying something different and making some profit out of it?'. Capitalism here, it seems, might replace pedagogy as an underlying solution to educational failure.

In terms of MFL education, it comes therefore as no surprise that the languages studied in schools represent economic forces and markets. Very few mainstream state schools in the United Kingdom offer courses, for example, in Celtic languages outside of those particular respective Celtic nations or community languages from the Indian subcontinent. Beyond the United Kingdom, Kramsch (2008) refers to the sense of shame felt by immigrants from Yucutan when speaking Mayan in San Francisco. This is because the language has no socio-economic value in the public domain away from a domestic setting. Instead, languages that are taught represent major world historical and/or current political, economic or diplomatic forces, for example the languages of France, Germany and Spain. Equally it is of interest that many educational commentators have recently called for the teaching of Mandarin in schools because it is the main language of China, which is set to become the world's largest economy. The Department for Education (DFE) itself is pressing for Mandarin to be offered as part of schools' curriculum because 'Mandarin is vital for the economic future of our country and is increasingly a world language. Several primary schools already offer some basic Mandarin teaching.' (DFE statement updated 27 February 2013). Further to this statement Education Minister Elizabeth Truss states that 'Mandarin is the language of the future – it is spoken by hundreds of millions of people in the world's most populous country and shortly the world's biggest economy' (DFE website 27 February 2013). Schools Minister Nick Gibb had already made a much earlier statement saying, 'China is at the centre of the global economy which is why it is important that our young people understand its culture and language' (Schools' Minister Nick Gibb, DFE website 15 March 2011). Of course English itself, in terms of languages generally, is world leader because of its socio-economic and sociocultural capital portable throughout the world due to the powerful economic reach of the USA.

I argue that although national systems of education have economic agendas, this should not be the primary concern of MFL education. This is because economic instrumentalism in MFL based on functional linguistic transactions may not have, as its driving force, the cultural embrace of 'Otherness' of the target language communities and of the language itself. MFL ought not to be learnt for profit as a primary motive much as schools should not be run for profit. Instead, I argue that a foreign language and its culture reside in the concept of 'Otherness' which, despite containing similarity to ourselves in the construction of a common humanity, is nonetheless different from ourselves. Notions of 'Otherness' or 'alterity' are philosophically grounded in the works of Derrida (1967) and Levinas (1969). The regard for another culture is of an ethical nature, stated as follows,

'Face à face avec l'autre dans un regard et une parole qui maintiennent la distance . . ., cet être-ensemble comme séparation précède ou déborde la societé, la collectivité, la communauté. Levinas l'appelle religion. Elle ouvre l'éthique. La relation éthique est une relation religieuse' (Derrida 1967: 142).

'Faced with the other in regard and in speech which maintain distance . . ., this being-together as a separation precedes or transcends society, collectivity, community. Levinas calls it religion. It opens up ethics. The ethical relationship is a religious relationship.' (author's translation).

Rather than operating at the level of words, phrases and surface skills-based language necessary to fulfil business transactions, Gieve (1999) points out that MFL should be taught at the level of interactional discourse, acknowledging difference in behaviour and social practice. The rationale of this would be to teach language as a cultural discourse encompassing a notion of alterity or otherness rather than as narrowly located decontextualized surface language. Ortactepe (2013) argues that more research is necessary at the level of interactional discourse to 'explore how power relations influence the nature of interactions between language learners and target-language speakers' (2013: 226). This is because, within interactional settings, there are issues of target language speaker acceptance and validation by the host community as well as the target language speaker's eagerness to explore the target language culture.

Here discourse is, of course, much more than language. As we shall see, discourse consists of language, social practice, social relations and culturally embedded behaviours including, as mentioned above, relations of power.

Discourse is defined differently by different theorists. Foucault (1972) regards discourse as a totalizing phenomenon which determines the way in which individuals and groups construct knowledge and themselves as human. Nothing exists outside of discourse and if, over history, discourse had taken a different path, the nature of existing knowledge about the world and ourselves would have been different.

Fairclough (1989, 1992) however views discourse as one social practice, albeit a major one, among others. There is a dialectical relationship between discourse and other social practices such as economic production, religion, education, advertising etc and this, as an outcome, shapes identity. Socio-economics forms part of the identity of individuals and institutions because the societal economic Orders of Discourse (Fairclough 1989) are a major driver in Western society.

For Gumperz (1999), an interactional sociolinguist, discourse involves indexicality as the phenomenon where individuals, within their everyday interactions, reach out to wider discourses for meanings to incorporate into their more localized interactions. Indexicality, therefore, is a term which reflects the notion of everyday interactions pointing towards or indexing characteristics containing cultural–linguistic phenomena in wider societal discourse. These wider shared linguistic–cultural meanings reinforce localized meanings and place them within a larger shared cultural picture. Everyday interactions are therefore always located within larger and more powerful discourses.

Consequently, the meanings for MFL teaching, including programmes of study, lesson planning etc do not take place in a vacuum but are informed by more powerful ideologies. The transactional language of socio-economics often then becomes a default setting for MFL education, more so since it seems to be without 'authentic' cultural content beyond its lexical and grammatical form. Cultural content is mainly located within school text books. This often appears contrived and stereotyped in terms of, for example, a standardized Frenchness or Spanish identity proposed by the publications' teams of editors. The cultural content often seems an easily accessed backdrop where the cultural identities of the lives portrayed are simple, finished products, playing a secondary role to the language itself rather than being integral to it.

Examples of such perfunctory cultural contexts occur in the presentations of family identities where the standard family grouping is harmonious and without the problematized narratives of separation, divorce, family break-up or children in care. There are no images of reconstituted families or same sex partnerships, all of which arguably are features of modern complex family lives.

In a similar way, daily routines in MFL text books seem superficially stereotyped where everyone performs similar tasks within similar time scales. (cf. Metro 2 coursebook 2000; Chapter 2, daily routine; Chapter 3, family; school coursebook reference).

Identity in language learning

I propose that there are three main issues of identity in MFL education: first, the cultural identity of the language and pedagogy; secondly, the cultural identity of the learner; and thirdly, the dialectical interaction, if any, between these two identities. Lantolf (2000) points out that even if students in the same class are undertaking the same activity, they may well be undertaking it for different motives. Some, for example, may feel compelled to fulfil, or perhaps reject, the local requirements of the lesson and the teacher's demands while others may look beyond this regulatory discourse towards seeking a cultural content for the language itself. Students then may be enacting very different learner identities.

An example of this difference in learner identities can be seen in the following extract of a research observation of a year 11 French lesson in a large secondary school in the south of England. The students are 15–16 years old and the author's dual role was both as researcher and as teacher of his own class. The learner identity differences in the following extracts appear to be gender based. All names of participants have been changed.

> *As we come into the classroom Zara and Alicia greet me in French saying 'bonjour Mr Evans, tu vas bien j'espère? (greeting and asking me if I'm well). I reply to them in French and, again in French ask them what they have done that morning. As this is a Wednesday morning before break they tell me in French the subjects they have already done and sometimes complain how boring it was and how bad the teacher was. I reply by saying 'Mais Monsieur X est très gentil et très intelligent'. (But Mr x is very nice and very intelligent), to which they reply 'ah non il est grincheux et pas sympa' (oh no he is grumpy and not friendly). I feel that professionally I have to stick up for the teacher or else the students might think I am colluding with them. Because the exchange takes place in French it has an air of playfulness as if we are re-defining and appropriating the world in a different language, however superficial that may be.*

> The rest of the students settle into their places but I don't extend this initial exchange to to them because I know that my interaction has now got to be formalized with the terms of the lesson procedures. The group of girls at the front are the only ones to initiate conversation in French. The other students need to be questioned with support from the lesson context in terms of objectives and the reviewing of preceding lesson material. Many of the boys sit down the side. . . . As the lesson moves on, they lose concentration and begin to talk amongst themselves. . . . (end of extract)

A gender difference is visible here in this classroom interaction where the female students seem more involved with the language than with the formality of the classroom procedural discourse.

A similar phenomenon occurs in a year 9 class of 14-year-old students where a group of girls are involved with the language whereas a group of boys use the lesson space for their own 'off-task' activity. This is an extract from a Spanish class which the author was observing as researcher only in the same south of England secondary school.

> *Lizzie and Georgina are working on vocabulary asking the teacher how to say 'my parents are called' in Spanish. The reply is 'mis padres se llaman'. Next question 'How do you say "they are divorced?"' The teacher's reply is 'estan divorciados'. Meanwhile at the back of the class George is playing with a football by bouncing it against a table. Mitchell is at the back talking to George and Adam and Fred are tying a white scarf around Mitchell's head* (end of extract)

Again a gender difference in learner identity is apparent. The group of girls is immersed in the lesson language content while a group of boys remains disengaged, inevitably waiting for the teacher's eventual remonstrations.

The issue of the cultural identity of the language and pedagogy concerns how teachers, in their pedagogical discourses, frame learner identity since their programmes of studies are likely to be based on the way they themselves perceive the needs of students and how they construct their identities. The second identity issue is interrelated with the first concerning the way in which students discursively construct themselves as learners. This is because their construction of their own identities as learners has a relationship with how they are viewed and defined, not only by their teachers but also by the school system. Therefore pupil/student discourses are shaped by a hybridity of voices including the way in which education and foreign language education are regarded by their families and communities. This hybridity is furthermore constituted by how individual learners actively play out their own classroom identities, shaped by the larger identity constructions of community, family, social class, gender, ethnicity, school culture.

The teacher construction itself, of student identity within teacher professional discourse is equally problematic. It may very well not be a simple homogenous, unitary construction due to the heterogeneity and hybridity of discourse itself. Wertsch (1991) refers to this composite nature of discourses as heteroglossia. This means that any one identifiable discourse may well contain many voices. Elements of more powerful discourses are likely to penetrate and even colonize weaker discourses with the result that MFL classroom teacher professional discourse may contain not only a linguistic–cultural, socio-economic voice but also bureaucratic, performative and regulatory voices. The teacher may well be representing the culture of the foreign language in the classroom but is at the same time regulating attendance, behaviour and also attending to performance and assessment issues. These voices and others constitute official teacher discourse and interact dialectically with pupil/student discourses. An example of teacher hybridity of discourse is the regulatory discourse seen in the following lesson observation extract, where the MFL teacher is attempting to resist a year 7 female pupil's persistent request to leave the lesson for a toilet break.

> *pupils from different classes often pre-arrange toilet visits at certain times and then meet up for a chat or for a smoke. This is often difficult for the teacher as some pupils may really want the toilet and so it comes as no surprise to me when the teacher says 'Kayleigh, you can go to the toilet a little later when I've seen that you have settled down to do some work. I want to see you working for 10 minutes'. The reply is as follows, 'no miss please I'm desperate, say 5 minutes' After 5 minutes she is allowed to go.* (end of extract)

Heteroglossia in terms of these extracts is then the hybridity of discourses and identities where social actors are traversed by multiple voices simultaneously, so that there is no one unitary teacher or pupil discourse. There is therefore an ongoing negotiation of identity between notions of cultural determinism and the free will of individual agency.

The third identity issue as the negotiation of identities

According to Bakhtin (1981), language, meaning and culture reside on the border between oneself and the 'Other'. Bakhtin refers to language as 'ideologically saturated' (1981: 259). This dialectical interface within language between oneself and the 'Other' is referred to by Bakhtin as dialogized heteroglossia. As mentioned already, heteroglossia is the notion of multiple voices within a discourse and dialogized heteroglossia is the voice of the interlocutor within the voice of the speaker within dialogue. Consequently, one takes account of the voice of the 'Other' within one's own discourse and the voice of the 'Other' permeates into one's own voice.

Therefore this third identity issue mentioned in the last section arises from the dialectical relationship between the subjective cultural process of one's own voice and objective cultural product contained in the 'Other'. This means that individuals process the meanings of others because words are already half the property of the voices of others as seen in the notion of heteroglossia (Wertsch 1991). One has to personalize language by imbuing it with one's own intentions – making it one's own. We will see later on how Kramsch (1993, 1998) advocates the appropriation of foreign language for one's own needs and ideologies. Furthermore Bakhtin states, 'The ideological becoming of a human being . . . is the process of selectively assimilating the words of others' (1981: 341). Within the individual, therefore, a constant struggle is taking place between his/her own meanings and those of language external to the individual. The resulting division is between cultural identity as an ongoing, active process generated by the individual on the one hand and culture as a product on the Other, external to the individual and apparently objectivized. A linguistic-identity example of this is the interface between an individual's own community-based language identity, such as an urban dialect and Standard English language legitimized by the notion of 'Queen's English'. This is often resolved by a movement of convergence in incorporating the standard language into one's own way of speaking and, of course, identity. This convergence is encouraged by the valorization of the standard language by institutions such as schools, media etc (Pavlenko and Blackledge 2004). Consequently, the interrelationship between process and product means that the individual draws upon the ideological cultural product of the external world to shape his/her identity. Given that the individual may inhabit various contexts in diverse social settings, s/he may negotiate multiple sociolinguistic identities as opposed to one unitary identity. Individuals may therefore develop a linguistic expertise in standard language as well as regional class-based dialects.

Norton (2000), drawing on the work of Bourdieu and Passeron (1977), argues that language use in the dominant standard mode is a widely accepted cultural capital and, rather like economic capital, language can be regarded as a strong or weak currency.

Learner learning identity as a process is therefore shaped by cultural capital and value since to learn something is to attach a value to it. As already argued, it is generally culturally more valued to learn Standard French, for example, rather than a Celtic language or Mayan because of historical reasons of power relations and socio-economics. It is also by logical extension more valued to learn Standard French than it would be to learn a French regional dialect or slang.

Ortactepe (2013) points out that second language social identity theories focus on three key concepts in language learning: Norton's (2000) social investment, Bourdieu's (1977) cultural capital and Miller's (2003) audibility. The latter concept concerns second language learning in the target language community rather than in the classroom where, in the former, the learner's participation in naturalistic settings needs to be legitimized by a sympathetic community.

Socio-economics and social investment as a motivating ideology in language learning

Norton (2000) argues that learning a socially desirable language is an investment in the individual's social identity which offers possibilities of accruing cultural capital for a return at a later date. She refers to this as the social investment model for language learning attached to a cultural interest in the language itself. This combines Gardner's (1985) instrumental and integrative motivations into a single model. Gardner was an earlier theorist in MFL motivation who advocated integrativeness, as the desire to integrate with the MFL target language community. This was seen as a strong form of motivation and much more long term than instrumental motivation. The latter was a short-term motivation for the achievement of goals external to the language, learning the language to pass an exam or gain promotion at work. Once the surface-level socio-economic instrumental goal had been achieved, Gardner argued that, without an integrative motivation, there would no longer be a reason to continue to learn the language.

Although Norton's social investment model seems to provide a strong learner identity because it combines interest in the foreign language and culture with the desire to tap into powerful socio-economic forces, there still remains the question of what happens to the learner identity once socio-economic instrumental goals have been achieved. It could be argued that Norton's social investment model is too economically and culturally deterministic in attaching language–culture interest to socio-economic self-interest.

Cultural capital

Bourdieu's (1977) notion of cultural capital is the underlying theory expressing a view that language forms part of a cultural capital. Language then is a cultural and symbolic resource and certain types of language, such as standard dialect is highly valued. Halliday (1978) maintains not only that highly valued discourses are only available to those who perform a standard language but also that local dialects can only access low status discourses. Therefore a regional dialect or urban dialect would have a low value cultural capital in the wider society. Norton expands this view by proposing that a foreign language such as French, German or Spanish which have a high socio-economic value also have a high cultural capital and socio-economic return on the social investment of learning.

Audibility

Audibility is also a concept, proposed by Miller (2003) which is built on Bourdieu's notion of cultural capital. Audibility suggests that in order to progress in the second language one's attempts at language use will have to be legitimized by target language community members. This would mean that one's use of the foreign language would have to converge on the dominant, standard dialect in order for the language learner to be accepted and therefore make further progress. The corollary of this is that learners who are excluded from participation in host language contexts do not acquire sociocultural capital to make further progress. This theory however relates more to learners in a naturalistic language setting where, in spite of being in a country for a very long time, fail to attain proficiency in the language and perhaps seek support from within their own native language–based communities.

Dornyei's theory of imagined future selves

Dornyei (2009) relates the much earlier integrative motivation of Gardner (1985) back to individual identity rather than to socio-economic self-interest in his social psychological theory of imagined future selves. He focuses integrativeness or the desire to be a part of the target language community back onto the self-concept of the learner as he/she moves forward into the future.

Here he acknowledges that identity contains an element of the future and also that the mastery of a foreign language is an activity that projects well into the future. Therefore in Dornyei's theory of future selves, learner identity contains the possibility of a vision of how one could ideally become if one could achieve one's MFL goal. This involves envisioning an ideal future self with mastery of the language. The implicit view of learner identity is then the representation of self to oneself when confronted with learning activities and that this has possibilities for the future. Dornyei also includes in his motivational system, a task-based situational motivation which in mainstream schools consists of classroom activities. However, this is a shorter term motivation and regulates the optimum disposition for classroom learning. Nevertheless Dornyei acknowledges that good teaching may not be enough by itself at classroom level if the 'bigger picture' is not culturally supportive. This means that a supportive wider discourse containing possibilities for the future is necessary for success. Anecdotally, Dornyei recounts how, in growing up in Hungary, he and his contemporaries were obliged to learn Russian which was considered to be the language of the oppressor. Consequently, due to lack of motivation in the wider picture, he states that 10 years of Russian lessons at school resulted in hardly any effect on him and his contemporaries.

Therefore the two identities that are major drivers for success in MFL are the perceived cultural identity of the language to be learnt and the cultural identity of the learner with a significant possibility for future self-concept. The next section examines how language identity and learner identity might interrelate in the context of a proposed cultural theory for language learning.

A cultural theory

A cultural theory for language learning ought not to completely discount previous theories concerning future selves or social investment but rather incorporate them within an eclectic model of MFL learner identity. The is because one could still acknowledge Dornyei's argument that identity contains possibilities for imagined future self-concept, or Norton's social investment as a future-oriented theory of delayed socio-economic return. However these ideas of motivation and learner identity, useful as they are in invoking future possibilities, are not predicated enough on the present and on how the individual in the present can construct meaning and culture from their own current situation.

Culture cannot be denied in terms of its larger narratives, larger than the lone individual. Lantolf regards it as 'history in the present' (2000: 171) and cultural identity as the totality of past and present resources to which the individual has access.

However Kramsch (1998) proposes a dialectical relationship between this cultural identity as historical product of history in the present and our own subjectivity. Dialectical here means that this interaction between product and process produces a new situation which she refers to as a third place. Intriguingly this third place, according to Kramsch can be alluded to but cannot be defined because it relates to the uniqueness of the learner. The next section outlines the notion of third place and how this might be applied to a learning context.

The third place

Skills-based language is language for 'doing things with words' (Kramsch 1993: 240). As already mentioned it is surface language and puts into operation the dominant ideology without questioning its underlying rationale. Skills-based language does not therefore raise cultural awareness but reflects the transactional utility of the language and by default normalizes its economic ideologies. The third place alluded to by Kramsch is by contrast a space where the learner finds his/her own cultural meaning and purpose. She argues that this can be subversive because learners will constitute their own reasons and interests set against those of the state or institution. Learners therefore can construct their own learning culture through the meanings they create by adapting the language of the 'Other' to their own needs and ideologies. An example of third place is in the following research interview with a male student Robert and a female student Jasmin, both 16 years old, where they construct learning and knowing the foreign language and people in a context of personal development.

> Robert: . . . *you would be socializing and you'd be growing on their ideas.*
> Jasmin: *Especially if you had someone of your own age, then you could compare stuff.*
> Robert: *As you grow older you could still keep in contact.* (end of extract)

Here there is still a notion of imagined future selves in the reference to 'still keep in contact' over time. However, essentially the view of learning language is very much a personal third place construction.

A further example of third place is the research interview with Bella a year 7, 11-year-old female student:

> Researcher: – what about your hobbies? What do you do in your spare time out of school?
> Bella: – Well I've tried French in my bedroom and I've got maps and I like finding out stuff and I draw in my bedroom. (end of extract)

The third place is therefore a cultural hybridity created on the cusp of subjective and objective cultural identity. It reflects the learner's own particular representation to the self of external reality, and because of its uniqueness, it can only be described by the individual him/herself rather than defined a priori for all cases.

Exploration of identity in MFL learning

The notion of third place offers a cultural model of MFL pedagogy from the learner's point of view. From a social constructivist point of view it offers an explanation of language learning where the learner is not only an interpreter of meaning but also a maker of meaning. The view of language involved is not just as a labelling device to describe the world but also as a social artefact that constructs and creates the world. Cole (1996) maintains that the entire world is a social phenomenon and that the objects and ideas are not only represented to us by language but also constructed by language. It is therefore argued here that language is a major tool in the construction of thought and, by extension, self-concept.

Dornyei (2009) states that successful study of MFL involves taking on different cultural identities. This is more than the surface language of words and phrases but rather the idea that we position and re-position ourselves as we speak and use language and signs within discourse. Again it must be re-emphasized that language is not a decontextualized phenomenon but is a cultural artefact situated within discourses of social relations, cultural ideology and power. To speak a language and also a foreign language is to become a part of this 'ecology', as expressed by Van Lier (2000). Pavlenko and Blackledge (2004) allude to a participative metaphor in language use. These ideas of 'language ecology' and 'participative metaphor' of language use refer to one's own language use as being part of a wider language cultural identity. Kramsch's notion of the language user constructing the world from his/her own cultural position should therefore form part of a wider journey of language. This will allow the user to embrace a wider cultural identity and move the user's cultural identity forward from perhaps a narrower cultural starting point. Kramsch maintains that 'desire in language learning is the basic drive toward self-fulfillment – the urge to escape from tedious conformity with one's present environment to a state of plenitude and enhanced power' (2009: 14). This journey forms the basis of a notion of MFL learning as creative and emancipatory.

Language users are therefore automatically part of a wider community since language is constructed within cultural discourses. This raises the notion of belonging to a community and since, according to Lave and Wenger (1991), learning and identity are bound up in the same process, the journey towards language fluency involves moving forward within new identities. The final stage of the argument in this chapter is to posit foreign language teaching as an exploration of new cultural identities, not as a form of plagiarizing already existing foreign language cultures but a way of finding new third places.

Self and 'Other'

It has already been stated that two mutually interactive identities are those of the learner and the language-culture. The third place was discussed regarding the individualized space of the learner from where the exploration of identity could take place. However, we need to further examine identity of language-culture itself.

Discourse has been a strong theme so far and it has been seen how socio-economics permeates into education from wider orders of discourse, thereby influencing the choice of languages to be studied and much of the content. However, other less powerful discourses might be explored relating to the notion of 'Otherness' of MFL as opposed to notions of socio-economic or future identity self-interest.

The rationale for this is a journey from self and socio-economic self-interest towards cultural 'Otherness'. It cannot be assumed that a foreign language-culture is for example Englishness or Britishness in translation but rather a different way, however slight, of thinking and behaving constituted by a different language.

Smith and Carvill (2000), echoing earlier references to Derrida and Levinas, frame this journey towards 'Otherness' as a moral–spiritual journey towards embracing alterity. Smith and Carvill argue that we need to see the 'Other' as 'truly other and not just as an imperfect version of ourselves' (2000: 102). They view MFL education as the cultivation and practice of hospitality towards the stranger and define hospitality as the creation of a space where the 'Other' can feel temporarily at home. This obviously refers to the cultivation of an empathic attitude towards alterity when the foreign language is used to welcome the 'stranger' in one's own country.

This view of alterity accepts 'Otherness' as objective rather than as a subjective extension of one's own identity. The 'Other' is therefore essentially different, objective and exists independently. It is approached and understood by using the language of the 'Other' since the use of one's own language would contain and constrain it within one's own terms of reference. This would be tantamount to the assimilation of the Other into one's own vocabulary and perhaps ultimate colonization of the Other.

This frames MFL as not only a cultural journey but also a spiritual–moral one and while this could exist alongside socio-economic investment identity, it is ultimately centred on the Otherness of language/culture rather than on its socio-economic exploitation.

The chapter began by arguing that MFL study is often linked to larger socio-economic discourses that are powerful enough to project the idea, through programmes of study, to teachers and pupils that it is perfectly normal to have employment and economic transactions as motivations for language learning. It has also been argued that this can be interpreted narrowly as a reductionist instrumental motivation external to the language itself as opposed to a wider language/cultural process. As socio-economic arguments are powerful, they can be easily communicated and easily understood. This argument, however, promotes nothing deeper or higher than the transaction and therefore has to be accompanied by a much wider learner identity to reflect MFL as a cultural expression and a means of making culture. Foreign language, as all languages, occurs through the process of living and simultaneously expresses and produces social life. It cannot be separated from the cultural process and should be taught as culture within discourse. Agar (1994) refers to this close connection as 'Languaculture' to convey the notion that culture resides within language as well as expressing it. Therefore an interest in grammar, vocabulary and pronunciation can be framed as culturally focused where these linguistic features are seen, not as isolated, but rather as constituting a cultural and meaning-making context. We have seen in Chapter 2 how culture comes to be encoded in lexicogrammar in Halliday's (1978) systemic functional linguistics.

This chapter therefore has the intention of framing students as cultural learners and, as we have seen in the last section, this can also contain a spiritual and moral content. Therefore, learning transactional language for only economic reasons does not position language in its wider cultural context but takes a short cut to an end result without bothering about 'the cultural bit' in the middle. Metaphorically, this would be showing more concern for the goal rather than for the beautiful game. Of course, embracing alterity of culture and language can result in an accumulation of cultural capital (Norton 2000) as a practical outcome but this is not the same as limiting MFL to transactions without the cultural commitment to transcend the surface language.

Conclusion

It is therefore possible to frame MFL within a culturally critical pedagogy rather than an economically performative one. Byram (1989) points out that communicative competence has meant an exclusive emphasis on language as a behavioural skill. He goes on to identify three strands in MFL education as follows: language use, language awareness and cultural understanding. Bennett (2003) also argues for an integrated development between foreign language and culture so that MFL learning is not simply 'bolted onto' an ethnocentric view of 'Otherness' based on one's own language.

It is proposed here that foreign language education ought to serve a dual and yet mutually related purpose: first, the understanding of the 'Otherness' of language and culture and, secondly, the journey towards Otherness through the use of language within the notion of 'third place'. The notion of 'third place' is vital as a cultural home for the student to take ownership of his/her skill and understanding. However, MFL education is also a journey towards that which is different and 'Other' from ourselves, and in this respect, MFL education, in working towards the valorization of difference, should be seen as both a cultural and spiritual–moral endeavour. This inevitably involves our own identities, as learning always engages our own subjectivities. Lemke (2002) views individuals as constructing their own identities when 'speaking different languages or different dialects of the same language' (2002: 78). The MFL journey is therefore a dialectical relationship between the discovery of 'Otherness' and the development of identity which should be underpinned by cultural and moral–spiritual ways of being human. This could furthermore be also seen as a metaphor for other areas of the curriculum where education is emancipatory, liberating individuals from culturally and narrowly situated instrumental discourses.

References

Agar, M. (1994), *Language Shock. Understanding the Culture of Conversation*. New York: William Morrow.

Bakhtin, M. (1981), *The Dialogic Imagination: Four Essays*, ed. M. Holquist. Austin: University of Texas Press.

Ball, S. (2008), *Education Guardian*. 29th January 2008.

Bennett, J. (2003), 'Developing Intercultural Competence in the Language Classroom', in D. Lange and R. M. Paige (eds), *Culture as the Core*. Greenwich, CT: Information Age Publishing.

Bourdieu, P. (1977), *Outline of a Theory of Practice*. Cambridge: Cambridge University Press.

Bourdieu, P. and Passeron, J. (1977), *Reproduction in Education, Society and Culture*. London: Sage.

Byram, M. (1989), *Cultural Studies in Foreign Language Education*. Clevedon: Multilingual Matters.

Cole, M. (1996), *Cultural Psychology: A Once and Future Discipline*. Cambridge, MA: Harvard University Press.

Derrida, J. (1967), L'écriture et la différence. Editions du Seuil.

DFE website. 27 February 2013. Department for Education.

Dornyei, Z. and Ushioda, E. (2009), *Motivation, Language Identity and the L2 Self*. Clevedon: Multilingual Matters.

Fairclough, N. (1989), *Language and Power*. London/New York: Longman.

Foucault, M. (1972), *The Archeology of Knowledge*. London: Routledge.

Gardner, R. (1985), *Social Psychology and Second Language Learning: The Role of Attitudes and Motivation*. London: Edward Arnold.

Gibb, N. (2011), Department for Education website. 15 March 11.

Gieve, S. N. (1999), 'Learning the Culture of Language; Intercultural Communication and Second and Foreign Language Learning'. *Literature, Media and Cultural Studies* issue 18.

Guardian Newspaper. Education section- interview extract with Prof Stephen Ball. J. Shepherd. 29 January 2008.

—Wednesday 1 February 2012.

Gumperz, J. (1999), 'On interactional socio-linguistic method', in S. Sarangi and C. Roberts (eds), *Talk, Work and Institutional Order: Discourse in Medical, Mediation and Management Settings*. Berlin/New York: Mouton de Gruyter.

Halliday, M. A. K. (1978), *Language as a Social Semiotic: The Social Interpretation of Language and Meaning*. London: Edward Arnold.
Kramsch, C. (1993), *Context and Culture in Language Teaching*. Oxford: Oxford University Press.
—(1998), *Language and Culture*. Oxford: Oxford University Press.
—(2008), 'Ecological Perspectives on Foreign Language Education'. *Language Teaching* 41: 389–408.
—(2009), *The Multi-lingual Subject: What Foreign Language Learners say about their Experience and Why it Matter*. Oxford: Oxford University Press.
Lantolf, J. P. (2000), *Introducing Sociocultural Theory*, in J. P. Lantolf (ed.), *Sociocultural Theory and Second Language Learning*. Oxford: Oxford University Press.
Lave, J. and Wenger, E. (1991), *Situated Learning: Legitimate Peripheral Participation*. New York: Cambridge University Press.
Lemke, J. (2002), 'Language development and identity: Multiple timescales in the social ecology of learning', in C. Kramsch (ed.), *Language Acquisition and Language Socialization in Ecological Perspectives*. London/New York: Continuum.
Levinas, E. (1969), *Totality and Infinity: An Essay on Exteriority*. Pittsburgh: Duquesne University Press.
Norton, B. (2000), *Identity and Language Learning: Gender, Ethnicity and Educational Change*. London: Longman.
Nuffield Languages Inquiry (2000), *Languages: The next Generation*. London: Nuffield Foundation.
Miller, J. (2003), *Audible Differences: ESL and Social Identity in Schools*. Clevedon, UK: Multilingual Matters.
Ortactepe, D. (2013), 'This is called free-falling theory not culture shock!', in *Language, Identity, and Education*, Vol. 12, no. 4, Routledge, pp. 215–27.
Pavlenko, A. and Blackledge, A. (eds) (2004), *Negotiations of Identities in Multilingual Settings*. Clevedon: Multilingual Matters.
Smith, D. I. and Carvill, B. (2000), *The Gift of the Stranger: Faith, Hospitality and Foreign Language Learning*. Grand Rapids/Cambridge: Wm. B. Eerdmans Publishing Co.
Van Lier, L. (2000), 'From Input to Affordance: Social-Interactive Learning From an Ecological Perspective', in J. P. Lantolf (ed.), *Sociocultural Theory and Second Language Learning*. Oxford: Oxford University Press.
Wertsch, J. V. (1991), *Voices of the Mind. A Sociocultural Approach to Mediated Action*. Cambridge, MA: Harvard University Press.

11

English Language Teacher Identity: A Framework for Teacher Learning and Professional Development

Richard Kiely

> ### Editor's Introduction
>
> Richard Kiely examines how teacher identity is discursively constructed through cultural performance. This is a progression from a former technical–rational teacher discourse of subject knowledge. Richard advocates a development discourse of teacher identity where pedagogy relates to the whole person rather than a disembodied technical brain. In this development discourse, knowledge and skill are co-constructed in a teacher–student partnership dialogue where identities are not static and complete, but ongoing and evolving.

Abstract

This chapter explores identity issues in the work and learning of English language teachers. It sets out ways in which the identity prism can serve to understand the work of teachers, and to sustain ongoing teacher learning and professional development. In many education contexts, English language skills proficiency has become a curriculum development focus at all levels, from primary school to university. Despite investment in syllabuses and materials in recent decades, curriculum goals are often not achieved. One reason often proposed for this is the effectiveness of teaching: teachers are viewed as ineffective in achieving desired curriculum outcomes and reluctant to innovate. While this representation is undoubtedly not the whole story – there are important issues of the limited agency of teachers in the wider social and cultural framing of foreign language learning – it is important to explore ways in which teachers can develop personally and professionally so that their work is more fulfilling, recognized and effective. This chapter explores these issues through an identity lens. Drawing on studies of English language teacher identity within Applied Linguistics, and the *communities of practice* framework of Wenger, I explore the learning dimension of English language teacher identity. There are two specific challenges faced by English language teachers. First, current methods in English language teaching, within a broad communicative language teaching framework, emphasize language use and interaction rather than grammatical accuracy. In this approach, the subject content knowledge shifts from the grammatical and other dimensions of the language system to the learning process. This constitutes a challenge for teachers who align with a transactional and instructional approach to classroom pedagogy, and for teachers whose expertise rests on their mastery of the grammatical system and on culturally situated features of English language use. Second, current teaching strategies require classrooms which are student led, exploratory and unpredictable, with students taking responsibility for directing and shaping their own learning experiences. Teachers, therefore, have to extend their expertise from a focus on knowledge of the language system to skills in managing people and interactions. These challenges are often unmet, with teachers focusing on sentence-level accuracy, both in performing their own expertise and teacher identity and in focusing students on learning. Teacher development activities focus on skills and techniques, which often do not have an impact on practice. Teachers and students are often working with received identities, which limit learning, and constrain the role of imagination in learning. Further work in curriculum development, whether in the skills of teachers, the rolling out of technological innovation and other learning materials, can only have limited impact while the fundamental teacher identity remains unchanged. The chapter ends with some examples of teachers doing identity work, in ways which contribute to personal and curriculum development, and with suggestions for incorporating an identity perspective in teacher learning, both for the individual reflective practitioner, and for teachers who are involved in organized learning activities.

Introduction

Over the recent decades the work of English language teachers has increased in terms of volume and of complexity. English has become established as a global language, as the language of commerce, media, science, and technology, and as a consequence, the contexts of teaching and learning have expanded. In many countries and educational systems English has moved from optional foreign language status to a key skill in the core curriculum. At university level, English is a required subject for all students in many contexts, reflecting workforce policies of embedding English proficiency as an essential learning outcome. This increase in the level of activity is matched by the increasing complexity of the teaching task. Research-informed curriculum development and advances in theory have reconceptualized the nature of instruction. The use of tasks within collaborative learning classrooms and the exploitation of a range of multimedia tools for promoting learning beyond the classroom have required teachers to move beyond the lesson plan and established instructional materials and engage the students in communication-led, autonomous learning.

The realization of these changes has not been as successful as intended. While the volume of learning has been established, the more qualitative changes are less evidenced. There are perceptions and reports of inadequate learning outcomes in many contexts both in terms of workplace needs and in terms of examination results. These are particularly prevalent in the media, though research and government reports in contexts such as Malaysia and Hong Kong reflect a need for improvement and further innovation in English language teaching and learning. Responses to the need for greater effectiveness have included the reform of syllabuses, materials and examinations, the investment in new and innovative multimedia technologies and initiatives to improve the education and certification of teachers. These initiatives in curriculum planning and resource enhancement are likely to have a limited impact, without a corresponding level of investment in change by teachers themselves (Markee 1993; Lamie 2005; Hall 2011).

A key contributor to educational effectiveness is the contribution of the teacher: the extent to which the teacher invests in the curriculum and leads engagement of the learners and innovation and change in learning practices (Edge 2006). Thus, teachers can contribute to student motivation, and better learning outcomes. To support this development, a range of theories, ideas and concepts have been elaborated to strengthen the curriculum. Within teacher development, reflective practice and practitioner research promote teacher investigation as the basis for curriculum effectiveness (Allwright and Hanks 2009).

There are two enduring limitations here. First, the direction of travel in the area of assessment of learning and language proficiency has been one towards the use of standardized assessment framework designs and tools. This means that whereas teachers might be motivated to implement different instructional strategies as a result of their own investigations, reflections and learning, they are likely to feel constrained by standardized examination formats. The students are also likely to be focusing on the tests and managing their investment in learning in order to achieve success in these examinations. Second, the nature of the teacher's work is based on an age-old construct of instruction – a combination of transmission of knowledge and control of behaviours of the learners. These factors shape professional identity: they represent teaching as a mechanical input–output process and the teacher as the operative implementing approved techniques to deliver the curriculum. One strategy to begin to change this is to develop an approach to the development of teacher effectiveness which focuses on teacher identity.

In this chapter I argue for such an approach. I review the literature on English language teacher identity, and drawing on the seminal work of Jean Lave and Etienne Wenger in the role of identity in situated learning in workplace situations, I propose language teacher identity as a valuable area of study in both theorizing identity in general, and in the specific area of language pedagogy and Applied Linguistics. Finally I set out some recommendations for taking this issue forward.

English language curriculum development and the role of the teacher

The development of a theory and an empirical research programme in Second Language Acquisition (SLA) in the 1960s and 1970s led to major innovations in language curriculum design. Instead of basing a language learning programme on an analysis of language forms, typically grammatical structures and phonological features, the programme could be based on an analysis of learning processes. The dominant approach from SLA research was learning by doing: using the language to communicate as the key language learning activity (Krashen and Terrell 1983; Long and Porter 1985). This led to the development of the communicative approach, which emphasizes communication as both the goal of learning and the process of learning (McDonough and Shaw 1994). The classroom should be a context of exchanging messages, rather than of teacher modelling, explanation and drilling. The focus on language forms – grammar and pronunciation – should be partnered, even replaced, by a focus on developing the skills of language use, typically through emphasis on the four skills – listening, speaking, reading and writing (Hedge 2000; Hall 2011). More recently, the task-based approach to language teaching and learning (TBLT) (Skehan 1998; Ellis 2003) has further emphasized this shift in curriculum focus. In this approach, the role of the teacher is not so much to instruct or to model, but rather to set up real-world language use tasks, manage interaction and provide students with the feedback which sustains and promotes continuing learning.

These developments in the planned curriculum for Teaching English to Speakers of Other Languages (TESOL) are further complicated by three factors:

i. Where English is a required subject through all levels of schooling, including university, teachers need to work with unsuccessful as well as successful learners. Thus, the curriculum has to work for those who have had repeated failures and setbacks as well as the elites who find language learning easy. The response here is for teachers to individualize learning, so that the curriculum meets the needs of each learner. Individualization involves additional demands for teachers: as well as setting a range of goals and activities inside and beyond the classroom, the teachers have to establish and manage learning relationships with students.

ii. Teacher accountability processes have increased. In many contexts where there is a drive to increase efficiency and effectiveness, teachers are required to document their work, and are monitored through classroom observations, scrutiny of test results and course evaluation returns. One impact of this has been a tendency for teachers to remain cautious and conservative in their practice, in order to have a defence when their professional practice is questioned.

iii. The introduction of new technologies have changed practices within classrooms and extended learning beyond the classroom. The use of internet resources and multimedia materials create new challenges for teachers, not least, dealing with a greater level of expertise among the students. Like English itself, technology is not for the elite or self-selected hobbyists, but for all teachers and learners.

These developments have generated a range of tensions for teachers. The general requirements, in terms of approach, suggest a move away from traditional instructional practices based on transmission of information and control of behaviour to greater emphasis on realizing a learning process based on interaction and communication. To achieve this shift the teacher needs to be a researcher and analyst of learning needs, and a reflective practitioner committed to building success through identification of problems and development of creative solutions to deal with them. However, the diversification of instructional practices implicit in this development is counteracted by the impact of teacher accountability measures and the demands of preparing students for standardized tests. So even where the test is not an appropriate goal for students, the teachers are likely to feel it is the goal to work towards. The technological developments are often seen at the policy level as a set of tools which enable teachers to meet their different pressures to diversify practice in ways which align to the set curriculum. However, for teachers this may seem impracticable, with use of multimedia tools for learning in the classroom and beyond, adding to, rather than reducing, workload, especially where students are not inducted and supported in autonomous learning (Kern 2006).

To resolve or at least manage these tensions, teachers need training and skills development. At one level, professional development activity, such as training workshops and conferences, experiences of mentoring and shadowing and opportunities for further study, can meet this need. However, two other dimensions also need development. First, at the personal–professional development, teachers need to explore how they might be a different kind of professional: investigative, reflective, creative in supporting learning at both individual student and class levels; second, at a work context level, a sense of community which establishes a collaborative work culture that supports investigation, reflection and creativity. One strategy to build these capacities is to focus on teacher identity. Recent work in this area suggests this is relevant in both understanding the complex dynamics of classrooms and helping teachers imagine a trajectory to more creative, rewarding and ultimately more effective work (Tsui 2003; Leung 2009; Burns 2010; Borg 2006).

The role of identity

Language teacher identity has been understood in three ways, relating to language, to professional status and to learning. Thus, the identity of the language teacher can be conceptualized as shaped primarily by the language as the subject taught, by the pedagogic stance and classroom performance and by the dynamic process of extending skills and career development.

Early perspectives on language teacher identity (though these would not have used this term) viewed the teacher as a language expert and instructional technician. In line with other subject teacher identities, the teacher is an expert in the subject taught. This included a particular expertise in language, whether from an L1 teacher perspective – intuitive knowledge of what is correct and acceptable in language use – or from an L2 perspective – an expertise in how the language system works, including key contrastive analysis points relevant to the language classroom. The work associated with this teacher identity involved promoting language study, often, though not always, at the expense of developing proficiency for language use in social settings. The expertise underpinning this linguistically oriented teacher identity derives from language subject knowledge and language awareness (Hawkins 1999; Andrews 2007).

Perhaps the most salient identity factor for English language teachers is whether they are an L1 (native speaker) or L2 user of English. This salience has two sources. First, a long-established discourse in language pedagogy centres on the superiority of the native speaker as teacher. This is an oppressive discourse for L2 teachers, and has endured in part through L1 English language teacher global mobility, and preferential working terms and conditions in many work environments (Pennycook 2001; Holliday 2005). Second, the TESOL Applied Linguistics literature shows awareness of the issue, from a sociolinguistic, social justice and language pedagogy perspectives. Rampton (1990) debunks the 'myths' of 'native speaker' and 'mother tongue', illustrating that their claim to represent some clear and distinct boundaries relevant to language learning and language teaching is both incoherent and ideologically grounded. He suggests that instead of these terms, the concepts of *expertise, inheritance* and *affiliation* should be adopted and developed in both sociolinguistic and language pedagogy discourse. Medgyes (1994) and Kiely and Rea-Dickins (2005) explore the challenge and futility of comparative studies of the effectiveness of L1 and L2 teachers. Holliday (2005) revisits the issue of the predominance of the discourse of 'native speakerism' in the language teaching profession, illustrating the difficulty in moving on from this convenient but inadequate marker of English language teacher identity.

A key element of moving on from the native speakerism as a key marker in language teacher identity has been a focus on pedagogic expertise: the teacher as a professional is skilled in implementing techniques and methods in the classroom. Drawing in particular on research in the field of SLA, the teacher is constructed as a technician working with a deep understanding of how second language are learnt, and facilitating the kinds of activity believed to support the learning process. General methodology handbooks (e.g. Hedge 2000; Harmer 2001) and guides to specific pedagogies (such as Skehan 1998 and Ellis 2003) for TBLT emphasize this dimension of the teacher role. While characterizing the teacher as a professional has facilitated a move away from the fixed attributes of 'native' or 'non-native' speaker, it also has limitations in terms of identity. It can align professional performance with student teacher performance – good practice involves conforming to fixed criteria in lesson planning and implementing techniques in the classroom – and thus, not recognize the values of creativity, criticality and social responsibility which are inherent dimensions of the identity of the autonomous professional (Leung 2009).

More recent accounts have developed a more relational, performative and holistic view of teacher identity. Miller (2009) observes that

> thinking, knowing, believing, and doing are enacted in classroom contexts in a way that cannot be separated from identity formation. What teachers know and do is part of their identity work, which is continuously performed and transformed through interactions in classrooms. (2009: 175)

A range of studies have developed the 'performance' of teacher identity as a way of understanding what teachers do. These accounts build in many ways on the seminal work of Butler (1990, 1997) and Gee (1999), who posit that all human action and activity is meaningful and purposeful, and in the performance constructs a social identity in an agentive way.

Pennycook (2001) illustrates how teachers negotiate macro- and micro-political issues in their work as teachers: they perform to establish themselves as part of the social and educational systems in which they participate. Varghese et al. (2005) outline three ways in which classroom discourse can be seen as 'performance of identity'. First, they draw on Tajfel's (1978, 1981) theory of social identity to understand how teacher identity can be understood as membership of a particular group: teachers align with their culture ethnicity and particular professional situation. A major issue emerging from this focus on teacher background was the non-native status of the teachers – L2 users of English. Second, the develop an analysis of teacher identity using Wenger's (1998) communities of practice framework. Here, current and emerging community membership, participation and ongoing learning are emphasized, with the non-native-speaking teachers constructed as 'bilingual' teachers, and with membership of overlapping communities enriching their sense of purpose and their practice. I return to the potential of the Wenger framework later in this chapter. Third, an image–text approach, drawing on Simon (1995), explores identity as a function of the situated relationships between students and teacher as they develop in the classroom and other social locations. In this view, the pedagogy, particularly interactions which have some affective dimension, constructs the identity of the teacher, and shapes the practice in classrooms and ongoing professional learning. The discussion of Varghese et al. is valuable in demonstrating the relevance of wider identity theory to understanding the work of teachers in terms of teacher background and group affiliation, in terms of role and status within the organization and in terms of learning relationships in the social space of the classroom.

Richards (2006) draws on identity theory to analyse the ways in which classroom interaction is social and conversational as well as instructional. He uses Zimmermann's membership categorization analysis to demonstrate how teachers in classroom interaction shift between *discourse, situated* and *transportable* identities to sustain the social nature of the classroom. *Discourse* identity reflects the moment-by-moment roles played in the use of language, such as 'speaker, listener, questioner, challenger, repair initiator' (2006: 60). Identity here derives from the often teacher-led organization of talk in the classroom, as the instructional and the conversational strands of discourse are developed. *Situated* identity refers to the ways teachers align with assigned roles and expectations. This is always powerful in the case of the teacher, since we all have a deeply embedded stereotype of 'teacher' as the one who knows, who instructs, who evaluates and who controls. In TESOL this teacher role has become inflected in recent decades with notions of coach, facilitator and learning guide. *Transportable* identity is, in Richards' view, 'the least predictable': it reflects those individual features or insignia, related to size, age, gender, ethnicity tastes, hobbies and philosophical positions, which in interaction we can chose to reveal or reference. This analysis explores the interface between the technical and the personal in acts of teaching. It illustrates the ways in which emotional, moral and belief issues find a place in classroom discourse, and the ways in which a performative view of identity can contribute to understanding the work of the teacher.

What is evidenced in these studies of teacher identity is the richness of the intellectual seam of performance of identity in classrooms. However, the second dimension outlined by Miller – how language teacher identity is transformed (2009: 175) – has been less developed. Specifically, how does an identity lens on understanding teachers' work contribute to professional learning? How does a focus on identity contribute to a learning process in which teachers improve their performance? How does it inform on ways organizations can support teacher learning, such that being a language teacher is not just a process of implementing effective lesson plans year after year, class after class? Following Clandinin (1986), Connelly and Clandinin (1988) there has been greater attention to holistic approaches to teacher learning and development, emphasizing the importance of personal qualities as well as professional skills and instructional techniques. Golombek (1998) concludes her study of how teachers develop their teaching by calling greater attention to the 'role of emotions and moral beliefs in teachers' sense-making processes' (1998: 462). Leung (2009), discussing what 'professionalism in TESOL' means, suggests teacher professionalism can be understood in two ways. First, through qualifications and role (akin to Richards' situated identity), teachers are recognized as sponsored professionals. Second, they need to develop independent professionalism, 'a commitment to careful and critical examination of the assumptions and practices embedded in sponsored professionalism, with reference to discipline-based knowledge and wider social values, and to take action to effect change where appropriate' (2009: 53).

The use of a teacher identity perspective to transform teachers' performance and contribute to more effective language pedagogy and better learning outcomes is however still a largely underdeveloped field. The emphasis has been on understanding classrooms and classroom interaction rather than on improving, on documenting and on describing rather than evaluating and taking action on the basis of such evaluations. There is a need to link the performative and the transformative, so that teachers, through understanding of the characteristics and impacts of their work in classroom interactions, are empowered to transform them, to learn and to extend their capacity for a better practice.

This view aligns with the seminal perspective on identity articulated in Butler: identity is not something fixed and assigned; rather it is imagined, dynamic and expressed through performance. The performance can involve alignment with established norms, or resistance to these to articulate novel imagined meanings. This is a view of identity which accords a high level of agency to the individual: in addition to unconsciously representing an identity, an individual can adopt, inflect and perform an identity in a developmental and transformative way. The role of agency of the individual is insufficiently problematized in many discourses of English language teaching and teacher development. Within policy and institutional frameworks, a teacher is encouraged to align with an established view, implement a specific methodology, and even conform to set ways of interacting with and supporting students. While such constructions of the work of the teacher are often intended as supportive, helping teachers in meeting the needs of students, protecting them and the institution against charges of poor or inappropriate practice and contributing to the professional development of teachers, there is a real possibility that they are in fact constraining. They frame professional decision-making in a way that compromises the teacher ownership of the teaching, and deny the creative engagement and investment that make an essential contribution to effective teaching.

Identity, learning and communities of practice

The notion of identity is central to Wenger's social theory of learning, envisaged as a negotiated trajectory of participation in practices:

> As trajectories, our identities incorporate the past and the future in the very process of negotiating the present. They give significance to events. . . . They provide a context in which to determine what, among all things that that are potentially significant, actually becomes significant learning. (1998: 155)

Within this view we are always learning, as a dimension of our social nature as human beings: we participate in a range of activities, for example, when watching TV with family or friends, playing a sport or undertaking required tasks in work or as a student. While we can participate in a mechanical, unthinking way, we are more likely to notice, reflect, connect, create, such that our participation in the activity changes the way we feel and think. Even where the activity seems totally unthinking – where the task has become routine, and completed in an instinctive, intuitive way – performance reflects learning, though this may not be recognized for, in Wenger's term, significance.

There are two particular ways in which the Wenger conceptualization of identity is relevant to understanding language teacher identity and how their work can be developed. First, the notion of professional identity derives from membership of a particular group and participation activities in order to articulate and develop this membership. An important aspect of this view is the notion of legitimate peripheral participation (LPP), 'the process by which newcomers become included in the community of practice' (1998: 100). This is problematic for teachers, whose induction is through qualification and licensing rather than graduated apprenticeships. From the start, teachers work in classrooms, demanding social spaces in many ways, but isolated from their professional colleagues. Thus, as a default setting, the novice teacher works in isolation, without the rich framework of participation and activity which Wenger posits as beneficial for the construction of the professional identity.

Second, a key dimension of professional identity is learning identity. For Wenger, this is the view of self which maximizes the impact of participation in activities on developing understanding and skills. The process of learning is also what progresses the trajectory from LPP to the centre, in terms of expertise and recognition. And as evident from the strapline to the title of the book, it is not just learning from doing, or learning through doing, but learning *in* doing. This is problematic for English language teachers because essential professional learning is assumed to be in place before work. The conflation of professional qualification and professional learning means that in many contexts, teacher learning is viewed as addressing skills deficits (Harland and Kinder 1997).

The diagram developed by Wenger (1998: 5) is a useful way to understand this form of learning and the role of identity in it.

There are four dimensions to learning within the theory: *practice*, *community*, *identity* and *meaning*. These can be related to the understanding of language teacher identity as follows.

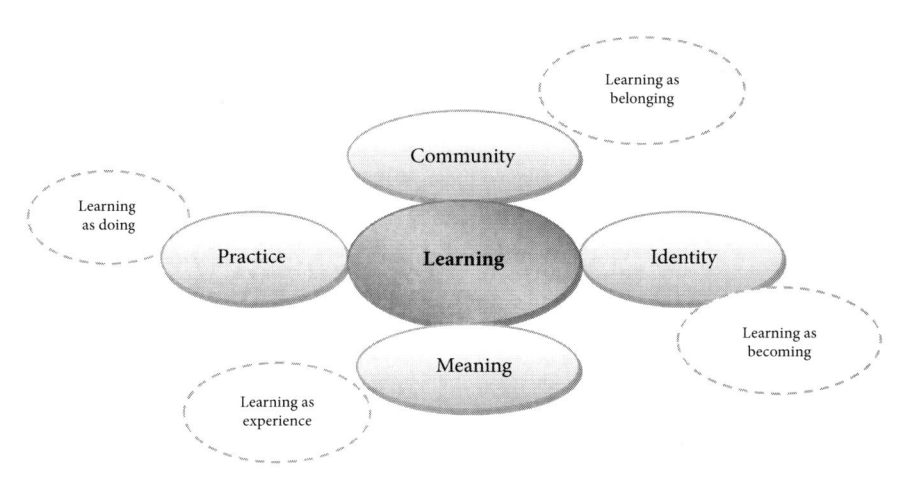

Figure 11.1 Components of a social theory of learning: An initial inventory.

Practice

Learning through a focus on the practice, learning as doing, can be understood as experiential learning. This view of forming a professional identity is in many ways recognized and documented in other theories (Dewey 1933; Freeman 1998; Moll et al. 2001) and could be seen as aligning with perspectives such as reflective learning (Schön 1983) and learning as craft (Sennett 2008). For Wenger, practices are more than just ways of doing things:

> collective learning that reflect both the pursuit of our enterprises and the attendant social relations. These practices are thus the property of a kind of community created over time by the sustained pursuit of a shared enterprise. (1998: 45)

Traditionally, practices in TESOL centred on analysis of language structures, and a capacity for accuracy in language use. More recently, the capacity to implement groupwork, to elicit, to foster communication in the classroom have become practices which are valued and which push the limits of creativity of teachers.

Community

Learning is the accumulation of the understandings and skills which establish membership of a particular community. Here again the perspective of Wenger aligns with a range of other perspectives on identity in general, and on language identity in particular (Tajfel 1978; Block 2007; Miller 2009). Our social nature, starting with immediate family and expanding through life to include belonging to groups on the basis of ethnicity, work, hobby etc is reflected in community membership. In TESOL, many communities are shaped by geography, institution type, student type and teacher language background, as well as recognized professional bodies and associations. In many contexts the multiple options for belonging may add to isolation, the loose professional framing combining with the solitude of the classroom to limit opportunities for learning. Core professional activities such as planning, student monitoring, assessment and reporting are carried out in an isolated way as well. The richest opportunities for professional situated learning in the Wenger approach is through working together and talking through the tasks, decisions and consequences – what Wenger labels mutual engagement, joint enterprise and shared repertoire.

Identity

The focus on learning as identity emphasizes on learning as becoming. Thus, in Wenger's conceptualization, we can, in a learning view, take our identity from the future, not just from the past. The becoming is driven by the imagination: the identity of the individual is shaped by what that individual imagines for himself or herself. This novel insight from Wenger allows us to understand a key issue in language teaching. It may not be adequately driven by a notion of imagination and becoming. In addition to features of the TESOL profession outlined above – licensing as a professional from the outset and subsequent isolation, and a transmissive, practice-as-theory-applied approach to professional development – the phenomenon of apprenticeship of observation (AoO) can limit the processes of becoming. In the absence of an environment which nurtures learning and the construction of a strong, confident, professional identity, and a recommended form of practices which work effectively, many teachers revert to what they know. They implement what Lortie (1975) calls the AoO: implementation of practices which they participated in as students in classrooms over many years. This phenomenon of AoO illustrates on the one hand, the power of participative observation for learning: through being students in classrooms, students gain an understanding of the teacher's work sufficient to generate their own practice. On the other it suggests the weakness of the transmission curriculum which teachers encounter in their pre-service and in-service training programmes. In addition, it suggests that the professional work of teachers is not a dynamic learning process which pushes the imagination of possibilities and the construction of the strong confident professional identity.

Meaning

The focus on meaning relates to the experience of work as situated learning. Thus, 'meaning' is not some content knowledge or theory to be understood and then applied; rather it is a kind of pre-requisite for knowledge and theory. Teachers, through working in classrooms as part of an institution and community, gain understanding and deep insights over time into how the activity connects with other aspects of individual's lives. For some participants, colleague teachers and students alike, the participation may be goal driven, relating to educational qualifications or career progression. For others it may be a primarily social space, where they have opportunities to interact with others. For yet others, the activity may be primarily an act of belonging, articulating an identity through alignment with expected norms. The situated learning of a particular teacher derives from understanding these perspectives, and finding and articulating a personal sense of purpose in that context. Thus, meaning is determined by the sense of purpose which guides participation and investment. It can be shaped by initiatives in professional and personal development, not as a process of knowledge and skills accumulation, but as a process of understanding the wider, more social purposes of TESOL through observation and participation.

Wenger posits three dimensions along which the trajectory of learning and identity formation develops: mutual engagement, joint enterprise and shared repertoire. The last of these – *shared repertoire* – can be conceptualized as language terms which teachers, their colleagues and their students share as they work together. There may be different fields here, from linguistic and methodological terminology in the classroom to teacher talk in the staff room: for example, in the classroom labels for the tenses in English and activities such as group work and listening comprehension. When teachers talk they use terms to refer to the syllabus, materials and examinations and the use of techniques such as 'information gap', 'running dictation' and talk of how groups 'gel'. At the level of repertoire, the situated learning of a novice teacher is likely to be speedy and evidenced in performance: the repertoire used as an initial stage of participation and alignment with norms.

The other dimensions are more challenging to achieve in language teaching and to evidence in data. *Mutual engagement* reflects the participative social nature of work and learning. It means understanding and responding to the particular perspective of the other, whether a colleague or a student in the classroom. *Joint enterprise* involves sharing a goal and implementing a shared strategy to achieve this. These dimensions of communities of practice can be illustrated from examples from a recent research study into teacher learning in TESOL: InSITE.

InSITE

The InSITE (Integrating Systematic Investigation in the Teaching of English) project was an initiative carried out in a Further Education College in the United Kingdom. The project involved implementing a continuing professional development programme with teachers in order to identify features of effectiveness in teachers' practice, and extend these by raising awareness through analysis of classroom episodes and reflection. Twelve teachers participated in two cycles over 2 years. The principal activities were classroom observation, identification of critical learning episodes (CLE) in recorded classroom interactions, reflective comment on these by the teacher and researcher and finally workshop discussion of the CLEs with all participating teachers. In addition the process was documented as a research initiative to understand teacher learning through such organized continuing professional development (CPD) activity. This involved constructing all episodes, reflections and workshops as data sets, and in addition interviewing the teachers on their experience of the process (Davis et al. 2009; Kiely and Davis 2010; Kiely et al. 2010).

The predominant single theme in these data was the meaning of work for the teachers. In the interviews and workshops, and in commentaries on specific episodes, they sought to explain what they were doing, in planning and in classroom interaction and in interviews which took a more general perspective on teaching. These voices emphasize the social nature of classrooms and teaching, the complexity of the task, particularly the elusive nature of success and the level of personal commitment and investment in efforts to make it successful. These themes reflect a Wenger-type view of situated learning such as that which characterizes communities of practice. The themes reflect in particular the notions of *mutual engagement* and *joint enterprise*.

Mutual engagement

Mutual engagement emphasizes the two-way nature of social interaction. In classrooms this challenges the 'transmission' model, where the teacher's role as instructor involves imparting knowledge and provide instruction. A typical characterization of this is the 'triadic discourse' – initiation, response, feedback – (Sinclair and Coulthard 1975; Young 1992; Wells 1993) found in classrooms. Thus, the teacher asks the questions and the student responds, and then the teacher provides an evaluation. An example of mutual engagement is in the opening of one CLE, where the teacher is introducing a letter-writing activity:

1. Teacher: It was my daughter's birthday last week
2. Students: Oh, How old was she?

This simple exchange illustrates three points about mutual engagement. First, the teacher is developing a genuine social interaction with the students. This is with a pedagogical purpose, but it does involve the bringing in of her transportable identity (Richards 2006) as parent. Second, the students (several speaking together) respond with a typical social response, showing interest in and engagement with the aspect of family life introduced by the teacher. Third, such mutual engagement at a social level does not surface easily in classrooms. The default setting is transmission and evaluation, where the teacher asks the questions, the students answer and the teacher evaluates (triadic discourse). So where in a random classroom observation, such mutual engagement is evidenced, it is reasonable to assume it reflects something of the nature of the classroom. Thus, the classroom has a social learning quality, where the teacher engages with the students to develop an effective pedagogy, and in turn, through creative effort, extends her own learning about effective practice in this situation.

In another CLE from the InSITE database, a teacher interrupted a pairwork activity to correct a student on a somewhat minor grammatical issue. The students were discussing which movie to go to in a local cinema as part of an activity to extend the interactive speaking skills. In the workshop discussion on this episode, the teacher explained that he would not normally interrupt a communicative activity in order to correct a grammatical error. However, he did on this occasion, because he felt that it would be beneficial to and appreciated by the student: she was very good at grammar, and invested a lot of time and effort at developing a deep and comprehensive knowledge of the grammatical system of English. The episode data illustrated that this was the case – the student double-checked the correction (mindful that the teacher may have got it wrong), then thanked the teacher and noted the correct form in her notebook. This episode illustrates a key feature of mutual engagement. The teacher's decision to interrupt and correct took into account the preference of the particular student, and in this case, this overrode the more generic principle of not interrupting a fluency activity. Thus, the teacher's action was informed by a whole-person analysis, not just a characterization of the student as a language-learning machine.

These episodes illustrate how classrooms work at a social level when decisions and actions are informed by consideration of individual students' and teachers' needs. Mutuality is central to how participants engage, with the teachers' pedagogic actions being fine-tuned by students, and students' learning opportunities being shaped by teachers.

Joint enterprise

Joint enterprise, where participants work together to achieve a shared goal, might be considered rare in the communities of TESOL. In the community of the classroom, teachers teach and students learn, teachers control and students comply, teachers assess and students are assessed. However, a dialogic, transformative (rather than transmissive) view of pedagogy emphasizes the need for classroom talk to be jointly constructed (Young 1992; Van Lier 2007), rather than in lecture format. The examples from the InSITE project in the previous section illustrate this jointness: the teachers' contributions are shaped by the way the students participate. And most importantly, a core feature of the classrooms is the students' understanding that such joint enterprise is the way the class operates.

In the staffroom, a locale where teachers form a professional community, there is a form of joint enterprise in the ways teachers support each other at an emotional level, and in maintaining the stability of the institution. Joint enterprise, however, involves more than 'just a stated goal' (Wenger 1998: 78): it can also be understood as part of the negotiation which is part of working together. Data from the workshops of the InSITE illustrate the potential of teachers to develop a sense of joint enterprise. The paired reflections showed a capacity to be understanding and supporting. The episode centred on the teacher's response to a student question:

| S1 | *(asking T)* | What's 'hang on though'? |
| T | *(to S1)* | You're a good language learner! I was just going to talk about that. |

Episode from the InSITE project

In their joint reflection on this episode, the teacher (T) was concerned if her praise for S1 could have a negative impact on other students. Her buddy led the joint analysis, showing that there was little support for such a conclusion, and opening up other dimensions of this interaction. An aspect of the buddy's focus throughout was emotional support, dispelling her colleagues' negative feelings, by commenting insightfully and reflexively. (For further discussion of this data, please see Kiely and Davis 2010).

One teacher illustrated in interview how sharing joint responsibility with a colleague facilitated her participation in the research project. The research was a novel dimension of practice for her, and constructing her participation as a joint enterprise with a colleague facilitates her participation in it at an early stage, of what Wenger would label the 'reification' of practitioner research (1998: 57).

> I can't take it out of the social situation, and that's why these things these episodes on their own don't really sort of say much. . . . Without the dialogue with the teacher, they don't say much. The fact that I had another colleague working at

the same site who was doing the same thing was crucial as well, because we sort of chivvied each other along. If I was on my own, I would have been at a bit of a loss and we were able to discuss our episodes before we sent sort of them off, saying, is this an episode? What's [the course leader] going to say about it? Do you think it will do? And in fact, it was my discussion with [Teacher D] about his episode which made me think: I had one like that, I have had an episode and I went and wrote it up, whereas I hadn't really identified one in the class.

Interview with Teacher A, InSITE Project

Joint enterprise for these teachers afforded both emotional support and conceptual clarification. Teacher A shows how she benefited from having a safe zone to explore key meaning of the practice, and how shared work on clarifying what an episode involved was helpful in allowing her to identify one. (For further discussion of this data, please see Davis et al. 2009).

Conclusion

In this chapter I have explored the notion of English language teacher identity, and the use of this as a way of working with teachers to understand, extend and improve their practice. As a conclusion to this discussion, I summarize the argument in four points. First, a language teacher identity has a significant language identity component: language teachers are socially defined by that subject expertise, and may affiliate with communities of users of that language. The English language identity issue for teachers often centres on whether the teacher is an L1 or L2 user of English, a discourse that can be limiting and oppressive (Holliday 2005). L1 language teachers may be viewed as having no expertise other than their intuitive L1 user knowledge, and L2 teachers considered in deficit terms because they lack just that.

Second, the language identity dimension has been complemented in recent decades by the emergence of a stronger professional identity. In English language teaching in particular, widely recognized professional qualifications at certificate and diploma levels constitute a licensing scheme that affords recognition as a professional. This recognition, however, does not always foster a learning identity. Institutional quality management processes, including alignment with examination formats and outcomes data often consign teachers to lessons implemented as pre-ordained, mechanical routines. In such situations, teachers find it difficult to own and invest creatively in the curriculum in ways which foster learning and development.

Third, the Wenger framework of identity formation as a process of situated learning within a community of practice is set out as a way forward. It takes an *identity as becoming* perspective, where imagination and investment drive learning along the trajectory from periphery of the community of practice to the centre. The notion of community is complex – it involves both the classroom and the staffroom as different 'localities of practice' (Wenger 1998: 122), for example, and the practices – 'the property of a kind of community created over time by the sustained pursuit of a shared enterprise' (1998: 45) – require description and analysis in each locality. The key drivers of learning in the Wenger framework of professional learning – shared repertoire, mutual engagement and joint enterprise – do not activate in some default way. It is necessary to push the pendulum, to act to enhance the working environment, so that the conditions for positive and continuing learning are facilitative.

Fourth, the potential of a focus on teacher identity and the particular use of the Wenger framework do not mean there is an easy mode of using it for teacher learning and professional development. It almost certainly cannot be achieved through the established practice-as-theory-applied notions which have informed transmissive notions of teacher learning in the English language teaching field. We need to develop awareness among teachers and the institutions in which they work of their practices, in terms of provenance, meanings and possibilities for change. Such awareness can be a platform for understanding the potential of a learning identity within each community of practice.

References

Allwright, D. and Hanks, J. (2009), *The Developing Language Learner: An Introduction to Exploratory Practice*. Basingstoke: Palgrave Macmillan.
Andrews, S. (2007), *Teacher Language Awareness*. Cambridge: Cambridge University Press.
Block, D. (2007), *Second Language Identities*. London: Continuum.
Borg, S. (2006), *Teacher Cognition and Language Education: Research and Practice*. London: Continuum.
Burns, A. (2010), *Doing Action Research in English Language Teaching. A Guide for Practitioners*. New York: Routledge.
Butler, J. (1990), *Gender Trouble: Feminism and the Subversion of Identity*. New York: Routledge.
—(1997), *Excitable Speech: A Politics of the Performative*. New York: Routledge
Clandinin, D. J. (1986), *Classroom Practice: Teacher Images in Action*. Philadelphia: Falmer Press.

Connelly, F. M. and Clandinin, D. J. (1988), *Teachers as Curriculum Planners: Narratives of Experience*. New York: Teachers' College Press.
Davis, M., Kiely, R. and Askham, J. (2009), 'InSITEs into practitioner research: findings from a research-based ESOL teacher professional development programme'. *Studies in the Education of Adults* 41(2): 118–37.
Dewey, J. (1933), *How We Think*. Boston: D. C. Heath & Co.
Edge, J. (2006), *(Re)locating TESOL in the Age of Empire*. Basingstoke: Palgrave Macmillan.
Ellis, R. (2003), *Task-based Language Learning and Teaching*. Oxford: Oxford University Press.
Freeman, D. (1998), *Doing Teacher Research: from Inquiry to Understanding*. Boston: Heinle and Heinle.
Gee, J. P. (1999), *An introduction to discourse analysis theory and method (2nd ed.)*. New York, NY: Routledge.
Golombek, P. R. (1998), 'A study of language teachers' personal practical knowledge'. *TESOL Quarterly* 32(3): 447–64.
Hall, G. (2011), *Exploring English Language Teaching*. London: Routledge.
Harland, J. and Kinder, K. (1997), 'Teachers' Continuing Professional Development: Framing a model of outcomes'. *Journal of In-service Education* 23(1): 71–84.
Harmer, J. (2001), *The Practice of English Language Teaching*. Harlow: Longman.
Hawkins, E. (1999), 'Foreign language study and language awareness'. *Language Awareness* 8(3&4): 124–42.
Hedge, T. (2000), *Teaching and Learning in the Language Classroom*. Oxford: Oxford University Press.
Holliday, A. (2005), *The Struggle to Teach English as an International Language*. Oxford: Oxford University Press.
—(2006), 'Native-speakerism'. *ELT Journal* 60(4): 385–6.
Kern, R. (2006), 'Perspectives on technology in learning and teaching languages'. *TESOL Quarterly* 40(1): 183–210.
Kiely, R. and Davis, M. (2010), 'From transmission to transformation: teacher learning in ESOL'. *Language Teaching Research* 14(3): 277–96.
Kiely, R., Davis, M. and Wheeler, E. (2010), *Investigating Critical Learning Episodes*. Reading: Centre for British Teachers.
Kiely, R. and Rea-Dickins, P. (2005), *Program Evaluation in Language Education*. Basingstoke: Palgrave Macmillan.
Krashen, S. and Terrell, T. (1983), *The Natural Approach: Language Acquisition in the Classroom*. Oxford: Pergamon.
Lamie, J. (2005), *Evaluating Change in English Language Teaching*. Basingstoke: Palgrave-Macmillan.
Leung, C. (2009), 'Second language teacher professionalism', in A. Burns and J. Richards (eds), *The Cambridge Guide to Second Language Teacher Education*. Cambridge: Cambridge University Press, pp. 49–58.

Long, M. and Porter, P. A. (1985), 'Groupwork, interlanguage talk and second language acquisition'. *TESOL Quarterly*, 19(2): 207–28.

Markee, N. (1993), 'The diffusion of curricular innovations'. *Annual Review of Applied Linguistics, Vol. XIII: Issues in Second Language Teaching and Learning*, 229–43.

McDonough, J. and Shaw, C. (1994), *Methods & Materials in ELT*. Oxford: Blackwell.

Medgyes, P. (1994), *The Non-Native Teacher*. London: Macmillan.

Miller, J. (2009), 'Teacher identity', in A. Burns and J. Richards (eds), *The Cambridge Guide to Second Language Teacher Education*. Cambridge: Cambridge University Press, pp. 172–81.

Moll, L., Amanti, C., Neff, D. and Gonzales, N. (2001), 'Funds of knowledge for teaching: using a qualitative approach homes and classrooms'. *Theory into Practice* 31(2): 132–41.

Pennycook, A. (2001), *Critical Applied Linguistics*. Mahwah, NJ: Lawrence Erlbaum.

Rampton, M. B. H. (1990), 'Displacing the "native speaker": expertise, affiliation, and inheritance'. *ELT Journal* 44(2): 97–101.

Richards, K. (2006), 'Being the teacher: Identity and classroom conversation'. *Applied Linguistics* 27(1): 51–77.

Schön, D. A. (1983), *The Reflective Practitioner*. Aldershot: Arena.

Sennett, R. (2008), *The Craftsman*. London: Penguin.

Simon, R. I. (1995), 'Face to face with alterity: Postmodern Jewish identity and the eros of pedagogy', in J. Galop (ed.), *Pedagogy: The Question of Impersonation*. Bloomington, IA: University of Indiana Press, pp. 90–105.

Sinclair, J. M. and Coulthard, M. (1975), *Towards an Analysis of Discourse: The English used by Teachers and Pupils*. London: Oxford University Press.

Skehan, P. (1998), *A Cognitive Approach to Language Learning*. Oxford: Oxford University Press.

Tajfel, H. (ed.) (1978), *Differentiation Between Social Groups: Studies in the Social Psychology of Intergroup Relations*. London: Academic Press.

Tsui, A. B. M. (2003), *Understanding Expertise in Teaching*. Cambridge: Cambridge University Press.

Van Lier, L. (2007), 'Action-based teaching, autonomy and identity'. *Innovation in Language Learning and Teaching* 1(1): 46–65.

Varghese, M., Morgan, B., Johnston, B., Johnson, K. A. (2005), 'Theorising language teacher identity: three perspectives and beyond'. *Journal of Language Identity and Education* 4(1): 21–44.

Wells, G. (1993), 'Reevaluating the IRF sequence: A proposal for the articulation of theories of activity and discourse for the analysis of teaching and learning in the classroom'. *Linguistics and Education* 5: 1–38.

Wenger, E. (1998), *Communities of Practice: Learning, Meaning, and Identity*. New York: Cambridge University Press.

Young, R. (1992), *Critical Theory and Classroom Talk*. Clevedon: Multilingual Matters.

12

Conclusion

David Evans

Language, discourse and identity have been the central themes of this book. The emphasis between language as a closely bounded phenomenon and the much wider sociocultural notion of discourse has varied from chapter to chapter. However, identity, in terms of being either relatively stable or ever-changing and fluid, unitary or multiple, has been a constant feature of each chapter. In respect of the nature of identity for instance, there is an immense difference between the relatively stable identity of the Mandarin-speaking Han majority of China or the minority Uyghur population by comparison with the individual unicycling youngster experimenting with alternative ways of being. Yet both extremes hold identity in terms of a self-concept, the latter is more existential with little historicity, constituted in the moment while the former has a more essentialist historical nature yet still subject to development and evolution within sociopolitical struggle. Both sets of identity are shaped by language and discourse; the former by sociopolitical linguistic capital and the latter by an alternative cultural capital, with unicycling being central to a discourse of gesture, music, fashion and a way of being.

Of course discourse is more than just the words, phrases and sentences of language. As Halliday (2003) points out, language is both ideational and relational. Taken together these two elements constitute a notion of discourse that encompasses language, signs, semiotics, relationships and the socialcultural power to make and communicate meaning.

Chapter 2 looked at identity on the inside of language and on the outside within discourse. Chapter 3 analysed the way in which social reality is contained within language through and within concepts that are constituted by language.

Chapters 4, 5, 6 and 7 of Part 2 looked at the varying emphases between language-marginalizing identity through sociopolitical constraints and language-liberating identity through new opportunities.

In Chapters 4 and 5 we saw the opportunities offered to widen identity through the possibilities of learning English as lingua franca and passport to economic success and yet we also learnt of the culturally invasive effects of the encroachment of Mandarin in the Uyghur province of China. We have seen in the book how identity emancipation and constriction revolves around language and its use.

Although the word 'discourse' is not always used in these chapters, it is, in my view, often the 'elephant in the room'. Language radiates outwards from its lexicogrammar towards sociopolitical identity through discourse accumulating political capital en route. Halliday (1978) shows this in his Systemic Functional Linguistics as do Chouliaraki and Fairclough (1999). In short, language is a sociopolitical and economic currency and in these terms some languages are more globally valued than others; witness the rivalled choice between English and French in Montreal, in Chapter 4.

Set against this, there are minority languages which are heading for demise and death and this means the death and demise of cultures. To combat this, we saw in Chapter 7 how former Amazonian tribal languages and cultural identities have been restored in Brazil.

A vital issue to be addressed is whether the dominance of a particular language has to result in the death of its minority neighbour. Marije van Hattum in Chapter 6 pointed to dual dialect identities among the Irish diaspora in Australia and furthermore Chapter 5 also points to possibilities of trilingualism within the Uyghur population between the Uyghur, Mandarin and English languages.

In Part 3 notions of multiple identities within pedagogy and teacher–student identity mirror the multilingual possibilities for identity in Part 2. We saw how identities are constructed within sites of interaction in the language and discourses people use, rather than identity simply being imposed from above. Students find, or should be encouraged to find, their 'third' place, be this in language learning or unicycling. Teachers need their autonomous identity for a creative pedagogy alongside students in the co-construction of knowledge-skill as a joint enterprise, as proposed by Richard Kiely's Chapter 11.

Future research might therefore be in the areas of multilingual and multicultural identities to enable individuals to navigate language, identity and culture in a world of an increasing migration of populations. Every chapter in this book describes a learning situation and a possibility for each person to be a learner of different languages, cultures and therefore identities.

Index

agency (of individual)   4–8, 12, 13, 16, 17, 19, 22, 24–9, 32–4, 134, 195, 208, 216
allophones   55–63, 77, 78
alterity   6, 7, 12, 13, 191, 203, 204
Amazonian (jungle, tribes, Indians etc)   4–10, 230
anglophones   30, 57, 58, 63, 65
ANOVA   65–9, 72
Arandic   40–2
attachment (language)   57, 61, 65, 74, 75, 77

Bakhtin, M.   6, 7, 11, 25, 195, 196
bilingual   62–6, 88, 89, 94–100, 116, 215
Bill 101   59, 60, 73–6
Bourdieu, P.   4, 30, 32, 152–7, 161, 196–8
Brazil   4–10, 124, 127–40, 230

capital
   cultural   4, 30–2, 152–61, 196–8, 204, 229
   sociocultural   191, 198
   symbolic   4, 31
Catalan   48
Catalonia   48
Chomsky, N.   16, 17, 18, 19, 21, 27–33
Chouliaraki, L.   23, 26, 28, 31–4, 230
civic identity   76
construction (of knowledge, identity)   6, 8, 12, 15, 16, 17, 23, 32, 145, 154, 158, 191–5, 201, 218–20, 230
critical pedagogy   4, 7–11, 13, 14, 204
culture   5–10, 11, 12, 13, 39–46, 60, 74, 81–4, 91–8, 124–40, 146, 147, 152–80, 185, 189–91, 195–204, 212, 214, 230

death of language   5
Derrida, J.   16, 19, 20, 21, 163, 169, 191, 202

Descartes   16, 18, 19, 22, 24
dialogic (dialogical, dialogism)   6, 7, 11, 25, 134, 139, 224
diaspora   9, 10, 230
discourse   3–9, 11, 12, 13, 14, 16, 17, 18, 22–9, 31–4, 100, 133, 135, 154, 170, 173, 188–205, 213–16, 222–5, 229, 230
   linguistic   3, 11, 170
   socioeconomic   203
   sociopolitical   5, 27
dominant (culture, discourse, ideology language)   7–10, 11, 12, 13, 23, 32, 86, 95, 125, 133, 155, 189, 196, 198, 200, 210
drama   12, 44, 168–80, 185
dual (identities)   10, 25, 31, 172, 193, 204, 230

economy–economic(ally)   5, 7–9, 14, 27–32, 56–60, 64, 72, 78–83, 88–100, 112, 124, 125, 136–8, 152, 188–92, 196, 197, 200–4, 230
English   5, 8–10, 13, 30, 31, 37, 40–9, 55–66, 69–77, 82, 83, 89–93, 97–9, 100, 106, 108–20, 134, 139, 170, 173, 177, 191, 196, 207–26, 230
episodic buffer   38
epistemology   5, 18, 19, 24
ethics   6, 191
ethnic diversity   56
ethnic identity   82, 95, 99

Fairclough, N   3, 5, 16, 23–8, 31–4, 189, 192, 230
Foucault, M.   5, 16, 22–4, 130, 146, 154, 192
francophones   55–65
Freire, P.   4, 7–10, 13, 127, 131, 134–9
French   5, 8, 9, 28–31, 44–8, 55–66, 69–78, 162, 166, 170–5, 178–83, 193–201, 230

globalization 60, 83, 100, 125, 139, 155, 156, 189
globalized identity 10
grammar 3, 8, 9, 13, 16, 17, 19, 20–32, 39, 46, 105, 127, 179, 203, 211, 223
grammatical 15, 16, 19, 23–8, 34, 108, 115, 170, 192, 208, 210, 223

habitus 32, 152
Halliday, M. A. K. 3, 8, 16, 17, 28, 29, 34, 198, 203, 229, 230
Han (China) 9, 10, 81–6, 90–100, 229
Heidegger, M. 16, 20, 22, 163
heteroglossia 23, 195, 196
hybrid (identities) 11, 12, 155, 167
hybridity 11, 194, 195, 201

identity
   cultural, sociocultural 10, 11, 13, 15, 25, 82–8, 94, 96, 100, 189, 193–6, 199–202
   linguistic 20, 31, 107, 111, 112, 196
   marginalized 4–8, 13
   multiple 7, 10, 13, 16, 230
ideological 4, 7, 9, 16, 17, 19, 25, 30, 34, 99, 196
ideology 5, 14, 25, 30, 58, 91, 135, 189, 197, 200, 201
immigrants 8, 9, 31, 56–63, 69–78, 106, 119, 190
immigration 57, 58, 78
intentionality 4, 8, 13, 19, 25, 27

Kant, E. 22
Kramsch, C. 167, 169, 189, 190, 196, 200–2

language culture 7, 12, 13, 167, 185, 191, 197, 202, 203
language education 12, 13, 99, 167, 194, 204
Levinas, E. 6, 7, 191, 202
lexicogrammar 5, 8, 28–34, 203, 230
linguistic (cultural) 4, 5, 10, 11, 30, 31, 192, 195
linguistic capital 31, 229

linguistic-sociolinguistic 3–10, 11, 12, 13, 14, 17, 19, 22–34, 37, 56–62, 73–6, 82–6, 92–4, 106–20, 124, 126, 145, 163, 169–73, 177, 179, 191, 192, 196, 203, 213, 221, 229
Logos (as divinity) 20

matched guise experiment 61–79
MFL (modern foreign languages) 12, 169–74, 178–84, 188–99, 201–4
minority languages 6, 7, 13, 82–9, 230
Montreal 5, 8, 9, 55, 56–66, 72–7, 230
Mundurucu 44

neural 42, 45
neuro-imaging 45
neuropsychological 8
neuroscience 39

Other 6, 7, 11, 12, 13, 191, 196, 200–3
Otherness 6, 12, 13, 189, 191, 202–4

pedagogy 4–10, 11, 12, 13, 14, 167–76, 184, 190–4, 201, 204, 208–16, 223, 224, 230
   banking system 4, 8
   third culture 167, 169
performance
   as discursive ideology 5, 13, 26, 151, 171, 195, 213, 214–16
   as enactment of behaviour 27, 149, 167, 168, 174, 178, 217, 221
performativity 13
poststructuralism 16, 22
poststructuralist 19, 22, 23, 146, 152
power (as concept) 4–9, 16, 22–5, 30–2, 82, 91, 130–4, 153, 191, 192, 197, 201, 202, 229

Quebec 8, 9, 30, 55–66, 73–8
Quebecers 57, 61, 74, 77
Questionnaires 61, 62, 94

Sapir-Whorf hypothesis 8, 36, 37
Saussure, Ferdinand de 20–2
self concept 3, 11, 15, 108, 198–201, 229
social justice 4, 7, 8, 213
social practices 5, 22–6, 192
socio-economic(s) 7–10, 12, 30–2, 60, 73, 94, 188–92, 195–203

socio-political   4, 5, 9, 10, 30, 31, 82, 125, 229, 230
spatial cognition   39–49
spatial relations   39–41
structuralism   16, 19, 21, 22, 26, 33
structuralist   21, 26
syntax   31, 46, 125, 153
systemic functional linguistics   8, 16, 26, 203, 230

third culture   167, 169
third place (as concept)   7, 11, 12, 169, 200–4
third space   11
trilingual (identities etc)   7, 83, 98, 100
trilingualism   10, 100, 230
t-tests   65

unicycling   11, 12, 146, 146–63, 229, 230
universal Grammar   17–19, 25, 27

urban dialect   31, 196, 198
urban identity   157, 163
urbanization   58, 59, 106
urban leisure   11
urban spaces   4, 151, 154, 163
Uyghur, province of China   4–10, 81–100, 229, 230

Verlan, social dialect   31
visuospatial   38, 42
Vygotsky, L.   16, 25, 33

Whorf, B. L.   8, 36, 37, 50
Whorfian   49, 50

young people   11, 73, 145–52, 155–7, 162, 163, 172, 191
youth
    culture   147, 162
    urban   151